December 1999

For Kate and Cindy —
Keep the faith
Love, Maryo

GRASSROOTS THEATER

A search for regional arts in America

Robert Gard

GRASSROOTS THEATER

A search for regional arts in America

With a foreword by David H. Stevens
and with an introduction by Maryo Gard Ewell
THE UNIVERSITY OF WISCONSIN PRESS

The University of Wisconsin Press
2537 Daniels Street
Madison, Wisconsin 53718

3 Henrietta Street
London WC2E 8LU, England

5   4   3   2   1

Printed in the United States of America

Library of Congress Cataloging-in-Publication Data
Gard, Robert Edward.
Grassroots theater: a search for regional arts in America /
Robert Gard : with a Foreword by David H. Stevens ; and with an
introduction by Maryo Gard Ewell.
pp.   cm.
Includes index.
ISBN 0-299-01234-4 (alk. paper)
1. Little theater movement—United States.   I. Title.
PN2267.G3   1999
792'.0223'0973—dc21   99-28781

for Maryo and Arthur

Contents

Foreword

At times we have the good fortune to come upon studies in American life that are unique. These have no formal patterns, no asserted aims of reform in the social, political, or cultural life of the people. One such work is the edition of Aldo Leopold's journals recently published under the title *Round River.* At the time of his death Leopold was a professor in the University of Wisconsin. But he was much more than formal teacher, hunter, and conservationist; he was a unique observer of nature and of education. When he referred to "the present educational marathon in memorizing" the data of science, he was preparing the path for his readers toward "some understanding of the living world."

In the present book, Robert Gard follows a similar ideal. His materials, however, are not out of physical nature but out of people. He uses drama as a vehicle for the interpretation of American life, but without fixed patterns. His people move and speak in a living world. They are guided almost anonymously until they give to audiences their several environments of North America through themselves. Before Professor Gard, like Aldo Leopold, settled in at the University of Wisconsin, he too did his work far afield. In this, then and now, he has had only one interest—to help people to express themselves under light touches of a hand that knows the feel of dramatic techniques but which is not endued by them.

His journeys in search of such learning about the people of America covered this continent northward from Mexico. Lately a leisurely tour of Great Britain has made drama on that side of one ocean also familiar to him. That was an advantage. It enabled Mr. Gard to appreciate how government can foster the arts successfully. Our country, by contrast, has lived under a political administration of such dull density, aesthetically and humanly, as to hamper the arts by varied mixtures of insensitiveness and ignorant righteousness. Only one exception has occurred in our time. Then it was another midwesterner who blazed a trail. Harry Hopkins came out of Iowa. He will be remembered in some part for his foresight in fostering American arts through the people, in spite of hindrances from persons fearful of something that they could not understand. For that nationwide projection of the arts many teachers of drama in colleges and universities gave their talents, as Mr. Gard and others are doing today, toward the good of their country.

Any review of experiences that are sources of this book will rest, in simplest terms, on four American environments known to its author. Mr. Gard, on whom the title of "professor" rests lightly, began observing people in Kansas. Later he increased his technical skills by study at Cornell University under a great teacher, Alexander Drummond. From that director of studies and of original productions he learned to leave his "artists" free, as people. They were helped to be themselves, within loosely drawn lines for technical progression, all the way from outlined sketches to footlights. Next, in Alberta he showed his ideas on drama so successfully that an entire province of Canada gained an enduring awareness of its place in a living world. I know of no demonstration more swiftly executed in a merging of history, folklore, and people for a unique expressiveness of an environment.

The dangers in uniqueness are real. Like conformity, this is a quality easily overplayed. Uniqueness may yield nothing more than samples of idiosyncrasy for us to bear silently to the limits of our cultivation of tolerance. Or, as in the present instance, uniqueness may produce a fine blend of elements to give permanence through art. It can deliver, with a hallmark of excellence, the characteristics of people as individuals living in their own times and places under the aura of certain beliefs, customs, and loyalties. This book by Mr. Gard illustrates the use of formal principles. It proves how to economize in impression by using formal rules while still saving the spirit of human experiences. Structure and theory are made to reveal, never to rule. On both sides, of theory and practice, he has made choices that open the ways of drama into American life. His success comes from a regard for the individual that is greater than for any finished regularity of product. Some of this power in selection, to create a dramatic unity in the fourth dimension of American life, appears in the pages of this book.

DAVID H. STEVENS

Acknowledgment

This book would not have been written had it not been for the Humanities Division of the Rockefeller Foundation. To Charles Burton Fahs, Director of the Humanities Division, and to Edward D'Arms and John Marshall, Associate Directors, my sincere thanks. To the staff of the Wisconsin Idea Theater past and present I owe gratitude for loyalty and personal sacrifice. Leslie Brown, Junius Eddy, Jack Curvin, Martha Van Kleeck, Edward Kamarck, Ronald Gee, and Georgia Pulvermacher have worked tireless hours in the cause of the arts in Wisconsin.

Finally, my simple gratitude to my editor, Vernon Sternberg, who has seen this book through from first to last.

ROBERT GARD

Madison, Wisconsin
May, 1954

Introduction

This book is a warrior's handbook. If you mean by "warrior"—as I do—a person with a clear vision and with ceaseless determination to live that vision in every moment of his or her life, then this book is one that you should read.

This book is for people who draw strength from the place they live and the people they live with. ". . . the knowledge and love of place is a large part of the joy in people's lives. There must be plays that grow from all the countrysides of America, fabricated by the people themselves, born of their happiness and sorrow, born of toiling hands and free minds, born of music and love and reason" (33). Do you care about the place you live? Then this book is one that you should read.

This book is for people who believe in American democracy. Within the term "democracy" I include concepts of broad citizen participation in shaping the way that we live; of the value and responsibility of every human being to think, speak, and act; of the value of community dialogue. If you are concerned about these things, then this book is one that you should read.

This book is for community workers. Regardless of whether your work is in the social services, community development, or community-based art, if you have a vision of how your home place and its people can be made more healthy, more beautiful, more interesting, then this book is one that you should read.

This book is for people who work in the arts. If you secretly write poetry, if you administer a broad community arts program, if you direct a theater, then this book is one that you should read.

I suppose you could say that I grew up with *Grassroots Theater.* In fact, my father wrote it during my earliest years, and it was published when I was eight years old. I remember hearing it read over WHA-Radio in Madison, Wisconsin, on "Chapter a Day." I have read it many times, and it was one of the forces that helped me decide, like my father, to make a life blending the arts and community work. I have thought that I knew this book pretty well; yet every time I reread it, it speaks to me differently, gives me something new to think about.

Yes, it was published in 1955. Yes, the central figures tended to be white males on university faculties. Yes, most of the examples are rural examples. Yes, there is an assumption that people make their home in the same place for many years. America, fifty years later, faces different issues. Our demographics, family structure, and workforce are dramatically changed. "Rural" no longer necessarily means "agricultural," as urbanites move to small places to telecommute, live in a second home, or retire. People are mobile and may change communities as often as they change careers.

Before I read *Grassroots Theater* again yesterday, I assumed that a large part of this introduction would be devoted to arguing how this chapter or that one was really a metaphor for dealing with a contemporary situation. I assumed that I'd be pleading with the reader to look beyond some now-quaint example to the universal. I assumed that I would be explaining to excess how you can liken your own creative community work to Gard's work in the arts.

Not at all. Yesterday, I realized anew what a modern book you hold in your hands. It takes no effort to make the case for the freshness, the utter relevance, of the ideas here. The vision of an individual's creativity—of his or her relation to place and to people—transcends technology, current events, and changing demographics. This book is relevant for the Asian American contemplating his or her cultural roots, for the worker in a strife-torn urban neighborhood, for the city manager of a small community, most of whose population is new. Below are a few of the things that I see in *Grassroots Theater* (and I have read it at different times with each in mind). One of these, or all of them, may be your reason to read it.

First, it is a spiritual autobiography. I spend most of my life—as I suspect most people do—in the world of action. I generate ideas, attend meetings, write memos, manage projects, finagle funds, and write final reports. As I update my résumé I briefly ponder the chain of events that has led me to where I am now and then rush off to a meeting. It is too easy to forget to examine regularly my soul to see whether I am still on course, to see whether I can even articulate that course, to see how the course may have evolved. *Grassroots Theater* makes me stop dead, insists I revisit those things that are so deep within that I rarely dare say them to other people for fear that it will make me too vulnerable. I believe it can do that for others as well.

In a letter that Robert Gard wrote to the Rockefeller Foundation as a graduate student in 1939, he articulated what he hoped to do with his life:

> I ponder more and more the question: in this great American growth of a non-commercial theatre . . . a theatre of the people . . . what will be the outcome, the goal? And increasingly it seems to me that the answer may be in the development of a . . . drama in which the . . . life of a community might be crystallized into dramatic form by those best able to do it: those who lived and been a part of that legend and life. . . . The true "people's theatre," as I see it, will be the creation for the community of a drama in which the whole community may participate. . . . That isn't a new idea, but perhaps I can help make it work in New York State. Anyway, I'm going to try.

Grassroots Theater was written when Gard was in his thirties and forties—old enough to start turning these vague ideas into reality. Ten years later, in 1967, he received the first rural-oriented grant from the National Endowment for the Arts; the well-known *Arts In The Small Community,* written with Mike Warlum and Ralph Kohlhoff, was the result. Later in other books, such as *Prairie Visions* or *Coming Home to Wisconsin,* the ideas were further expanded. And, in a speech he gave at Cornell University just five weeks before his death in 1992, Gard acknowledged that he never lost sight of that fundamental 1939 vision. There must be "a new concept of native roots, local awareness and folklore as well as a new consciousness of the possibility of an American drama depending on themes and subjects beyond [the merely] superficial. . . . A concept of theater must be broad enough to include many things. . . . Writers must be encouraged throughout the region. The people of the region must be let in . . ." (*From the Ground Up: Grassroots Theater in Historical and Contemporary Perspective* 1993).

Though he never lost sight of his big vision, within *Grass-*

roots Theater the development of specifics can be seen: the initial ideas from his young Kansas days growing through his student days, being tested, rejected, accepted, refined in New York, Alberta, and finally Wisconsin.

This is a wonderful look at the growth of the soul of a man who has devoted his life to creativity and community. For those of us who say we are too busy to take time to search our souls, it will stop us short, make us ask why we do what we do, force us to articulate our own answers. For those of us who sometimes, in dark moments, doubt the ultimate value of our work, it will restore faith in ourselves, though perhaps not the old faith we thought we had. I think you will see something of yourself here.

The second point I see in *Grassroots Theater* pertains to those interested in community arts: it is a rare chronology of a too-little-known part of your history. This is a story of remarkable people whose university-based community arts development work spans decades from the 1910's to the 1950's. It introduces Thomas Dickinson who shook the academic world in 1910 by teaching the first course in contemporary drama at the University of Wisconsin—though the University still would not allow the production of plays on campus. It introduces one of Dickinson's students, Zona Gale of Portage, Wisconsin, who wrote the famous play, *The Neighbors*. Quoted in this volume, she said, "I should be very glad that the play be given without royalty in country theatres when the play is given for the benefit of any civic or other social enterprise . . ." (15). We meet Edgar "Pop" Gordon who in 1922 with WHA-Radio ". . . organized and broadcast what is without doubt the first music appreciation course ever to be heard on the air. In those days, of course, people listened with headphones, and many listeners wearing their phones sang under the leadership of Pop's friendly voice" (92).

The intriguing fact that so much of this work was being done through the College of Agriculture is revealed. Deans and Extension Agents and rural sociologists are presented—individuals who, recognizing the natural and crucial role of personal creativity in the home and the community, induced nationally known visual artist John Steuart Curry to come to the College of Agriculture as its resident artist. And who, *because* they were in the College of Agriculture, furthered Gard's drama work. This may seem astonishing.

Yet the chronology goes deeper. *Grassroots Theater* connects all of this arts development to the Wisconsin Idea, an extraordinary populist social and political vision in which the workings of state government and the University of Wisconsin were deeply intertwined. Concepts of "democracy in the arts" or "the arts in the everyday life of all Wisconsin people" were derived from the Wisconsin Idea.

Grassroots Theater does not only chronicle this arts movement in Wisconsin. Gard introduces other larger-than-life figures doing similar work elsewhere. Indeed, I became so intrigued by his brief introductions that I have begun my own research into the broader populist arts movement in America in the period from 1920–1960. Let me tell a bit more than Gard does.

The "intellectual lineage" that was Gard's began, it seems, at Harvard at the turn of the century when George Pierce Baker began to expound the radical idea that there should be a body of American dramatic literature, and he encouraged his students to start writing plays. Two of his students, Alexander Drummond, later of Cornell University, and Frederick Koch, of the University of North Carolina, started play-writing movements of extraordinary proportions in their respective states from the 1920's through the 1940's. The principle behind these movements was, "Write what you know." They believed that there could exist no real record of American culture until "ordinary" Americans began to write their own stories: stories about themselves, their cultures, their real-life issues, their communities.

By advertising in the *American Agriculturalist* magazine, Drummond identified scores of rural New Yorkers who had stories to tell: stories of aspirations, broken hopes, poverty, community folklore, land-use conflicts—not at all the generally vapid stuff available for community theater production at the time. Drummond and his students assisted these individuals in conceiving their stories in dramatic form, in writing the plays, in producing the plays for their neighbors or at the New York State Fair, in making the plays available for wider use in the state. One of Drummond's students was Robert Gard.

In North Carolina, Koch was doing the same work. The scores of "Carolina Folk Plays" that were penned by his students—including Thomas Wolfe and Paul Green—were real stories drawn from experiences lived. They were stories of sharecroppers black and white, of women in the Mexican revolution, of mountain life. One student, Mrs. Lorretto Carroll Bailey, an African American, took these ideas to Shaw College where she attempted to do the same work in predominantly African American communities.

Meanwhile, concurrent with Drummond and Koch, Alfred Arvold was working in North Dakota. A Wisconsinite himself, perhaps bitten by the Wisconsin Idea bug, Arvold spent a half-century in Fargo developing the concept of the "little country theater." According to Arvold's idea, each tiny community should use its spaces—town halls to home basements—as settings for drama. Though these words are Gard's, they espouse Arvold's idea as well: "[and] when plays cannot be found to fit the needs of the people, someone or some group must make up a play; in such playmaking there is a wonderful freshness" (135). Meanwhile,

Arvold presented in Fargo all of the great American artists who toured at the time, from Paul Robeson to Kirsten Flagstad to Artur Rubenstein to the Trapp Family Singers; and he presented, in collaboration with the Masonic Lodge, historical pageants telling the story of the Dakotas using literally thousands of community members.

Gard carried the work into the next generation, taking the idea further. While his predecessors stimulated play-writing and presenting almost as ends in themselves, Gard connected this writing process to community-building (though he does plenty of soul-searching in *Grassroots Theater* about that concept). His work was paralleled by that of Baker Brownell, a Northwestern University philosophy professor. Brownell was invited to Montana to help stabilize small Montana communities left economically stranded by the post-war copper bust. Brownell's idea of community-building expressly included the making of community dramas, written about, by, and for citizens to help work out their issues and, in doing so, articulate their desired future.

Gard also thought that the arts could be crucial in developing leaders for rural communities. Indeed, he and John Barton—a rural sociologist—and Brownell together devised a six-week summer training program for community leaders. It is detailed in a letter from Gard to the Rockefeller Foundation. The curriculum that was never carried out, when funds ran dry, looked like this: In the mornings for the first three weeks, students would work with Barton on the topic "American Community Behavior"; in the afternoons they would work with dramatic artist, Alan Crafton. In the mornings for the fourth through sixth weeks, students would work with Brownell on the topic "A Philosophy for Community Arts," and in the afternoons they would work with visual artist-in-residence, Aaron Bohrod. (Oh, to have the opportunity to carry out this kind of curriculum—perhaps someone who reads this book will.)

The Rockefeller Foundation, under the leadership of Humanities Vice-President David Stevens, supported all of these men (except Arvold, who was offered support but chose to turn it down). In a memo preserved at the Rockefeller Archive Center, Stevens stated his belief "that if we are to have a characteristic American culture we must give our people easy access to their own cultural traditions. . . . a cultural map [which] leads to its resources for spiritual adventure and for the creative expression of their meaning." In this historical community arts drama Stevens is a sort of stage manager, for he enabled these individuals to experiment with their big dreams. In an interesting way this support has come full circle as I have received funding from the Rockefeller University allowing me to use the Rockefeller Archive Center to do this research.

Still this exciting history, touched on in *Grassroots Theater,* leaves the reader with so many questions, chief among them: Why is the truly revolutionary work of these men unknown in America, while the work of their contemporaries like Eugene O'Neill or Tennessee Williams is well known? Thousands of "ordinary" citizens, writing *of* their lives and often making very good plays, breaking down the lines between idea-generator, writer, actor, audience: these were larger-than-life, incredible new ideas. Master playwrights writing *for* anonymous audiences—this was not a new idea. Why do we not know of the former?

Gard and Brownell took the Drummond–Arvold–Koch work of mass playwriting to the next stage. Without losing the original idea, they *also* saw possibilities of connecting this writing to "youth at risk," conflict mediation, and community planning—to use the 1990's vernacular. What, then, is the next stage, the stage that *we* workers are undertaking? And what setting, in turn, do we want to leave those who come after us to take the work further? We must look back in order to look forward. Gard says, "Not to know the past of a region is like viewing the setting but never seeing the drama" (126). Change the word "region" to "our shared history" and you have another reason to read this book. Perhaps, at last, the time has come when we can hear these people who were but voices in the wilderness in their own time.

The third aspect of *Grassroots Theater* that makes it a great resource is that it is full of wonderful project ideas to make your own. There is at least one elegant fundraising idea I had not heard of before. There is also a wonderful story of using drama to mediate a very intense public meeting. An extraordinary research scheme for understanding the role of culture in small community life is presented, and it seems so contemporary that one might read it twice, just to make sure it is being read correctly. The birth of the Wisconsin Regional Writers Association is described, a group that literally had thousands of Wisconsin people trying their hands at writing poetry, plays, and novels for the first time.

The fourth and final item I wanted to highlight from the book is the presence of cultural themes of extraordinary power. I have read *Grassroots Theater* just looking to expand or clarify my own ideas on some of these themes, to borrow good language and stories about them. I am tempted to illustrate each, to quote wonderful passages about each—but read for yourselves:

- Community-building, community development, community self-awareness
- The relation of the arts to place
- The role of arts in society
- The role of arts in American democracy

- The correct understanding of excellence in community-based arts
- Leadership development
- The development and retention of a personal faith
- The understanding of creativity in the "ordinary" individual
- The interrelationship of the arts, education, sociology, philosophy, anthropology with daily life

Well, all of this is from my perspective, of course. My hope is that you will add to my list of themes and find your own. That you will make this book your own.

Having told some reasons why this book is timeless, and why I hope that you read on, let me now tell what I hope will be done after the book has been put down.

I hope that you will walk or bicycle or drive through your town or neighborhood as though you were visiting for the first time, seeing it with the eyes of the newcomer, marveling, reveling, being puzzled by, reacting to what you see and hear and smell and wonder about. Notice how natural things lie, how manmade things are arranged. Maybe take along a Polaroid or a digital camera and photograph things that interest you and maybe create, afterwards, a little exhibit of your place. Maybe invite your neighbors to look at your exhibit and respond to what they see. Talk to folks about why they live there, and where they came from, or why they stayed. Take nothing for granted—either the things you love or the things you hate. Why are they the way they are? Revisit the places you love anew. Visit places or folks you always meant to visit, someday.

How does your place influence you? How do you derive strength from its landscape, buildings, layout? How do you derive strength from your neighbors? Or how might you? Play a game of "three whys": Ask yourself why you live there.

And then ask "why?" of that response. And then ask "why?" of *that* response. What do you learn from answering these questions?

Then reflect on the people who helped shape you: the people that you found to be larger than life, to whom you would apply the word "great." Reflect on the events and social and political milieus that helped you articulate your idea of the way people are, of the way things are and can be. Can you articulate—as though for the first time—your personal and social roots?

Think of Gard's teacher, Miss Lynn: "She said I probably had some good materials but that until I developed a philosophy of writing the materials would not do me much good" (9). To what extent is your work only your skills, rather than the drive in your soul? What are your own big ideas, those ideas so terrifyingly pure to you that you are sometimes afraid to say them even to yourself? Which brings tears to your eyes because they are so powerful to you? Try articulating these. Write them down. Dare to say them to someone. Perhaps try the "three whys" on these as well. Eliminate other people's slogans. Eliminate techniques. Stand in front of your spiritual mirror: Whom do you see?

And then, armed anew with your place, your people, your culture, your chronology, create your own "Grassroots Theater."

Through your life, give new life.

Reflect. Burn. Speak. Act. Create.

Maryo Gard Ewell

Gunnison, Colorado
1999

GRASSROOTS THEATER

A search for regional arts in America

Chapter one

A FEELING FOR PLACES

I know that a great deal of the joy I have felt as a worker in
back-country American theater has sprung from my feeling
for places. My father loved our part of eastern Kansas and
perhaps transmitted to me his intimate knowledge of towns
and prairies. Or it may have been my early association with
things on and about our Kansas farm that has made a search
for the flavorings of America one of my greatest pleasures.

There was our local river, for instance, the Neosho. The
Indians called it that; it means rapidly rising water. In flood
time it would reach out across all the lowlands, and from our

3

upstairs windows the whole north and west would be a great brown sheet in the morning light. On the Santa Fe railroad tracks that cut east of the river the folks would sometimes gather to watch the flood water rise or to just silently watch the young corn leaves swirl around in the rapid water and come loose from their rootings. On the bridge where the Missouri Pacific crossed the river there would usually be a crowd of white and negro boys with fish lines, hoping to drag in a mud catfish. About once a year a boy would slip off the bridge and into the muddy water and would be sucked down and lost. Then the whistles at the water works would blow, and a search would go on into the night until the body was pulled out—usually down below where the river made a sharp bend. And when the flood receded the corn stalks would be lying flat against the earth, frayed and brown, and the whole earth would give off a musty smell, and cracks would begin to grow until the earth was a pattern of twisty brown cracks.

It seemed to me that the men of our town and countryside were shaped by the river and that the river knew and held their destinies. It crushed at will and gave at will, too, because in good years corn grew in great, tall stalks in the bottoms, and the ears were often half as long as a man's arm. And in good years the women's faces were serene as they sang hymns in the kitchens while their menfolk stood at nightfall leaning on pigpen fences listening to the soft grunting of hogs and thinking, perhaps, of the corn that would fatten the pigs.

There was the river, and there was the earth along the river all plow-broken except for a prairie acre or two where there was a tangled burying ground. I saw that our earth like our river shaped men's lives and that in dry years the earth whirled away from the roots of the corn and our

4

neighbors' faces grew long and solemn and the women quit singing hymns in the kitchens and the men praised God in small voices with the edges of questions sticking out.

The river, the earth, the sky. In the sky at dusk the night-hawks swooped and boomed, crying as they crisscrossed the air, and after a hot day a coolness would come out of the ravine that ran down to the river—a coolness and a loneliness. There were sweet singers in the bottoms along the river and on the uplands too. They sang of Scotland and Holland and Ireland and of Illinois and Indiana. There were lips that could be kissed under the rustling corn leaves, and there was sweating work to be done in the heat of the day heaving the heavy alfalfa onto the hay racks and then pitching it off in long ricks.

My observations of the life around me were pure waves of sensation which beat against me and tossed me this way and that on billows of pleasure that had no other meaning. Good and evil were inextricably mixed, and I did not care to separate them. I sensed that the river was cruel, but when I slipped the saddle off my mare and shrugged off my clothing and swam the horse across the river in the early morning hours, the water, the smooth movement of the swimming horse, and my own careless appreciation were welded into a wordless poem. There were mists that rose from the lowlands and stimulated my night-time imagination, and I was a void, an opening, a space into which sensations poured in confusion.

Looking back, I can see how these things helped to give me a taste for the flavorings of places, but a taste for theater came my way through the purest chance. Certainly, my father gave me no leaning in that direction. He was a country lawyer, a Kansas pioneer who set great store by the economic development and welfare of the countryside, but he had little sympathy at all for cultural matters. To him the arts were participated in by women or the weaker members of society and had no real place in dynamic community development.

Though he was a self-made and almost completely self-educated man, he encouraged me to go to the University of Kansas where he hoped I would become interested in law or business. I disappointed him by floundering around for a couple of years with no noticable inclination for a profession. The nearest I came to it was once during a visit to Kansas City, Missouri, when a handwriting expert at the YMCA told me that I had a modest amount of literary ability. I could attach no possible value to his judgement, and neither could father. So I wandered America for a while in the middle of my college career, just as many other Americans were wandering and seeking during the early depression years. I returned to Kansas University for my junior year no nearer a career than I had been before but with a keen remembrance of people and places I had known and seen and a deep liking for a wandering life.

Now it happened that there was a professor of speech and drama at Kansas University named Allen Crafton. He was small physically, as men go, with bright blue eyes and a thin nose that looked as translucent as a mellow clarinet reed. But there was so much about him that was legendary— tales spun by students which grew with the telling—that my characterization of him can afford to be extravagant and perhaps sound a bit like a legend.

Crafton was a pagan-god figure whose lips were stained with the juices of barefoot-tramped grapes. He had steel in his hands and art at his fingertips. He could paint a magnificent landscape or write a poem of mighty tone or of aching, small joys. He was capable of turning out—and did turn out—a novel in a week or a play in ten days. It didn't really matter that they were not published. He seldom tried the publishers.

Women tended to follow him like dogs, and good men shoved for a place at his side. He was regarded as a wit, a philosopher, a roarer of bawdy ballads, but he could be as sensitive as harp strings in a soft wind. He was a staunch friend, and he would fight for friends like a demon. He savored the unusual, but tolerated the usual and found it useful. He loved and was a judge of good liquor and good smoke, but he was grateful for inferior stuff if a poor man offered it to him. He lived the life of Everyman; yet he kept a personal integrity and was at once malleable and impregnable. He seemed to live a man's full lifetime every day. He rode the sun like a chariot. He had a quick mind capable of whipping out at sensation and fact and gathering them into a child's wondrous pattern of imaginative grace.

Crafton had imbibed the goodness of places. He had traveled to the far cities of the earth, and he spoke of them in their own fashion. He turned back the landscapes he viewed like the pages of a book, seeking the sights and sounds of old generations.

His friends said that Crafton was undoubtedly a genius but that he would perhaps die unsullied and unknown. So there is poetic truth in all that I have written about him. And it is with gratitude that I look back on the time in 1937 when I stood with him one afternoon on the south side of Mount Oread at Lawrence, Kansas.

The prairie grass grew lush where we were standing, just as it had when the great Wakarusa Valley lying before us was the carpet of the pioneers. The grasses rustled gravely in a slow wind that seemed to blow from a wild spot on the

7

opposite hill where the bones of men killed in Quantrill's raid on Lawrence in '63 were lying in prairie graves. The big University buildings were at my back and the whole scene was laced through with nostalgia, for I was leaving Kansas and I knew that Kansas would never be my home again.

I first met Allen Crafton when I was a junior in the University. That was 1933, a bad time for everybody. Students I knew were living in chicken houses or in the back seats of Model T Fords. They were tracking down cockroaches in the University buildings at night and selling these quick insects to biological companies. They were doing most of the manual work of the city of Lawrence, and they were endlessly pleading with suspicious merchants and heartless landladies for credit. The struggle was primitive, too, and the highlight of the week might be a hike on Sunday night along the Union Pacific railroad and the Kaw River with twenty cents worth of hamburger for five fellows and a few matches to light a fire.

It was a bad time and a sad time. Often some sensitive spirit got too tired and leaped from the Kaw River bridge, or gagged and burned his throat and belly with poison. But it was a good time for militant ideas and pleasures of mind clashing with mind. It was a time when sham and unreality dropped away and when the girls looked deep into the eyes of their men for the soundness of soul that was in them.

Allen Crafton opened his home and often his purse to the Kansas students, but his generosity alone was not the reason for his popularity. He was an extremely able teacher. Among his course offerings was a course in playwriting. This course interested me. I had never quite forgotten what the handwriting expert at the Kansas City YMCA said, and I had been experimenting and dabbling with writing during my early college years.

I wrote some short narratives for a good teacher named Margaret Lynn who knew and loved the prairies and had written books about them. My writings, I remember, were all brief episodes about people and places I had seen in my wanderings. Miss Lynn said the sketches were good but that they were merely impressions and had little central idea. She said I probably had some good materials but that until I developed a philosophy of writing the materials would not do me much good. Although I was completely ignorant of every aspect of dramatic writing and although I had seen only a few plays in my life, I thought that a course in playwriting might do me some good and help me learn the philosophy of writing Miss Lynn had said I needed.

In 1933 when I decided to take Professor Crafton's playwriting course the depression was at its peak. There were more breakdowns caused by malnutrition, and our Chancellor, E. H. Lindley, decided that something drastic must be done. He assembled a lot of the cases of what students were doing to keep alive and went off one day to Washington to see FDR about American college life. The result of Chancellor Lindley's visit was the CSEP—"College Student Employment Project"—which created jobs in American colleges and paid students a small sum per month. To most students the money was a profound godsend. It broke the tensions. It rippled away the drawn tightness on the faces. It started up new fires and creative hopes. The CSEP was certainly not the greatest thing that FDR did, but it saved many young hearts from breaking.

I was one of the first students to apply for and receive one of these jobs. When the committee asked me what kind of work I would like to do which would benefit me and still allow me to earn the money, I replied that I did not know. I would like a day or two to decide. And it was during this small decision period that I first attended Crafton's playwriting class. He talked about character, and he had the great dramatic characters of world drama waiting at his lips to illustrate what he said. I listened with fascination, for I knew that he was talking about life itself and that the characters he was using as illustration were easily within my own comprehension.

After class, I walked over to old Fraser Theater. The heavy oak double doors were closed, and when I pulled them creakingly open the dim theater seemed very silent and lonely. I stood a moment looking at the empty seats and the silent blue curtain and the frame of the stage opening with its scrolls. There was a cold unreality about the place that made me uneasy. When I opened a door at the side of the stage, a curious odor came from the stage itself. Ahead of me there were six steps going up to the level of the stage, and in a moment I moved up them. There was an even deeper silence on the platform. A bare bulb burning high up cast a hard little light down upon the stage boards, and the curtains hanging around the stage seemed to move as if in a tiny draft. Ahead of me against a wall was a stack of scenery with a flat, dusty, dry smell about it, and high over head there was a small creaking and swaying sound as though a small breeze were swaying heavy ropes in wooden pulleys.

I put my hand on one of the curtains, and a filter of dust fell in the dim light. I walked out on the stage and wondered what I was to do here. I wandered around. There was a steep flight of steps at the left side going up into a high dimness. The floor around the stairs and near the walls was littered with pieces of crumpled kleenex smeared with lipstick and make-up, some odds and ends of clothing, and a pile of boards. I turned and stood in the center of the stage. It was the first theater I had ever taken the trouble to examine from the stage side of the footlights, and as I stood looking out at the seats that rose gently in front of me I tried to imagine the stage peopled by the characters Crafton had told us about. I found the experience pleasant, and I stood on the stage for a long while. The next day I saw the University committee and told them that I wished to work in the theater. They assigned me to Crafton.

He was rightly dubious at first, but after he found that I was willing to do any kind of work from scrubbing the stage to building scenery and acting we became fast friends. I got fifteen dollars a month for working with this master of stage design, lighting, painting, and costume. He was an excellent carpenter and a good sculptor and carver. He could write a play, if he wished, or act with wondrous art. But he was most magnificent of all as director of the play.

Every day of my last two years in college was a day of creative joy because of my association with Crafton. The mighty dramatic literature of the world came to life for me. I read everything, looked everywhere for ideas. Food and clothing did not matter. The theater at Kansas University was my playground and I worked and dreamed there day after day.

I enjoyed working for Crafton at least partly because of his deep love of Kansas people and places. I stayed on as his assistant for a couple of years after graduation, and we talked increasingly of a theater of the Kansas people based on the history and tradition that seemed to make Kansas unique. One morning after one of our talks I was working on the stage and a thick cloud of dust began to drift down from the heights of the stagehouse. I was building some flats, but I let them lie and climbed to the attic. I went to the windows, and as I looked westward out across the great valley it seemed to me that the valley was curtained with thick, black velours. The richness of the prairie country was blowing away, and the whole plains lay in a whirling, drifting torment. It was as though from the attic windows I could sense all America writhing and gasping as from a great wound.

My father had been a Kansas pioneer, but the frontier that he knew was ended. It could probably never return or be relived; the depression with its floods and hungers was the end, perhaps, of a scene that began with the push West and ended in the spiritual and physical torment of the American people. If the power, the drive, the call that had sent my father forth from Cumberland County, Illinois, to Kansas was now somehow responsible for young and old wandering futilely through the depression, then, indeed, I thought, we must seek a new, inward expansiveness that would enrich us, not so much in silver and gold but in our whole soul and feeling.

Crafton had said many times that this inward growing must be of the art that was in us and of a recognition by all people of the goodness of the stuff of America re-created in terms of theater so that theater might be an accepted part of our lives. In his own way, in his own theater, Crafton was making his belief live magnificently and was probably finding his own salvation. But I wondered how his idea could spread—how it could come to everybody.

As I stood at the attic windows alone with the great dust curtain curling around Old Fraser, it did not seem strange to me that, somehow, somewhere, I might become a tiny part of the spreading of such an idea. Afterwards, I began to wonder whether the people of America might be drawn closer together in tolerance and in joy in one another through their stories and songs, their presents and pasts told and sung in a theater whose stages were everywhere and whose actors were the folks in the cities and on the farms, in the crossroad places and in the back places where the American past lay quiet and undisturbed. I thought about it a great deal and talked it all over with Crafton.

Then, one day Crafton told me that if I were really interested in native American theater I should go to Cornell University to study with A. M. Drummond, who had made some big steps toward a New York State theater. I applied for a scholarship to Cornell, received one, and so at length I was standing with Crafton, as I have said, on the side of Mount Oread one afternoon in 1937.

There was silence between us, and my thoughts were reaching out beyond the valley to encompass my experiences in American places. I had heard American voices from the deep South, from the West and the Northwest, from New England and Texas and the middle country. I had heard a singing that was Mexico and had felt a vast, unspoken sensation that was Canada. Somehow I knew that these voices and feelings must relate themselves to a theater I earnestly desired to help create but could not really define. I hoped Cornell and Drummond would teach me American theater.

I got set up in a room on Dryden Road, Ithaca, New York, in September, 1937. Crafton had told me that Professor Drummond, who was the Director of the Cornell University theater, had already been interested in a theater of the New York State people and that he had started an interesting country theater at the New York State Fair in 1919. Crafton had told me, too, that Professor Drummond was quite unique, but he did not enlarge on that statement. I did not comprehend, when I arrived at Ithaca one rainy afternoon, that I was embarking on an experience that was to alter my whole life and that I was to make the acquaintance of a man whose ideas and examples were to be the actual groundwork of experiments in which I was to engage later.

As I think back over the leaders in American theater I have known, I am certain that Professor Drummond is the most complex of them all and probably the deepest thinker. Here is a man who made the Cornell Dramatic Club one of the outstanding college theater organizations of the country. He directed the club in outstanding productions of fine European plays, and in many cases his productions were the first in America of those plays. He set the standards of scholarly research in theater at Cornell and created a splendid program of graduate study. He made theater a respected area of study at Cornell, and the influence of his academic ideas, especially in aesthetics, spread far and wide among American universities. Yet this same man was able to feel the utmost elation in his New York State Fair experiment of 1919, when he took the Cornell Dramatic Club to the Fair at Syracuse and established a country theater which became widely talked about throughout America. He proved that he was at least as interested in helping to establish a taste for good theater among the country folk of New York State as he was in producing plays in his own theater at Cornell. His country theater was one of the really significant early demonstrations of what an excellent theater program could do in raising countryside drama standards.

Drummond's friend, George Pierce Baker of Harvard, wrote to him after the New York State Fair experiment: "If you can demonstrate to the people of the countryside how relatively easy it is to give plays well, and that it is just as easy, or easier to give good plays rather than poor ones, you will have done real service to both your community and the bettering of appreciation of drama in the country."

Professor Drummond did demonstrate these things. His Cornell Dramatic Club played to six thousand persons a week at the State Fair. The country theater, which was established in a wing of one of the older buildings, was packed for every performance. As Professor Drummond has written: "We had 400 seats, and 500 standing room. Both were filled." The country theater was open even when productions were not on just for folks to walk through and see, and there was always a crowd looking the stage over and asking questions about stage lighting, scenery, make-up. But, Drummond has recalled: "The audience were in a way undemonstrative. It was a 'demonstration' and they were serious. We even preceded every play with a short, informal talk on the idea of the thing. But in their undemonstrative way they laughed and nudged each other and beamed and wiped furtive tears and voted it good and stayed for more and sent their friends. There is something in it."

Zona Gale of Wisconsin was extremely interested in the New York State Fair theater and waived the royalty on her play *The Neighbors*, which was the Drummond headliner. She wrote to Drummond:

I should be very glad that the play be given without royalty in country theatres, when the play is given for the benefit of any civic or other social enterprise. We might come at something picturesque, with an appeal to the imagination.

The use of *The Neighbors* is offered free to any country theatre which will use a part of the funds so raised for the following purposes, or will prevail upon some member of the community to carry out the following:

To plant at least one long-lived shade tree in the community; or
To plant a fruit tree by the roadside; or
To plant a spruce or a balsam to be used, when so desired, as
a community Christmas tree.
One tree for every performance!
And if the producers wish to give really good measure for the
use of the play, it is recommended that they conclude the evening
with a community gathering, with community singing and dancing,
and a discussion of the things which their community needs.
Furthermore, it is understood that the producers, the cast, and
the audience at such a performance shall all be neighbors to everyone, as long as they live.*

I find it extremely interesting, looking back, to note that
Zona Gale had this connection with Professor Drummond's
country theater experiments and perhaps helped in some
way to formulate, or at least to confirm, some of his ideas
about countryside drama. Zona Gale's home town was
Portage, Wisconsin, and she had been very active in the
development of the Wisconsin Dramatic Society, perhaps
the earliest little theater movement in America. Professor
Thomas Dickinson, then of the University of Wisconsin,
founded the Society in 1910. On March 10, 1912, he wrote
to Zona Gale to ask her to do a short play which the Society
might produce. *The Neighbors*, which, incidentally, was
written in just a few days, was the result.

The love of home place is apparent in much of Zona
Gale's writing. Professor Drummond was impressed by the
honest, human qualities of her characters, and I have certainly been no less so in my work with the Wisconsin Idea
Theater. It is impossible to estimate the effect of Zona Gale's
writings on the feeling of Wisconsin people for Wisconsin
places, but it was perhaps the success of Zona Gale as a
playwright—her *Miss Lulu Bett* was a Pulitizer Prize win-

* Quoted in A. M. Drummond, "A Countryside Theatre Experiment,"
Quarterly Journal of Speech Education, VI (Feb., 1920), 46–47.

ner—which focused the great popular interest on her as a Wisconsin personality and threw playwriting and theater in general into a very favorable light in the state. Zona Gale's regard for regional themes, her interest in community development, and her success as a professional writer undoubtedly made subsequent drama development easier in Wisconsin.

Professor Drummond emerged from the State Fair theater with the convictions, which he stated in an article in the *Quarterly Journal of Speech* in 1921, that plays of high literary value do "go" in the country and that local groups can be stimulated to do acceptable work. He was positive, too, that there was great latent interest waiting to be aroused in the communities of New York State.

Years afterward, when I was established in Wisconsin, Professor Drummond wrote to me:

I am pleased with your efforts in the behalf of regional drama. Not so much that regional literature and drama needs help, as because your appreciation of and presentation of the life and idiom that spring from near the soil, and from common ways of feeling and expression, are the basic stuff of our best writing, and our best thought about the many types and attitudes that make up our varied country, its people and loyalties.

I think our best literature is in a true sense regional, and our greatest American writers and dramatists have done their richest work when they were rising from or returning to their native heath, folkways and sentiments.

The contemporary interest in regionally-based literature, both factual and fanciful, its success on the stage and in the press, encourages us to think that a new generation of American writers, dramatists, musicians and painters may be drawing content and style from native roots to challenge the merit of the American-bred writers of the Nineteenth Century.

And your encouragement of such an interest in your own region is a true if modest aid to some of those who will make American literature.

My personal debt to Professor Drummond is very large. It was his theories and ideas that drew my own into focus, just as it was the State Fair experience that probably made his own interest in regional drama development more keen. Drummond's personal interest in New York State was, of course, very great. He was born in Auburn, and his entire family relationship was calculated to make him extremely fond of his town, his familiar countryside, and his neighbors. He was educated at Hamilton College, Cornell, and Harvard. During his younger days he wandered into almost every corner of central New York country and established the intimate relationship which fixed so firmly his desire to see the theater arts flourish in the back-country places he knew and loved. Nostalgia, however, was not Professor Drummond's chief motivation. He felt a keen sense of responsibility to his region and hoped to motivate a movement that might breed a superior kind of home-grown theater.

Although Professor Drummond has never formally stated it, I believe his thinking about theater in the region centered around the hope of developing fine original plays authored by the people of the area. His course in playwriting at Cornell developed several well-known playwrights, the most outstanding of whom is Sidney Kingsley.

His theory of countryside playwriting was that writers should be encouraged to consider themes and subjects closely allied to their own places. Cornell, the leading educational institution of higher learning in the region, ought, he thought, to assume a leading rôle in stimulating local playwriting by drawing the promising subjects and materials to the attention of writers. Cornell should also stand ready to assist the local writers once they had their plays underway.

Drummond himself was a master play doctor. He believed that a body of highly usable original plays might be developed jointly by the authors and by someone like himself able and willing to straighten out the kinks in the scripts. These plays, once they were developed, would be of great service to local theater groups which, ideally, *ought* to be interested in the region where they existed and therefore *ought* to be concerned with doing regional plays.

I do not think that Drummond had any illusions about the various groups' obvious preference for Broadway plays. He simply hoped that the larger city groups might try an original play once in a while. It was the smaller rural groups which I am sure he had in mind as doing most of the original play production.

His theory about this body of regional plays was extremely sound. He planned to distribute the plays on a nonroyalty basis to help to counteract the excessively poor plays found in the commercial publishers' lists—the plays which rural groups left to themselves almost invariably selected. He did not expect to develop any great authors in his playwriting scheme. His chief desire was to see the theater come into its own as an interpreter of regional life.

The State Fair country theater, I am sure, led Professor Drummond to contemplate long-range plans for regional development in New York State.

It was three weeks after I arrived in Ithaca before I encountered Professor Drummond. During that time I noticed that students spoke of him with awe, sometimes with downright fear. When I finally met him I could see why. He is an immense man with great shoulders and a proud head. He holds his entire body more erect than any man I have ever seen. He usually wears a hat that is turned up a little at the brim and crushed down in an indescribable fashion on the crown. Behind his glasses are wonderfully alive eyes that can freeze you or warm you according to the mood of the man.

One day I was nervously waiting for him in his office when he entered slowly but with sure movements. He got his chair into exactly the position he wanted, sat down at his desk, and began straightening out some papers. Then he opened a drawer and looked for several moments among some files. He got up from his desk and went to his bookcase. He pondered over several volumes, finally took one down and laid it on the corner of his desk. He said, "Oh, dear!" in a sudden expulsion of all the breath in his lungs, and then he sat down. Finally he sighed, looked at me with a kind of glare that had a great deal of distaste in it, and said: "Well, what do you think I can do for you?"

I said, quite timidly, and a little pompously: "I want to work with you and for you, Professor Drummond. I am interested in a theater that will grow from the hearts and the everyday lives of the American people. I want to learn from you how such a theater may be encouraged."

He glanced at me quickly, then began to fiddle with some more papers on his desk. He picked up a letter and read it through carefully. I could see the date on the letter; it was about six years old. I thought that his careful reading of this old letter was eccentric, but later he made me understand that a fine letter, with all the ideas clear and the prose sturdy, was something to keep on one's desk and refer to and reread many times just for the sheer tonic of it. That was probably why Professor Drummond was reading the letter. Anyway, he finally put the letter down and said, "Well, I dunno," and began drumming the top of the desk with his fingers.

I got up to leave, thinking that he wanted to get rid of me. He let me get as far as the door of his office, then he said, "Oh, Gard!"

I turned around and he was holding out the book he had taken from the shelf. "Have you read Carl Carmer's *Listen for a Lonesome Drum?*"

I said, "No, sir."

"Well, you might look it over. Pretty good."

I took the book, thanked him, and got to the door again. He called me back several times to chat about seemingly inconsequential matters. I was puzzled when I left his office; yet I had the feeling that I had met a great man; that he knew a great deal about me; that I did not know anything, really, about him.

At Kansas I had learned the fascination of ideas. At Cornell I learned, among other things, the rigors of discipline. This was an ordeal by fire under perhaps the most terrifying master in America.

The method of this amazing man was so complex and painful that the agonized student did not really know what was happening to him until things had happened. Little by little, with stinging rebuke, calculated irony, or with fabulous, small whips of rhetoric he stripped the student of practically every bit of encumbering ambition, pride, eagerness, and initiative. With students who could take it, his method was directly brutal. He might provoke the student with the most amazing accusations, defamations, and deflations, and when the poor student rose at last in desperate self-defense he would never be able to get a defense underway. Little vanities and conceits were either tossed out of the window or the student, in endeavoring to keep them, submitted himself to the most horrible tortures. He was often stood up before his classmates and flayed until, hot with shame and futile anger, he was sent forth to study himself.

All this torment was of course hitched to learning. The man was so mature, so worldly wise, that he pushed no one beyond the absolute limits of endurance, and the whole result of the Drummond ordeal was not only a vast respect and affection for the man but was also an increased desire for the ferreting out of truth and a new and stimulating liking for scholarship. For, after stripping the student down to nothing, Professor Drummond, slowly, and with the utmost patience, began to build him up again. This was almost an unconscious process. It might begin with a single "Good!" scribbled on the front leaf of a paper over which the student had spent his blood; yet so meager had been the Drummond praise until this point and so vast the Drummond integrity that the student grabbed this tiny straw of praise and wandered about in an ecstatic daze showing the paper to his friends and truly believing that he must have written a minor masterpiece.

If the student were acting in one of the masterly theater productions that Professor Drummond directed in the Cornell University theater, a note written on a slip of cheap, yellow paper might be handed to the student by the stage manager. The note might say merely, "Smith, 1 per cent improved!" and the student would strive with all his might to make the part 2 per cent better the next night, just to get another one of those priceless scribbles. Professor Drummond could inspire superhuman feats of intellect and strength with a word or a gesture, simply because the student felt that a word or a gesture from Professor Drummond that was not ridicule or debasement meant that Professor Drummond considered the student worthy of some small respect. It was a kind of signal that a small part of the student's self-respect might be assumed again.

Professor Drummond was a man with a volcano burning inside of him. When the fire burned bright he was incomparable, wonderful, brilliant. He could tell stories beyond any living master of story-craft, or he could hold a group of keen intellectuals spellbound. When the fire burned low, however, he was grumpy, full of clichés and apt to complain woefully of his ills. He was, in other words, extremely human, with most of the human frailties that beset all of us. Some of his frailties seemed rather larger than ordinary, perhaps, because he was rude on occasion when rudeness did not actually appear necessary. He made little attempt to pay back the ordinary social obligations in the conventional way, much to the distress of hostesses who complained that he should certainly know better or that he was ungrateful for the attentions heaped upon him. He paid little heed to the complaints about his misbehavior, but he found his own way to return kindness.

With students he was training, however, he was completely generous. He almost always paid the check at restaurants or bars. If a fellow achieved any sort of respect in Professor Drummond's eyes, then suddenly that fellow might be left to pay the check, and if he went out with Professor Drummond for food or drinks thereafter, he had better look out for himself. If a student came to Professor Drummond full of real trouble, he would be taken behind a closed door where no one might hear or suspect and be given excellent advice or helped with money. God knows how many Cornell students survived through the opening of Professor Drummond's pocketbook or how many men and girls told him their involved private troubles.

The general principles upon which he taught had great

bearing on my feeling for places and for theater in relation to places. His principles were basic to the broad approach to theater I have tried to develop. This partial list of the Drummond principles is my list, not Professor Drummond's. I am sure that he never drew up any such list as this:

A man must have within himself the seeds of self-improvement.

He must not fear introspection; he must have an abiding faith in what he believes.

He must bring forth the best that is in himself in order to rightly understand himself and his works in relation to other men and to the arts.

He must respect knowledge and be able to discern and use wisely the best sources of learning.

He must respect people and must carry always a learning attitude toward any man.

He must respect place and the flavor of the countryside and develop fearlessly and poetically his regard for a familiar scene and remembered event.

He must be broad in outlook; he must not be a man pedantically interested only in the narrow, dusty corners of knowledge but one who is willing to carry ideas to the people everywhere.

He must see theater as a reflection of man; he must see drama not as a toy, a bauble, a plaything but as an instrument sensitive to all the sights and sounds of mankind.

He must have ideals but no rigid fixity of mind that might make him argumentative, impatient, and intolerant of other ideas or ideals.

He must savor and try the temper of America and acquire a thorough knowledge and understanding of her peoples, traditions, figures of speech, and historical trends.

Often the ideas that one discerned in Drummond's teachings of what a man ought to be and do were taught in the very awesome and wondrous presence of nature on top of a New York State hill, perhaps after a dinner at the Taughannock House, the Dryden Hotel, or some other country inn when the August northern lights were softly rolling the skies and the great valleys and wide stretches of the New York State land were mystically and faintly discernible. Then he was at his best. He would stand on the hill, a landmark himself, and point out the interesting places and scenes. At these times he was a poet, and the forgotten roads, the wild places where few persons went, the hulk of an old steamboat sunk in Cayuga Lake were the substance and subject of his poetry. He loved central New York above anything on earth. From him I learned a love for this soft, mysterious country of hidden drums and slender, deep lakes and long valleys.

If Professor Drummond liked any of the things I was doing at Cornell he gave little sign. During the first months I got no little notes on yellow paper, except the kind that made me wish to crawl into a hole somewhere and die. I wrote plays and passed them to him, and he passed them back with many suggestions, often, for revision, but with no indication whatever that the plays were good in idea.

Professor Drummond's famous course "66" was the place where students came face to face with dramatic theory. Wide reading was required. Searching questions addressed to the students brought them one by one to the front of the class to sit at the master's right hand where he demonstrated how feebly they grasped the meaning of Aristotle, Komisarjevsky, Gordon Craig, Evreinov, Jacques Copeau, Appia, Bakshy, and Jourdain. I did not comprehend then how greatly I was to rely on the ideas of some of these writers in my later work. Hardly a day goes by now that the *Poetics* of Aristotle does not come up somehow or that connections cannot be made with the theory of lighting advanced by Appia or with the theater-in-life idea of Evreinov. It seems logical to me now that if regional drama standards are to rise it must be through an acquaintance at least with the best thinkers in the field of dramatic and aesthetic theory.

I made scenery in the theater and helped work it for all the plays. Because I always spoke in tones so very low and so indistinct that many persons had great trouble in hearing me, Professor Drummond called me "the whispering Mister Gard" and generally worked on my sensibilities until along in the Spring, without any warning whatever, he suddenly cast me in the character of Captain Shotover in Shaw's *Heartbreak House.*

This part calls for considerable skill in acting; the character is a complex one; and the part calls also for a voice fitting a retired sea captain. I was numb with terror. Yet such was the personality and influence of Drummond that he drew a voice out of me. Little by little, with the most infinite care, my voice grew in volume and projection, and little by little Professor Drummond moved his rehearsal chair back in the auditorium. I had no idea, really, what was happening until suddenly during a dress rehearsal my curiosity as to whether or not I could be heard grew too strong to be contained. "Professor Drummond," I bellowed, "can you hear me?"

There was a short pause while the sound bounced between the theater walls, and there was a longer pause during which Professor Drummond seemed to be lost in a kind of wonderful self-admiration. "Gad!" he said, "the whispering Mister Gard has spoken!" And this was about the only comment I received. But in all the long years of our subsequent and comradely professional relationship I do not think anything I ever did pleased him half as much as my development of a voice. I developed a voice simply because Professor Drummond willed that I should.

Yet, despite the fact that this small encouragement came my way, I grew more and more despondent, because it seemed to me that I was slipping backward, that the freshness of the idea about theater I thought I had when I left Kansas was no longer good or powerful. I was conscious only of needing to know so much and of so often seeming to find myself incapable of mastering the disciplines of graduate study that Professor Drummond insisted upon. So I sank lower and lower, developed a very nasty disposition, and was on the point of chucking the whole Cornell affair. The Cornell library chimes that had seemed so lovely to me early in the year now seemed to symbolize the University's apartness from life. I was tired of books. I wanted somehow to be merged into a more direct life stream. I hungered for open country, machines, men, animals. I believed that I had failed to find at Cornell any semblance of what I had come there to find—sympathetic and expert guidance toward the kind of theater of people that I had dedicated myself to work for.

Then, too, I had written a play that I liked, based on experiences I had had, and I was proud of this work. Professor Drummond had been holding it for nearly three months, and I felt that he must have thought it pretty bad stuff. All-in-all, I was down in the dumps. So one morning in May I went to Professor Drummond's office and told him

I guessed I had better be leaving Cornell. There was silence for a while; then he said, "Who told you to go?"

"Nobody."

"Better think it over."

He obviously had more to say, and I sat and waited. "Better think it over," he repeated. "I've been working very hard for the past two months to get you a fellowship with the Rockefeller Foundation. I want you to stay and help me start a new theater project in New York State. Maybe we can learn something about stories and people and theater that will help the whole idea of American theater along."

I sat very still. The reversal was terrific. I felt like laughing; then I felt a great wave of affection for this big man who knew so exactly what to do. And I understood in that moment that everything I had experienced at Cornell, every debasement of soul, every moment of torment, every indication of faint praise, every book I had read had been calculated to make me a better worker, a more worthy worker for a larger scheme.

He said: "I had just this morning received a wire from Dr. David Stevens in New York. He would like to have you come down to the Foundation and see him."

I stood up. "I would like to stay at Cornell if you really think I could help."

He shoved the play I was so proud of across his desk to me. "I was going to send you back your play this morning. I'm sorry I kept it so long."

I took the play and saw that he had written on the cover: "This play has a real flavor of America that I like tremendously. Come and see me. I have some news for you."

That evening I dined with Professor Drummond at the Ithaca Hotel. The check lay between us on the table for a long time. Finally I picked it up.

There is good land for farming in New York State, but most of the hill land is poor. Its top soil has been spoiled by careless growing, and the wild growth is creeping back. In the hills I found people from Oklahoma, Dakota, and Kansas who had fled to the East, away from the sting and filter of the dust. I saw how the hope had faded from these Western faces and how thin the crops they grew looked against the futile soil. I knew many of these families, and in the time that I knew them they seemed to drift away, one by one, leaving the hills lonely and without laughter.

For two months I soaked up the sights and sounds and the lore of New York State. I walked among the grape harvesters working on the steep hillsides above the long, narrow lakes. I cherished the picture of the foliage greens and harvest purples and the bright kerchiefs of the pickers. I sat with old men and heard their stories of past days. I met a wonderful professor from Cornell—a jolly fat man with a bald head and thick glasses. He sang the ballads of the land in a beautiful tenor voice, and when he knew that I was not going to write a book and use his material he told me masterful stories of New York State people and places.

I traveled all over the state. I met the people everywhere. I heard yarns about outlaws, bogeymen, farmers, pretty teachers, milk strikes, revival preachers, murderers, buried treasures, race horses, haunts, wondrous cures, and probably hundreds of other things. I sat in crossroads stores, hung over back fences, sat on front steps, milked cows, chewed the fat with the boys at the Spit and Whittle Club at Dryden, New York, and generally engaged in any occupation that allowed for yarn swapping. It was a happy time, and all through it Professor Drummond left me quite alone. Then one day he sent for me.

I went to his office with acute hesitation. Surveying my

activities I could not actually see that I had accomplished much. I felt that what I had seen and heard from the people had point in the sort of theater I imagined might spring from the land and the people, but I feared that Professor Drummond would ask me what books I had read, and I knew that I could not impress him. I expected the ax to fall.

I went into his office. He was writing, and he wrote for a while. Then he said, "Well, what have you been doing?"

I blushed and said, "Professor Drummond, I have been hearing stories and swapping lies."

"Where have you been?"

I named two or three dozen places I had visited. He said, "Well, there's plenty to do."

"Yes, sir."

"You think this floating around is worthwhile?"

"Yes, sir."

He said, "I was hoping you would think so. It's the only way you ever get the real flavor of the region." He stood up. "I have my car downstairs. Let's go!"

Touring the central New York countryside with Professor Drummond was like being blind and suddenly seeing the unbelievable beauty of sunlight and landscape. It was like that, yet something more, for he seemed to endow the land with a mystic poetry that sprang from his sensitiveness to present and past. There seemed no back road that Professor Drummond did not know. There was no hilltop he had not seen and no valley to which he attached no mysterious significance. The land, the people, the winds and rains all added up to a complete and satisfying unity for Professor Drummond, and so perfectly were these things reflected in his observations that word pictures dropped from his lips like impressionistic paintings.

Sometimes at night we would stand on a high place called

Butcher Hill from which all the land seemed to drop away to the North, to Lake Ontario, and then all the grumpiness, all worldly disillusion, the entire burden of life rolled away from him and he would speak for hours of the legend and of the folklore of places.

As such talk went on and on, broken occasionally by excursions to eat wonderful country food in corners of the land that only Professor Drummond seemed to know, I fell more and more under the spell of the country. It was a bewitchment that stimulated fantasies of imagination and sapped creative strength. I lived every day as a mad kind of excursion, breathing into a subconscious creativeness everything I saw and felt and heard. I had no inclination to work. I rebelled against writing. The whole state was my stage, but I could not formalize the product of my senses into characters that were like life, nor could I merge the fantasy of ideas that rushed through me into the tight packets that were the plots and themes of plays.

There was a sudden stop to this madness. I visited a county fair one day at Morris, New York. In one tent a stage had been set up, and the tent was packed with people. They were old folks and young folks and farmers and city people. They were eager; they were in festival mood. They wanted theater, excitement. They wanted hearty humor, dramatic picture, furious impact. They had a right to expect such things, for the plays they were there to see were billed as being from rural life. Rural life to these people meant kindness, neighborliness, strong appreciations of land and wind and color. Rural life meant the strength of outdoor bodies, the good simplicities of food and work and neighborhood fun. Rural life meant songs and games, stout problems in land economics, education for the kids, and a savor of the things that were essentially part of their own place. Rural life meant a tiny thread of loneliness, too, and maybe a very occasional breath of tragedy. Rural life meant the neighborhood arts of careful canning, weaving, quilting. Rural life meant everything these people knew and understood—the whole goodness of their lives.

The plays were billed as rural life plays, and they were played by local young people and adults. When they began, I, too, was eager, for I had seen the broad, free life of American country places. But when the plays were over, I looked at the faces around me. Anticipation had turned to a solemn disinterestedness. There was no laughter, no tears—only definite exodus that was filled with vague irritation. There was no festival here—only the departure of an initial eagerness that had seemed very precious and deep.

The reason seemed to me then quite clear. The plays were not rural plays. True, they were supposedly set in the country, but their characters had no relation to the kind of country life I and the folks around me knew. They had very little relation to life anywhere. They were dreary in tone; they were filled with bad jokes lifted from a collection read somewhere or heard on somebody's radio. The characters were stereotypes of real people. They maundered on and on about poor housewives who had no pianos or washing machines or they talked in clichés about cruel fathers who would not let sons or daughters have boy or girl friends or join 4-H clubs. They hinted at shotgun weddings, and they dusted off the old conflicts between the farm and the city. They sawed back and forth on the fringes of obscene jests about the farmer's daughter and the city slicker.

I remember thinking, as I walked out of the tent into the autumn sunlight, that this was the only real theater the people in this place knew, that there could be only failure and disillusionment in such plays, and that such plays were evil and would kill any art that might grow here. I paused as I thought of the rural life that I knew in Kansas, of the wheat fields, of the mighty machines biting through the yellow grain, of the harvest parties, and of the wild singing and dancing. I thought of New York State grape pickers singing on a steep hillside, of a farm mother holding a little child against her breast, of the terror of a violent storm, and of faces full of suffering from pain and lost crops. As I stood thinking, the great Butternut Valley that was all around Morris turned golden in the afternoon light. I looked at the hills, and suddenly my spirit was filled and lifted with a clear knowledge. I knew that there must be plays of the people filled with the spirit of places, and my aimless activities assumed meaning. I felt the conviction then that I have maintained since—that the knowledge and love of place is a large part of the joy in people's lives. There must be plays that grow from all the countrysides of America, fabricated by the people themselves, born of their happiness and sorrow, born of toiling hands and free minds, born of music and love and reason. There must be many great voices singing out the lore and legend of America from a thousand hilltops, and there must be students to listen and to learn, and writers encouraged to use the materials.

The next day I went back to Ithaca and sought out Professor Drummond. When I told him what I had been thinking, he said, "I'm glad some of the ideas have been jelling for you." And we sat down at his table and made some plans for a playwriting project for the state of New York.

Professor Drummond said that there were probably a lot of people in New York State who wanted to write plays. He said that we would try to get in touch with these people and that the result of our efforts might be such a bloom of country-grown plays that the entire state would enjoy the aroma of up-country life. He said that outside the University playwriting classes, there had been almost no attempt to get the people to think and write dramatically of themselves. When I asked him how many people might try writing a play, he refused to estimate, but his eyes warmed up, and I knew that he was dreaming of a large number and that both he and I were hoping for sensational results. I suppose that when we were alone and remembered the soul-tormenting rigors of playwriting, we had some serious doubts, but these doubts did not in the least deter us from trying. Indeed, so great was our faith in the people, so real was our dream of a people's theater, and so confident was our belief in the goodness of the folklore and life of the region that it was almost as though some old central New York Indian god had endowed us with this dream as a special mission.

This dream soon became a reality. Our first task was the preparation of a letter which we circulated widely through the mails and got printed in papers and magazines. The letter pointed out that many persons, young and old, should be interested in writing a play about New York State, that as soon as good plays became available they would be circulated throughout the state, and that anyone might receive advice and perhaps assistance by writing to Professor Drummond or me at Cornell University. The letter stated also that we were eager to get in touch with folks who might have some good ideas for plays so that we might pass these ideas on to possible authors and that we wished people would get in touch with us who might like to present some of these plays in their own communities.

Perhaps Professor Drummond knew what we were letting

ourselves in for, but I did not. All I had was enthusiasm and a capacity for work. I needed both, for immediately our mail overflowed the boxes. There were letters scattered everywhere. Such a good thing as a secretary to help handle this spate of potential culture was a part of our dream that we had not dealt with. But every letter was answered, and the ideas, the encouragement, the offer of free publicity, good will, even love, made us believe that maybe, just maybe, we had touched a popular chord. The letters were filled, some of them, with a sort of fresh hope, as though a farmer or a housewife or a grocer or a country doctor after years of working and thinking and dreaming suddenly saw a chance to speak of the things he lived by. Some of the letters were neatly typed. Others were written in illegible scrawls with soft lead pencils. A few were written in foreign languages—in French, German, and Finnish.

There were letters that I remember particularly well. One was from a farmer's wife in Cattaraugus County, New York, Mrs. D. H. Chambers. She wrote that she was much interested in writing a play about the Dutch Hill war, a rather comic incident of the land troubles of the 1840's which took place on her farm. She wrote: "I have never expressed myself in the dramatic form, but I am willing to learn. I have a brother who has been fairly successful in dramatic writing and you may possibly have heard of him. His name is Maxwell Anderson."

There was a letter from a fellow up in the Adirondacks who caused me great concern. He wrote:

Was reading this day of your playwriting announcement in the paper. I wish I had until July to submit my contribution. However, I plan, or want to send, or make a contribution. I know a lot of women folks will try writing plays, and I want to try just to spite the women. I don't like the idea of giving women more chance or call for action over men, as women are not only first in nearer all things but has the world with a fence around it.

Now, has the story got to be submitted in play form, or will a story do the trick? Just what do you call a one-act play? I wish I could get a specimen copy just in case I must submit full form. Will be glad to receive any assistance, and I am obliged to ask you to hurry.

There is not a preponderance of women characters in my stories, and only some have several characters. Do you require many characters, or will as few as several be enough? Please explain matters out to me. I want to find out what you want, if I can. Will a one-act play permit of more than one continuous scene or scenery? How many or how few words would you say would suffice? Please tell me what constitutes a one-act play so that I can tell at a glance what it is like. A stamp is enclosed for reply. Such envelopes as I have are misfits. Don't see how I can send you the usual envelope, sorry.

P.S. What shall I write about?

This mountain man never wrote a play, though he sought and received plenty of information. But as the personal mail got less bulky, our boxes began to fill with larger envelopes, brown ones with first class postage, containing plays of every sort. These we read over and sorted out and mulled over, and soon again I was engaged in a tremendous correspondence, teaching playwriting by mail, offering encouragement, criticizing or praising what seemed hundreds of manuscripts. Overnight my job became almost completely office work, though I had no office and the manuscripts were apt to be spread over tables in any corner I might find temporarily vacant. Then people began to drift into Ithaca to see us about their work. A woman from Buffalo brought her play about Underground Railroad days at Niagara Falls. An old man with long gray hair came to see me with a jolly little play about antique collectors. A machinist from around

Rochester brought two scripts about workmen. A girl from the western part of the state brought her play about grape pickers. A thin young man came with his play about a schoolhouse that was painted in big red and white checks. (One faction in the community had once wanted the schoolhouse painted red, the rest of the community wanted it painted white. They had compromised.) Folks came from all points of the compass with plays that reflected many facets of regional life.

There was excitement in meeting these people and talking with them. They were new signs of an art expression that seemed to be springing up joyously everywhere, and so infectious was the spirit of this simple movement that Professor Drummond and I were caught up in it. We began to write, too, and several plays were our joint efforts. One of the plays I wrote grew out of an incident I had witnessed while wandering in the hill country of New York State. One evening I was on top of a high hill and I saw a thin old man sitting under a lone cedar tree strumming on a guitar. After a while he began to sing a slow song about a sad wind in a willow tree. I listened to him sing, and when he finished the song a wind came over the hill and brushed through the cedar. Then the old man stood up with a dream on his face and made a speech to an old friend who was lying in a cemetery grave a piece down the hillside.

"Tom," the old man said, "I can see you over yonder astanding up beside your stone. I expect you recall like me when these hillsides was green with crops and the young fruit trees tender with spring blooms. You kin see them light yellow colors in April and smell the earth new turned.

"Looka, yonder, Tom, down the line of the hill there, see them timbers sticking up out of the long grass? That was the Ervay house and the Barnes house was down below it. Who's that beside ye, Tom? Lucy, I expect. And is that Lally over in the corner holding her baby?

"Everybody is gone off the hill but me, Tom. Young pine trees is growing everyplace now. Recall my place that was so fine set against the far side of the hill? Them white columns on the front porch was good to see. Could see them from a mile away, and my fields back the house spread with new wheat.

"The state's went and bought my farm, Tom, and they're making a woods out of it. The land's wore out, they say. Yesterday the mail stopped comin'.

"Nothin' but the wind left. There's wind ablowing through the old cedar, and it's the night wind over the graves."

The old man put his guitar under his arm and walked down the hill. He lay down with his head up against one of the stones. The old man took his place, with his lyric speech and guitar, in a play that symbolized the New York wild country.

From the famous frontier preacher the Rev. Lorenzo Dow we fabricated a play in which the Reverend raised the devil from a flour barrel in a settler's cabin, and thereby converted the entire settlement of Schoharie, New York. We wrote radio scripts about the old 999, the New York Central engine that set a world's speed record, and about Colonel Tom Meachem of Oswego and his big cheese— biggest ever made. We fixed the frontier propensity for tall yarn spinning into a play called "Bill Greenfield's Legend."

We tried out a lot of new plays in the Cornell University theater and slowly began to build up some really actable scripts. Then we decided that we must write a long show that would set the temper of the thing we were trying to do. We hoped that such a play might draw the attention of the state to our project. For a subject we turned more or less naturally to one of the greatest of the New York State tales, the famous yarn of the Cardiff Giant.

Almost anyone, these days, knows the story of this hoax that took place in 1869 in the little village of Cardiff when a great stone man was uncovered by well diggers on the farm of "Stubby" Newell. The discovery of this figure aroused thousands of simple, God-fearing folk to fever pitch, for they believed the stone giant to be a religious manifestation, one of the Biblical giants of Genesis. Great scientists, too, were hoodwinked for a time and considered the find to be one of the important paleological discoveries of the age.

The hoax was actually fabricated by a cigar maker from Binghamton named George Hull. One day George was arguing with a preacher in Fort Dodge, Iowa. The preacher claimed loudly that there "were giants in those days" and Hull maintained there were not. The preacher did George down in the debate, and George went out and hired men to cut a great block of gypsum out of the river bank at Fort Dodge. Then George shipped this block of stone to Chicago where he got a tombstone cutter to carve the block into the form of a giant. George got the giant to Binghamton, then shipped it by wagon to Cardiff, the wagon traveling at night for secrecy.

George was first cousin to "Stubby" Newell. Stubby let George bury the giant on his farm. In the dead of night the deed was done. The giant lay buried for a year. Grass grew over the spot secluded under the shadow of a great hill. One day Stubby hired a couple of men to dig a well right on the spot where the giant lay buried. When the men encountered a great stone foot and dug a little more to see

39

what manner of creature lay buried there, they both tossed their shovels and ran to the village to spread the news.

In a few days Newell's farm was tramped over by seething humanity. A tent was erected above the giant's grave, and Hull, Newell, and company, which included by this time the famous Homer, New York, banker, David Hannum (later known fictionally as Harum), were coining money at the rate of 5 per cent on $3,000,000!

Everybody wanted to see the giant. Certain ladies viewing the sculptured wonder fainted dead away, for Hull's tombstone carver had left nothing to the imagination. A dentist, Dr. Boynton, pronounced the work to be of Caucasian, not Indian, origin and called it the noblest work of art that had come down to us. The Board of Regents of the state of New York came to view the colossus, bearing with them insurance in the words of the state geologist, Dr. Hall, who called the giant the "most remarkable object brought to light in this country deserving of the attention of archeologists."

And so it went. Preachers basing sermons on the giant gleaned converts like falling chaff. One fool from the Yale Divinity School identified the giant as a Phoenician idol brought to this country several hundred years before Christ. P. T. Barnum, recognizing the giant as a magnificent showpiece, offered to buy it for sixty thousand dollars, and when he was refused, went off to New York to make a duplicate. He displayed it as the only authentic Cardiff Giant.

Professor Marsh of Yale at last exposed the hoax for what it was—a crude and recently carved block of gypsum, something which President Andrew D. White of Cornell had maintained from the first.

While Professor Drummond and I were speculating about the Cardiff Giant as a potential dramatic subject, a dreamer from the south came to visit us at Ithaca. This was Paul Green, who long before had caught a vision of a people's theater, and who had been ever since working toward that end with Professor Koch of North Carolina University.

This tall man with the sensitive face and deep eyes made a profound impression on me. His plays were pointed out as the foremost regional dramatic expression in America. He spoke simply, yet like a poet, and everything in the earth and sky and of men had a philosophic meaning for him. He spent long hours talking with me. When he heard the story of the giant he began to grin and get excited and to walk up and down. He said the yarn demonstrated the universality of human folly, and he insisted that Professor Drummond and I start writing the play immediately.

So one day in the early Spring we drove up to Cardiff, up Highway 11 that runs north from Cortland to Syracuse, and we paused a little while on a great fill that the glaciers left across the Onondaga Valley like a high wall. We looked down the valley flats, across the salt well derricks, toward the little town of Cardiff near which the giant once lay. The valley was quiet and mysterious, with the hill they call Bear Mountain shadowing it from the west. It was a scene to inspire awe. Several years later, Professor Drummond writing the introduction to the published version of the drama, *The Cardiff Giant*, remarked:

The traveler south of Syracuse along Route 11 at close of day will sense mystery rising with the mile-long shadows from the great valley at Cardiff and with night coming down the dark slope of Bear mountain to the west, or off the star-crowned hills of Pompey to the east—mystery which could cause him to think some wonder might come upon us there, and he would, maybe, *believe*, as did Onondagans of the sixties.

For the Indians well knew this valley and these hills as places of old mystery: stone giants clanking through the underground;

great men of old striding across the hills; gigantic Indian prophets of centuries gone who had foretold the coming of the white men, and who had prophesied that they themselves, after death, would again be seen by their peoples.

The earlier whites actually exhumed bones of huge, prehistoric men along the hills of Pompey, and later where the first roads and the railways edged into the rocks on their routes into Canastota or Cazenovia! Mystery in the old days had possessed this land of solemn and rugged beauty; and so now from our "joy in believing" in a wonder, even the "American Goliath" is not perhaps so remote from some of us.

We found an old man in Cardiff, Mr. Nichols, who lived alone in a shack. He was the son of one of the fellows who had dug the well and uncovered the giant's foot. Mr. Nichols had seen the giant lying in its grave, and he had some yellowed photographs of the scene and the wonder. He took us to the exact spot where the hoax had taken place. From him we got the atmosphere and the flavor of the event. We found other old-timers who remembered songs that were sung at the revival meetings or who had poems that had been written to commemorate the find. We discovered relatives of Stubby Newell, and little by little we assembled a fine body of working materials.

Such materials included, in addition to the items described, notes made from the newspapers of the period, the *Syracuse Journal* and the *Ithaca Journal*, especially, from articles in magazines describing the wonder, and from actual statements gleaned from published lectures by various personalities involved. We also dug a bit into the backgrounds of Stubby Newell and George Hull, and we did extensive reading relating to the topics of the times and to the state of New York crops and climate in 1869. In other words, we assembled a fairly complete body of information pertaining generally to the region in the particular year we wished to set the drama.

During our work collecting materials, we discussed the form of the play. We believed that the play must be flexible in form to allow for the inclusion of many scenes and numerous characters. We wanted to draw a merry picture of country life in New York State with its color and variety—including the social "bees," the rural school, the church picnics, the political argufiers, and all the rest. To do this, we knew that we must think more in terms of a "show" than of a strictly plotted play. Therefore, with the excellent models of the ancient Chinese theater, the "living newspaper" dramas of the Federal Theater, and the newly produced *Our Town* before us we conceived a New York State show.

One critic, Professor Henry A. Myers of the Cornell English department, thought that we had been successful. He wrote in the Cornell *Alumni News* as follows:

> *The Cardiff Giant* will long serve as a model for advocates of native drama. It deserves, however, to be judged in the larger category of true comedy. In keeping with the homely simplicity of central New York in 1869, the authors see themselves as putting on a show rather than as presenting a play. They have done both. Rich as *The Cardiff Giant* is in spectacle, excitement and incidents that make a good show, it is fully as charged with the significance that makes a good play. The chorus of school-girls, the canal men, and the State Board of Regents, the showmen and farmers are the very stuff of which laughter is made, but in the laughter and behind it is the revelation of the human spirit through the medium of language.

I got up a first draft of the play which seemed pretty good to me, but Professor Drummond said: "Gard, this is too long. We'll have to cut it." And then he began to work on the play. He proved that he was a true lover of New York State and her stories, for he lengthened the play, added characters, scenes, and generally filled the whole thing with his intimate understanding of the people, their language, their music and poetry. The final draft of *The Cardiff Giant* had ninety-eight speaking parts. In the first production in the Cornell University theater I played nine parts myself. When the curtain rose to an enthusiastic crowd of New York Staters and the Narrator was on the stage saying, "You gotta imagine yer back in 1869; that's when the hoax jelled—in October, '69!" it was as if the spirit of central New York State had come alive.

And in the very first scene the folks all began to go to Cardiff to see the giant, and the Erie canallers sang their famous song:

> We was forty miles from Albany,
> Forget it I never shall,
> What a terrible time we had one night
> On the E-ri-e Canawal!

Politicians, Farmers, Merchants, Professors, Indians, rich men, poor men, beggermen, dogs! And the preachers began preachin', and the ladies of the Methodist, Free Methodist, Presbyterian, Baptist, Hard Shell, Spiritualist and all the other churches began singin' revival hymns, and Dave Harum, P. T. Barnum, Bob Ingersoll, the Board of Regents of the State of New York, the Bloomer Women, and the Yale professors all got on stage at once yelling that the giant was an honest-to-God sign from on high! Yes, sir, in the first scene there was a lot going on, but there was more to come, with the giant lyin' in his grave there on the stage, and crowds of people milling around and demonstrating lots of kinds of human folly!

When the audiences saw the big show they went away thinking that the New York State Plays project was sure off to a good start, and some of them went home and did some thinking about York State and sent us a lot of good yarns.

I can still feel the central New York State land calling me. When I close my eyes, the patchwork hillsides across the deep valleys are as vivid to me as though I stood on the Cornell campus on a May morning and looked west toward Mecklinburg. I might have lived and dreamed forever in the Finger Lakes country if it had not been for the war. But suddenly one day, there it was, and the course of our creative project in New York State was instantly altered. There was writing, yes, but it was frenzied writing on wartime themes, and when we looked about the land, there were no longer home-grown plays on country stages. Sadly we admitted that the dream must wait, and for me, indeed, the York State project is only a green memory. I have never lived in New York State since.

There were many ideas that I took away from Cornell. Most of these ideas were simply a part of the maturing of other, larger ideas and not definable in themselves. But the large ideas about regional theater that I took away were definable. Reduced to general terms they are these: A concept of theater must be broad enough to include many things. The traditional materials of the region, at least those having possible literary significance, must be assembled. Writers must be encouraged throughout the region. The people of the region must be "let in" on what the regional drama project is trying to do and a friendly public attitude toward the project must be established. The university should take the rôle of leadership in the theater arts not only on the campus but throughout the region.

These ideas became very important to me as I moved to Alberta, Canada, to help develop the stuff of a native cultural expression in the province and then to Wisconsin where an idea of theater grew and developed into an idea of place more than merely geographical.

45

Chapter two

FRONTIER IN CANADA

It was in 1942 that Professor Frederick Koch of the University of North Carolina decided not to return to the Banff, Alberta, School of Fine Arts where he had been offering a course in playwriting, and I was invited to take his place. I well knew that I could never really fill Koch's position, but the opportunity to carry on his good work in native playmaking in Canada was challenging. I went to Banff, therefore, in the Summer of 1942, and was greatly impressed by the sincere desire of the founders and organizers of the School to establish the arts and crafts as a necessary part of regional life.

46

The Banff school gave me an opportunity for the first time to see the arts integrated in an educational program having wide regional significance. The art instructors, for example, were westerners eager to make their students and the public more sensitive to the western landscape. Walter Phillips, internationally famous wood engraver and water colorist, and George Glyde, a young, British-born painter of remarkable power, did most of the art teaching. These men loved the West and were able to transmit to me through their personal approaches to painting a new feeling and regard for western places.

I walked with Phillips in the mountains and on the prairies, and from him I learned to appreciate landscape through an artist's eyes. He gave me an expressive understanding of the sharp beauty of grain elevators seen against the varied prairie backdrops, of washes and coulees, and of the stark fronts of stores and dwellings in the western towns. Through Phillips I developed a concept of painting and theater working together toward fine regional interpretation.

I consider, looking back, that this idea of combining the art expressiveness of a region was one of the most valuable ideas I gained in this period. It is an idea that I have never lost sight of.

And from the Banff students, too, I learned much about the West. Many of the students were westerners, and there was no false sophistication, no awkward self-consciousness in their use of familiar materials. They dramatized their own experiences—such as, for instance, the experience of a country schoolteacher faced by all the problems that a young, and sometimes extremely pretty, schoolm'am faces in the Alberta countryside.

The students wrote colorful plays about rodeos, prairie

storms and mangled crops, drought and dust, or about aspects of the life of the many nationality groups or religious beliefs. (There are 417 faiths in Alberta.) The plays were sincere and often quite playable. The students approached their subjects with a theatrical point of view. The traits of their characters seemed intensely real because, usually, the characters were drawn from life, boldly and without undue restraint.

At the end of the Summer of 1942 I found myself with a deep desire to remain in the Canadian West. I proposed to University of Alberta officials that a project devoted to the collection of the folklore of Alberta might have worth as a preservative measure before many old-timers who had actually settled the Province passed out of the picture, carrying their valuable recollections with them. I thought that such a project might do something to help playwrights, too, for I sensed that there was a great mass of uncollected regional lore which might, if it were assembled, be of value to writers.

In 1943, the Rockefeller Foundation and the University of Alberta set up machinery to make my wish possible. I taught the Banff course again in the Summer of 1943, and then stayed on in Alberta with headquarters at the University in Edmonton. My title was Director of the Alberta Folklore and Local History Project. "Local history" was tacked on to satisfy certain antiquarians to whom folklore meant total disregard for fact. There were no public archives in Alberta, either, and the University authorities thought that an emphasis on local history might do something to hasten an archives building.

The title of the project worried me deeply. I had no illusions whatever about myself as an authority on folklore or local history. I was interested primarily in creative aspects of the work and in the opportunity to test some of the ideas I had taken away from New York. It is needless to say that what I dreaded might happen did happen. The publicity the project received was too good to pass by. My rôle was cast for me. I was to be a leader, a missionary, a preacher in a kind of great revival meeting built on the argument that Alberta was God's own country, had the best yarns, the biggest liars, and the most glamorous history and the strongest winds that God ever created.

I had made one public address at Banff in which I spoke about the folklore of New York State. Immediately I was called by the press an authority on folklore. The Director of the Banff School—who was also the Director of the University Extension Division—soon bore me off, wildly protesting, on a round of public addresses about the folklore of Alberta. I was terrified, for I had hardly had time to read more than a book or two about the province. But I scrabbled around, did a month's work in a couple of days, and clinging desperately to a small sheaf of notes, was hurried off in a cloud of thick Alberta dust to begin my recitals of places and people about whom I knew so little.

It was my first experience with the bitter truth that a wide popular interest in native literature may be stimulated by a leader of a project such as mine only through playing a rôle—in my case the rôle of a kind of missionary with the sole aim of working up public interest in a region. In a way, I did not realize what I was doing. I went from town to town, mouthing the same stories because I knew no others, asking people desperately for yarns, materials about themselves and their places, shaking hands, uttering absurd platitudes.

It was a false rôle, for I knew that I was actually not at all like the rôle I was playing. I desired quiet, time to think, time to write, time to savor the countryside, time to appreciate the great prairies, smell the clean air, climb the hills, and time to look for the forgotten trails and search for bits of rubble where the old frontier forts had stood.

But these times seldom came. As I accustomed myself to my rôle I developed techniques that must have made me more palatable to my audiences. I picked up a wide repertory of Alberta wit, sayings, tall tales, weather lore, and assorted local history. I spread these far and wide. The laughter in the places where I spoke became more genuine, and my presentations became less desperate, but inwardly I was no less self-conscious, no less rigid, for I felt ashamed that I could not offer the people a warmth that could only come with greater intimacy with the region.

But even the shame left, little by little. I developed mannerisms in keeping with the materials I used in my lectures. I was able to stand on a platform and will an audience into a liking for its local traditions, and I became able to shake the hundreds of stretching hands, utter proper words, and to escape at the right moment.

It was all a great act applauded by the press and approved to a certain extent by the people. Not all of them by any means, of course. There were the native Albertans and the transplanted Albertans, the ones transported from down east or from the old country, who muttered that everything I was doing could be done better by a Canadian. And they were right. Absolutely. But I was an authority by this time, and their remarks could not touch me. I was riding high. Sometimes the press called me the Mark Twain of Alberta, and my ego fattened. I was invited to all the service clubs—a terrific honor. I attended banquets of hardware merchants and stock dealers. I fraternized with brewery executives, ranching magnates, and political personalities. Once I rode to one of my engagements in a private railroad car on the Canadian Pacific Railroad and drank expensive liquor.

It was ballyhoo, a capitalization on a people's desire to know themselves and to understand themselves. They looked on me as an authority who was to lead them. At first I tried to say that I was no authority on anything, that I was a simple guy, really, and that I only wanted to do simple things such as appreciate the region simply and honestly and be accepted by the people as one of them, but I was always on the outside because the people were trying to see themselves through me. And I was a false window, a glass that gave back only a dim, shallow image.

However, I had never been so respectable, nor so respected. I had the magic words. The prettiest girls smiled at me, and the strongest men were eager to shake my hand. In my work in New York State it more often had been the women that crowded around me. But in Alberta it was the men. For it was a man's land, and the stuff I had to say concerned men in their battles against nature. For a while I forgot the creative ideas I had developed with Drummond. I was caught in a kind of holy regard for tall tales and yarns that had little relationship to art. The rôle I was playing was the great thing. And my rôle was effective. It was a tremendous weapon, really, which I did not quite know how to wield.

I suppose that every man or woman who sets out to do a piece of regional work requiring a wide variety of public contacts must play a rôle. He becomes a leader for a certain idea, and he develops techniques which he thinks work. Sometimes the rôle becomes a mask, as it did for me, but sometimes, if one waits long enough, the mask wears away, and one finds, curiously, that the mask and one's own face are the same thing. The outward qualms, the shames are gone then, but inward scars remain. With some people it is the scars on a nervous belly, and with others it is the removal of a spiritual part that will never grow again.

I have found that I have always had to play a rôle to get the best results in my work. The Alberta experiment was the first brush at it but not the last by any means. When one attempts to be champion of a cause or a region he has to become a kind of symbol, like a statue almost, of the thing he believes, the single idea he is striving to put over. A symbol, blessedly, is often an unfeeling thing, just as a statue is, and one does not really mind. The people themselves will endow the symbol with spirit and the statue with warmth and life in terms of their own concepts of such things. And the statue may stride (full of the life people have given him) along his way, knowing that everyone loves rôle-playing and that crowds of women, especially, will follow after and idolize the best rôle player, just so long as he does not enter their private lives.

I do not mean to sound bitter. I am not bitter at all. For of late years I have grown into my rôle and will never again struggle against it. My rôle has changed, modified, and perhaps flattened out my creative skills and swept away my nostalgia for a homeland, a place in which I could become an old-timer like the ones I heaped with laurels for their frontier manliness. I know that such nostalgia is not for me and will never haunt me again.

But between speeches and hand shaking in Alberta some solid work was going ahead. Looking back, I know that my tests of ideas in Alberta were extremely valuable to me later. And the things we tried to do to encourage a home-grown Alberta literature were satisfying to me. I confirmed, too, the idea that public relations is an essential part of regional work in the cultural arts. We had known that, vaguely, in New York State.

In 1938, when I chanced to enter the picture in New York it had become apparent to Drummond that to be successful the whole regional concept of drama must encompass objectives other than mere playmaking. First and most essential was a study of the region and of the native source-materials of the region with an eye toward the collection of an authentic body of material that might be wisely and creatively applied to the dramatic form. In fostering this idea Drummond had the coöperation of Harold W. Thompson, always an interested scholar of the American scene, who had already compiled a collection of New York State tradition. Drummond's scheme to employ a dramatist to scan the Thompson and other materials and to use them as a basis for plays brought me into the picture as a beginning student of the whole affair. The New York State Plays project, as I have already related, was subsequently conducted at Cornell with moderate success. Plays were written and dispensed to the people, with, however, little real result becoming known because World War II interrupted our work.

As we worked at Cornell, Drummond and I became increasingly aware that we must somehow help to create or encourage a popular consciousness of the themes and traditions of the state. Home-rooted plays, we believed, were often eyed suspiciously because the producers or the audience, or both, were not really informed about the places in which they lived, or at least had no deep affection for them. We realized that a sympathetic attitude toward place and tradition could not be developed through plays alone or through books or pamphlets we might write.

We knew that the radio, especially, and other public organs must somehow be used in solving the problem of arousing interest in the state or region.

In New York we found it extremely difficult to reach the state as a whole. New York can never be considered as a closely-knit cultural unit. It is broken into many regions, each containing what might be considered a basic culture or tradition. We attempted a haphazard New York State radio series of plays, but the war halted our efforts.

In Alberta the job looked easier. The people, I soon discovered, were familiar with a sort of common lore of the region and were sensitive to the literary materials of the region. In other words, the stories the Alberta folks liked to tell best were distinctly regional in that they dealt with rains, hails, droughts, chinook winds, dust, various industries like ranching, dry-farming, oil, or with the whole memory of the frontier, which is quite a force still.

In Alberta, for instance, in the earlier days it was fairly easy to accumulate a lot of money in one year. There were oil booms and land booms and large ranching and wheat ventures, some of which paid off. One of my favorite stories is of a rancher who rushed into a Calgary store one day to buy a fur coat for his wife. He was dressed in an old green bowler, ragged trousers, and boots with soles flapping loose. The clerk who waited on this strange individual hesitantly took a fifty-dollar coat from the rack, stated its price, and had the garment thrown instantly back at him. The clerk brought out a five-hundred-dollar coat, and the rancher threw it on the floor and wiped his feet on it. The clerk then timidly offered the best coat they had in the store—a thousand-dollar one—and this the rancher said he would take. He asked whether the store would take his personal check. When the store said "No," the rancher whipped a check for $100,000 out of his pocket. The check was made out to the rancher and was signed by Pat Burns, the biggest meat packer in the province. The rancher had sold Pat Burns some cattle that day. He asked the store to take the thousand out of the check.

But if the frontier can produce such happenings, the Alberta climate can produce others no less wonderful. In the heart of winter the mighty chinook arch may form in the west and a soft spring-like wind may come puffing over the prairies, melting the snow with temperature rises of as much as sixty or seventy degrees in an hour's time. And usually there is plenty of snow to melt. Take the year of the Big Snow, for instance, when the snow was so deep it covered all of Morley Church except the tip of the steeple. Morley is over on the Indian Reservation west of Calgary. The old-timers tell me that the Indians would ride to church on top of the crusted snow, tie their ponies to the tip of the steeple, and go down into the church through a tunnel. One Sunday the Indians were terribly surprised when they emerged from the church to find that a chinook wind had come, melted the snow, and had left their ponies dangling from the steeple. That was the year, the old-timers continue, that a character named Dave McDougall traveled to Calgary by sleigh. A chinook slipped up behind Dave, but by whipping his horses he was able to keep the front runners on snow. The back runners, according to legend, raised a tremendous dust storm.

In southern Alberta, where the really strong winds blow, folks are said to walk around permanently bent over at forty-five-degree angles from facing into it. A rancher friend of mine from Macleod told me that he kept a heavy log chain tied to a post in his yard. This was his wind gauge. When the chain blew out at an angle of about thirty degrees there was a breeze. When the chain stood out at right angles the rancher figured he better tell his wife to get the clothes in before a gale hit. When there was a good steady wind the rancher's three boys practiced chinning themselves on the chain.

Such imagination, surely (or so say the Alberta newspapers), can flourish only in a section where the frontier "feel" is still strong.

Yet, I was not insensible to the fact that in our efforts to establish a home-grown literature of Alberta the frontier, or the memory of it, might be a chief antagonist. The Canadian critic E. K. Brown had just published his excellent essay in which he had observed that the "powerful obstacle at present to the growth of a great literature is the spirit of the frontier, or its afterglow." According to Brown:

Most Canadians live at some distance from anything that could even in the loosest terms be known as a material frontier; but the standards which the frontier life applied are still current, if disguised. Books are a luxury on the frontier; and writers are an anomaly. On the frontier a man is mainly judged by what he can do to bring his immediate environment quickly and visibly under the control of society. No nation is more practical than ours; admiration is readily stirred, even more readily than south of the border, by the man who can run a factory, or invent a gadget or save a life by surgical genius. This kind of admiration is a disguised form of the frontier's set of values. No such admiration goes out to any form of the aesthetic or contemplative life. The uneasiness in the presence of the contemplative or aesthetic is to be ascribed to the frontier feeling that these are luxuries which should not be sought at a time when there is a tacit contract that everyone should be doing his share in the common effort to build the material structure of a nation. That a poem or a statue or a metaphysic could contribute to the fabric of a nation is not believed. In a gathering of ruminative historians and economists, speaking their mind one evening in Winnipeg years before the war was imminent, the unanimous opinion was that a destroyer or two would do more than a whole corpus of literature to establish a Canadian nationality. The dissent of two students of literature was heard in awkward silence. If there were any belief in the national value of art or pure thought, the strong desire of the frontiersman that what is being built should eclipse all that was ever built before would make a milieu for art and thought that would at the root be propitious.

In a disguised form of frontier life what function can the arts hold? They are at best recreative. They may be alternatives to the hockey match, or the whiskey bottle, or the frivolous sexual adventure as a means of clearing the mind from the worries of business and enabling it to go back to business refreshed. The arts' value as interpretation is lost in the exclusive emphasis on their value as diversion, and even their value as diversion is simplified to the lowest possible form—a work of art must divert strongly and completely. It must divert as a thriller or a smashing jest diverts, not as an elaborate and subtle romance or a complicated argument diverts. In a word, Canada is a nation where the best-seller is king, as it is on the frontier.*

One could certainly not write off Brown's theories. Indeed, looking backward to my boyhood in Kansas, I knew that much that he said had great point; yet I had convinced myself that the theater and allied arts could be in themselves a kind of frontier and that their development could be a challenging, dynamic kind of pioneering which ideally might lead toward great spiritual satisfaction for many North American people.

Perhaps the painters do not paint on the street corners of Canadian towns as they do in Paris. And, it is probably true that there are not nearly so many pictures by native artists hanging on the walls of homes in western Canada as there may be in Norway. But the fact of the matter is that

*E. K. Brown, *On Canadian Poetry* (Toronto: Ryerson Press, 1943), pp. 19–20.

a movement is under way right now in Canada and in the United States that may well overcome the best-seller complex that Brown rightly attributes to Canadians.

It is easy to point out that the frontier has left a hangover of the success complex to dull Canadian and American interest in home-grown literary and art products, and the results of the drive of the frontier are easy to see. Observe the mess of tanks, stacks, furnaces, and stinks that lie along Highway 12 as it runs into Chicago from the east. Or drive along the Mississippi as she curves south from Galena toward Davenport and witness the factories on the shore and the barges in the river. Go across western Kansas in wheat harvest time and see the combines with twenty-foot platforms biting into the grain. See the herds of purebred cattle and the infinite lacings of wires and derricks in Oklahoma. Or go to the Leduc Field in Alberta and watch a great new oil development uncoiling.

These are easy to see. What is not so easy to see or to comprehend is the change that has come upon us of late years. It is a change so subtle that the farmer or the farmer's wife cannot tell you exactly how or when it came. All he or she knows, if they live in Wisconsin, for example, is that if he or she wishes to sit in the front yard and paint a picture, no one will think it unusual. Or if he or she wishes to write poetry it is not necessary to keep it a secret any longer because many of the neighbors are doing it. The native artist has been accepted in many communities in North America, and no accusation of nonvirility is put upon a man for expressing himself in any of the arts and crafts. This has happened partly, perhaps, because we have paused from our frontier success story and have begun to look inward for creative things. This inward looking has happened most successfully where there has been a leader of vision to interpret, to stimulate, to encourage, or to help the development of a native arts movement naturally from the materials at hand—the legend, folklore, tall tales, and the feeling of the people about their own places.

It could perhaps happen everyplace, for even as the people of North America have made the chief end of frontier struggle the success of an industrialized or mechanized society, so they may be capable of becoming an art-conscious people in a short time. We do things in a hurry, once we get the idea.

The seed somehow must grow from ourselves. And the way to make it grow is to create an attitude, a friendly attitude, in which the native things may flourish. I must go on to say, of course, that the surest way to create such a friendly attitude in the communities of North America is to see that the product of the native artists is good—preferably superb. I am not speaking now of the arts that are purely recreative. These have their place, and where the frontier hangover is strongest the recreative arts may be the farthest development we can hope for. I am speaking now of the native artists who will create a product that is well above the mediocre, that is outstandingly interpretative of the artist and the region. This, of course, brings up the point of how such native artists are to be developed. In the instance of the creation of a good home-grown literature, what are the writers to write about? Or what is the painter to paint? The obviously good advice is to write and paint what you see and know best. To most people this is the event and association of community life or the landscape seen in a twenty- or thirty-mile radius of the home doorstep. Such advice cannot be gainsaid; yet in its very goodness—to write and paint what you know—

lies the often bitter controversy of regionalism. For it is certainly true that the scholars and writers of the past seem to have divided the subject into battlefields and thus have greatly limited the scope of regional creation.

There were the "folk" specialists who held that good regional creative work must be related to the homely customs, sayings, and ways of the people who were vaguely classed as "the folk" of a particular region. From this interpretation grew many stage and literary stereotypes: the mountaineer with his cud of tobacco and his whiskey jug, the shotgun wedding, and the elaborate dialogue so often a poor attempt at phonetic rendition of the actual speech patterns of a certain type of character.

There were those who argued back and forth in foolish arguments that nothing regional could exist in a city. There were those who shouted that nothing of any literary worth could come out of a rural area. Some authorities maintained that regionalism could be only state- or, even, county-wide. Others said that geography was the true factor.

In light of a calm estimate of contemporary conditions most of these points of view seem slightly awry. Anybody can guess that "the folk" no longer exist as they once did. Communications have so broken the older patterns of society that only in the broadest and most general terms can the people of any region be called "the folk." Folklorists who make a science of the collection of indigenous materials still desperately seek and classify such items, but as a creative force "the folk" idea is dead. Thus, "folk drama," as it was once defined, may be dead. And anybody can say with truth nowadays that rural and urban are so mixed and mingled that the edges of that old controversy have worn off.

How, then, is the writer or artist, looking at the things

about him, to approach his creative work? Perhaps with the argumentative statements no longer present to hinder and plague and classify creative talent, the author or the artist may strive for a sincere creative grasp of the things he knows and understands and which he may now interpret with universality. For in universality lies the soul of great regionalism. Our authors must show us our familiar landscapes; yet their characters must be so created in true patterns of human life that those characters may be recognized and understood anywhere in the world.

Somehow we must find in North American regions the few persons capable of achieving such creations, and we must give them every opportunity to create; for in such universal interpretation lies understanding of our own place and our region and understanding of us in other places, other regions, and other nations of the earth.

As I look at it now I can see that regionalism becomes terribly important to a project in drama such as the one I now direct in Wisconsin—the Wisconsin Idea Theater. It is tied financially, politically, and geographically to the general Wisconsin area. We have before us, as a result of research, the assembled materials—the backgrounds and themes—of this part of the American Middle West. Also, we know in general the extent in Wisconsin of the creative force that is the human impulse to act, paint, write, or to engage in some other related creative process.

Regionalism, from my point of view, therefore, seems to become the development of a popular art movement drawing its vital force from the cultural streams of the region but transcending the smaller limitations of subject matter and method. Within the popular art movement, of course, must be the few native artists of great worth.

All this may be a somewhat intuitive answer to E. K.

Brown's theories of the frontier as a chief antagonist to the creation of a great native art. In 1943 when I read Brown's essay, I perhaps considered only that if the frontier emphasized the golden things and placed a halo on success it called forth also a vast regional pride which bubbled constantly, in the case of Alberta, with extravagant statements and poetic rhapsodies on the wonderful qualities of the Alberta land. It seemed to me then that the legendary character the frontier in all its varied aspects assumed to the average Albertan could be one very direct source of the distinct feeling for home place that I could sense wherever I went in Alberta. And I believed that this common feeling for place might be used to win sympathetic regard for plays of the region.

There were then, as there are now, many opinions about the state of Canadian theater and Canadian plays. The recent Massey Report on the state of the arts, letters, and sciences in Canada presents in an amusing letter from "the correspondence of Samuel Marchbanks" to Apollo Fishhorn, Esquire, one such opinion.

Dear Mr. Fishhorn:

You want to be a Canadian playwright, and ask me for advice as to how to set about it. Well, Fishhorn, the first thing you had better acquaint yourself with is the physical conditions of the Canadian theatre. Every great drama, as you know, has been shaped by its playhouse. The Greek drama gained grandeur from its marble outdoor theatres; the Elizabethan drama was given fluidity by the extreme adaptability of the Elizabethan playhouse stage; French classical drama took its formal tone from its exquisite, candle-lit theatres. You see what I mean?

Now what is the Canadian playhouse? Nine times out of ten, Fishhorn, it is a school hall, smelling of chalk and kids, and decorated in the early Concrete style. The stage is a small, raised room at one end. And I mean room. If you step into the wings suddenly you will fracture your nose against the wall. There is no place for storing scenery, no place for the actors to dress, and the lighting is designed to warm the stage, but not to illuminate it.

Write your plays, then, for such a stage. Do not demand any procession of elephants, or dances by the maidens of the Caliph's harem. Keep away from sunsets and storms at sea. Place as many scenes as you can in cellars and kindred spots. And don't have more than three characters on the stage at one time, or the weakest of them is sure to get nudged into the audience. Farewell, and good luck to you.

S. MARCHBANKS

March 4, 1950 *

The report goes on to point out that while Canada is deficient in playhouses, as such, she is not deficient in theatrical talent, whether in writing for the stage, in producing, or in acting; but this talent at present finds little encouragement and no outlet apart from the Canadian Broadcasting Corporation which provides the greatest and almost unique stimulus to Canadian drama.

Radio drama may be an inadequate substitute for living theater, but the fact is that Canadians living away from the larger centers see few stage plays. There is an increasing movement in countryside theater in Canada nowadays I am told, but when I was in Alberta in the early 1940's the war had greatly reduced community play production, and the farmer or rancher found his greatest dramatic pleasure by simply turning his radio on in the evening and letting his imagination become his stage. For the great theater of Canada is a theater that comes out of the sky. Fine plays, both classics and contemporary original plays, wing out from the producing centers of the Canadian Broadcasting Corporation at Montreal, Toronto, Winnipeg, and Vancouver,

---

* *Report Royal Commission on National Development in the Arts Letters and Sciences 1949–51* (Ottawa: Queen's Press, 1951), p. 192.

directed by the finest radio producing artists in North America.

The CBC has shown an eagerness to let its writers experiment as they please, to try the unusual story, to break codes or taboos, and the result has been some of the most exciting radio drama heard in North America. The stir and discussion generated throughout the Canadian countryside when a radio play is produced which hits hard with idea and force of unusual treatment is comparable to the excitement that follows the *première* of a successfully shocking serious play.

In 1944, Andrew Allen, in Toronto, and Esse Ljungh, then in Winnipeg, both had a deep sense of responsibility for the faithful dramatic interpretation of Canada. Allen's famous "Stage" series carried then, as it does now, a fair amount of dramatic material highly pertinent to the Canadian scene, and Esse Ljungh was forever seeking new, poetic talent to interpret the Canadian West. The production studios of the CBC were opened, therefore, to the plays of many new writers.

When the Alberta Folklore and Local History Project right from the start was flooded by yarns about Alberta told by a rich variety of persons, I began, in the Fall of 1943, to utilize many of these Alberta yarns in the form of weekly radio broadcasts over station CKUA in Edmonton, done always at a certain, specified time when the greatest number of listeners could be assured. I had had no time to shape these yarns into radio dramas; so I narrated them straight, and through these yarn broadcasts I built up a large following of people who, from their many letters, seemed to have an intense regional interest.

The Prairie Regional network of the CBC became interested, too, and, recognizing that the Alberta stories were fairly typical of the entire Canadian West, made time available to me. I was then able to cover most of Canada with my broadcasts. I consider that the two years of continuous broadcasting in Canada made a deep and lasting impression and established an attitude that helped in the development of a native drama of Alberta and the West. For in my radio talks and in public lectures I made it a point to tell the stories which might be most readily adapted to dramatic form. I talked a great deal about the countryside heroes such as Twelve-Foot Davis, the Peace River Country hero of generosity and kindness to travelers, Dave McDougall, hero of the tall tale, and Bob Edwards, the great Calgary humorist and editor of the *Calgary Eyeopener*. And as stories about these and other dramatic figures were told and retold on the air and their dramatic potentialities emphasized, it began to be more apparent to the people of Alberta that they had a wonderful set of dramatic traditions ready to be turned into fine plays that they would like to see or hear.

My own attempts at playwriting when I finally found the time were largely in radio. To gather material for my broadcasts I frequented local gathering places. During the war years, beer flowed only during certain hours in the western Canadian beer parlors. Usually the hours were between three and six, with servings of beer at three o'clock, four o'clock, and five o'clock. The practice was for the men to gather in the parlors, wait impatiently for the trays of glasses to come around, and to collect as many glasses of the good Canadian beer as possible. Then the yarn spinning would begin. It was certainly not my chief purpose to haunt the beer parlors of Alberta, but from the parlors flowed, along with the beer, a virile brand of lore that I delighted to hear.

There was a shabby man with bright, small eyes and chin whiskers, for instance, who came each afternoon to the beer parlor in the MacDonald Hotel in Edmonton. His yarns of curious doings throughout Alberta, always with himself as a participant, were examples of the most masterful exaggeration I have ever heard. Yet his tales were fretted and scrolled with authentic flavor of the West. His friends quite frankly said that "Johnny" was 1 per cent man and 99 per cent straight liar. He narrated how he spent hours frozen into the carcass of a steer in which he had sought shelter from a plain's blizzard. His time inside the steer was phony, but his descriptions of the blizzard were brilliant. He told of the year when there was no Fall or Winter, when Alberta bloomed the year around under the soft fingers of the ceaseless chinooks. He told of the year when there was no Summer and of how the Big Ice crept within a stone's throw of Calgary.

His yarns I managed to frame into a radio play that I called *Johnny Dunn*. Esse Ljungh produced the script from the Winnipeg CBC studios, and the heroic Johnny of the play enjoyed a wide reputation for a time as the type of all Alberta tall tale spinners. I eventually turned the radio play into a stage piece which had its *première* at the Banff School of Fine Arts in 1944.

There were other radio plays, too. One afternoon it was quiet in the MacDonald Hotel beer parlor between the five o'clock and the six o'clock ration. Johnny Dunn had drunk all the beer he could hold and had stopped telling tall stories for a while. It was during this small lull that another man at our table, a neat, elderly gentleman, told me the dramatic story of the great Frank slide.

This slide was a mighty avalanche that swept away a small mining town called Frank in the Crow's Nest Pass in April, 1903. The yarn was told so quietly, yet with so much feeling—my old acquaintance had lived near Frank when the slide occurred—that I was quite carried away. A few days later when I was remembering the old man's tale of how the side of the old Turtle Mountain had slid away in the early morning hours and of how they had afterwards found an unidentified baby lying on a huge stone after the slide had passed and had named her "Frankie Slide," the words and music of a song came to my lips. When I had set the song down I called it "The Ballad of the Frank Slide." Later the song turned into a Canadian Broadcasting Corporation play. Andrew Allen produced it first in Toronto in 1945, and it has since been repeated on the CBC networks many times.

A little while after the play was produced on the Trans-Canada Network I received a letter from a lady who lived somewhere in British Columbia. She said that she was the baby girl who had been found on the rock.

Looking back, I can see that the chief value of the small series of Alberta plays that I did for the CBC lay in my conviction that dramatizing native materials for radio would always be an important part of my regional program. The success of the CBC plays certainly led me later to try the same idea in Wisconsin, where I created a weekly half-hour dramatic series called Wisconsin Yarns.

There were also some fine Alberta stage plays written. From the beginning of the Banff School in 1934 playwriting had been on the increase, and from Professor Koch's playwriting class at Banff had emerged at least one outstanding dramatist—Gwen Pharis. Gwen had been raised on a ranch in Southern Alberta, and her plays about prairie life, written sincerely and, often, poetically, were widely known in the province. Gwen's success as a playwright sprang directly from her intimate feeling for her native landscape. Professor Koch was so impressed by her sensitive first plays

67

that he obtained a Rockefeller fellowship for her to study playwriting with him for two years in Chapel Hill. When Gwen returned to Alberta it was to see her country through refreshed eyes. I asked her not long ago to tell me how she felt about the Canadian West. In her letter, which she graciously has given me permission to quote, perhaps lies the hope of developing the few native artists capable of deep artistic interpretation. In her letter to me she wrote:

You have asked me to tell you something about my feeling for my country since I completed my work as a Rockefeller fellow at the University of North Carolina in the Spring of 1939.

I always remember Chapel Hill as it looked in April, veiled in the loveliness of the southern spring. I remember a warm, fragrant April night when Rietta Bailey and I stood under the Bell Tower and talked for a long time about our plans and hopes and fears for the future. The depression was beginning to loosen its grasp. There had been a war in Ethiopia; there was a war in Spain; and at the World's Fair in New York City the room assigned to Czechoslovakia stood empty, its walls bare except for a nation's cry for freedom. *Mein Kampf* was on the book shelves and the shadow of World War II lay long across the world.

Fourteen years ago, when so many whom we loved were still alive and now are dead. I think of Thomas Wolfe's line "Oh lost, and by the wind tossed ghost, come back again." I suppose that has been the hard thing for all of us in these years—to remember them as they were, young and proud, and to know that they will not come again.

That night Rietta and I found ourselves dissatisfied with the world of the University. It seemed to us a cloister set apart from clamorous reality. We went down from the Bell Tower feeling that we must put away childish things.

And so after Convocation we left Chapel Hill and I have never been back. The two years under the "Humanities Division" has added much to the richness and fullness of life, and I realize now as I did not realize then, that it is perhaps in the "cloisters" devoted to the study of the Humanities rather than in the market place that the answers to the world's dilemma may be found. And some day in the spring I hope to go back to Chapel Hill with my husband and our four children, to show them all the places I loved and see again the people I hold dear.

I came home by way of New York. New York was the hub of the world. You felt like you owned it. In it you could feel the pulse of the continent, and when you could find your way around the subways, you had conquered a tiger. How could anyone be happy away from New York? You would hurry back to it, never leave it! That's how it was for the little while I was there. But as I began the long progress by bus across the continent, this passion for New York proved ephemeral, slipping away as we rolled past the stockyards of Chicago, the lakes of Wisconsin, the show windows of Minneapolis, the grain elevators of Winnipeg, almost gone as we travelled the long road across the prairie. Then I was home again. I was back in Alberta.

And since then I have been out of Alberta only for a short time, never out of the West. The men came home from overseas with talk of Paris and London and Dublin and Brussels and Rome and one feels in their talk now a longing to see these cities again in peace time. "When the children are older," we say, looking at the maps and brochures of holiday splendour. But in the meantime we have discovered Alberta, made it our own.

In the years during and since World War II, I think many Canadians have for the first time become strongly conscious of their national heritage. We no longer build homes with an eye to selling out and retiring to California or 'going home' to the Old Country. We may grumble about the winters or the freight rates or the price of coal but we like it here and we intend to stay. In the past, cultural achievement has been largely centered in the East, with sporadic developments elsewhere, but more and more through the Canadian Broadcasting Corporation, the National Film Board, the Dominion Drama League, the Society for Adult Education and other nationwide organizations, we are bridging the gaps of language and distance between Quebec and British Columbia and beginning to feel that what is important in one part of the country is important for us all. Our ties with the British Commonwealth and our ten thousand miles of borderline shared with the United States make it easier for us to think internationally than is true for more isolated countries.

And all across Canada our own writers and writers from elsewhere have begun to uncover our stories and legends, the beauties and strangeness of our countryside, the conflicts of our various social patterns. We see them with new eyes. Canadian painters and musicians are receiving recognition and support and are contributing to our understanding of Canada. At this time I believe we are about to see in Canada a period of sound and vigorous achievement in the arts, achievement which will be an expression of Canadian character without being an expression of a rigid or parochial nationalism.

For my own part, I have only a sense of Canada as a whole, a feeling for it. I do not know the length and breadth of my own country as I hope I may. But I know the Canadian West and each year I have come to a deeper appreciation of its many-sided character, its infinite variety.

. . . .

And for the most part these are the things I have written about. Most of my plays, I suppose, could be called "regional." *Marie Jenvrin* has its setting in the far north at a mining camp. *Still Stands the House, The Rainmaker* and *Dark Harvest* belong to the southern Alberta where I grew up. *Stampede* and *The Jack and the Joker* attempt to recapture a romantic period in the history of central Alberta, at the end of the last century. *A Fine Colored Easter Egg* is a comedy about Ukrainian-Canadian farm people and the oil boom. A new play *A Far Cry* is about liberalism in a small town.

I find I have written at length about the Alberta countryside, much of it familiar to you. But the fourteen years have brought no certain answers to the questions Rietta and I were asking that April night in Chapel Hill. They have brought an increased appreciation for the dear familiar landscape, an abiding joy in family and friends, and a kind of desperate optimism that the words "United Nations" will ultimately mean just that.

Gwen was closely associated with the Alberta Folklore and Local History project, and her advice helped to produce many new Alberta plays by authors who strove after the poetry so apparent in Gwen's work.

The Alberta Folklore and Local History project confirmed for me the theory I had formed in New York State that a collection of native materials can be of immense value in stimulating creative writing. The project confirmed, also, my belief that a public relations program using mass media could greatly enhance the appreciation of native literary works. These ideas and beliefs which I had tried out in New York and Alberta formed the basis of the work I was to attempt within the framework of the Wisconsin Idea.

In Alberta I deepened my feeling for place and, I think, became more sensitive to elements in regional life—elements which can make any region unique, a place of distinctive flavor. Association with such persons as Gwen Pharis helped me to develop these sensitivities. I became, in Alberta, aware of rôle-playing in my work and became conscious of a drive which stimulated and made possible my adventures in promoting regional arts and in gathering native materials. Spiritually at least I was ready to move to Wisconsin when the time arrived, even though the exact nature of my rôle there was not clear to me.

Chapter three

THE BOUNDARIES OF A STATE

One day late in August, 1945, I, a stranger, was sitting on the campus of the University of Wisconsin at the top of the Hill in front of Bascom Hall. It was afternoon: long shadows fell across the grass and there was a feeling of quiet loneliness everywhere. The summer session had ended, professors had departed, students had vanished, and I was quite alone.

My loneliness I knew sprang from sources deeper than the quietness of the campus. On this hill I was alone spiritually, without the steadfast bulk of a Drummond to bolster and inspire me as his presence had on many a New York State eminence. In Alberta I had been alone, but it was quite a different loneliness there. It was wartime when everything seemed speeded up, hectic. Also, I had been on a short-term project. But now I was to begin work as director of a new, long-term University regional cultural program. I had come to the top of Bascom Hill hoping to experience a first delicious feeling of curiosity, of belonging, of anticipation that a move to a new base had always held for me. I looked down across the slope to the foot of State Street, and at an angle between the trees I could see the top of the State Capitol. There was no breeze at all. A slow, faint sound of traffic wandered vaguely up the slope, but somehow that sound, too, seemed only a part of the general stillness.

Above me in front of the building stood a Lincoln statue. The quiet pose bothered me somehow, and I had a guilty sense that the figure was staring into me, seeking my reasons, my sensations, as I was myself.

I moved away from the statue to the front of the building and idly read a plaque that was fastened to the stone. It was a statement about academic freedom: "Whatever may be the limitations which trammel inquiry elsewhere, we believe that the great state University of Wisconsin should ever encourage that continual and fearless sifting and winnowing by which alone the truth can be found." It was taken from a report of the University of Wisconsin Board of Regents in 1894.

I thought about what the plaque said, and this too, bothered me. "Sifting and winnowing" was what I was doing a lot of within myself, and somehow this idealistic statement seemed to urge me on, to dare me to define my motives and my dreams. I moved uneasily away from the plaque onto the grass and sat down under a tree. What was to be my rôle here? I wondered. What was this Wisconsin experience to mean? The quiet, the peaceful campus, the contemplative mood of the place vanished. I was frightened, suddenly, for I sensed that quietness, solitude, moments of contemplation would soon be extremely rare for me. A tightness began in my belly, and, almost unconscious that I did it, I placed my hand on a sore spot near the center of me that had been present since I had left Canada a few weeks before.

Looking around, I realized for the first time how completely I was a stranger in this place. The realization was shocking, for I had been extremely conscious of one of the more superficial reasons for coming to Madison. This reason was twisted up with nostalgia. I had traveled constantly in Alberta; I had been on the move, in a way, since the depression days in Kansas; and I thought that I desired more than anything else a feeling of being at home, of soil where I could put down real roots, where I could live at peace and with an honest faith that the work I was doing had importance to the people about me.

I probably knew, too, that deep roots would not be easy for me to put down in any one soil, for the strange restless drive that had impelled my journeys and my drama-based discoveries of places and peoples would send me on a continuous search for personal gratifications arising from such seeking. Plumbing within myself, I knew that a part of the pleasure of my work in New York and in Alberta had been the movement about the region seeking the yarns and the flavors. My pleasure had been the changing colors on the land and the patterns of landscape. Perhaps my pleasure had been the few creative thrills I had received from seeing my own creative work used and from hearing the few utterances of public approval. I wondered whether much of the energy that had seemed so abundant in New York and Canada had not been motivated by fear—a hangover from my student days in the depression when often there was no job and no food.

I understood that I had a sincere liking for places and for people, but whether I could turn such liking into the kind of responsibility required to form an outstanding program in theater and allied arts in Wisconsin, I did not know. The Alberta experience, while it sharpened my appetite for the lore of places, had, perhaps, shown me my chief weakness, which was lack of an abiding faith in the worth and goodness of the work I had to do. As yet, my rôle-playing had not become a genuine thing, and the public aspects of my Alberta work were, I found, basically distasteful.

I had faith in my regional approaches; somehow I knew that I was on the right track, philosophically, for me, but a larger thing, a cause, a drive beyond restless seeking that might transcend all the weaknesses within me was vaguely felt but undefined.

I wished that I could experience a spiritual drive like the one that had carried my father into the Kansas lands in the '80's, determined, and without question, to see that a certain kind of human progress concerned with breaking, tilling, and building was carried forward. His problem of faith was easy, I believed. The rainbow was ever apparent to him and the gold was really waiting. There were irritations, delays, and obstacles, but these were regarded by father as romantic barriers to be swept aside with knightly charges and missions. Knighthood paid off for father in ways as simple and as definite as a wooden box six feet long or a bag of clanking pieces of money. The Grail was the land itself and the expanding nation.

Unhappily my problem was much more complex. I sensed

that America must come to her maturity through the cultural things, and I sensed that I must be a part of the bringing about of such maturity. But the things I must do were the things I feared. I had been brought to Wisconsin to do a certain job. There was concern at the University of Wisconsin over the state of the cultural arts. Cohesive forces, I had been told, were lacking in society as a result of the war. A new and integrated pattern for the cultural arts was necessary if the University was to continue to meet its obligations in the realm of cultural service to the people of the state. The University authorities felt that it was time to extend the University's services more completely into the field of the cultural arts and that the arts should be related directly to community life and made a vital part of the everyday experience of the people of the state.

My appointment to Wisconsin was somewhat surprising. In 1942, David Stevens of the Rockefeller Foundation made it possible for me to visit several American colleges in the hope that I might find promising fields for the development of native theater. One of the places I visited was Madison, Wisconsin, set down among four blue lakes with the great dome of the State Capitol and the main, pillared hall of the University facing each other across the city.

I had spent most of a day listening while a sociologist, John Kolb, and the Dean of Agriculture, Chris Christensen, told me about the Wisconsin people: the downtrodden peoples from Europe who sought freedom; the down-east Yankees and the farmers and tradesmen from New York State who sailed on the packet boats of the old Erie Canal and then came through the Lakes to Milwaukee where they spread out across the woodlands and the prairies like a wave.

They told me of the Indians who left their names and the mystery of their legends across the face of the Wisconsin earth, and I heard of the lumbermen who chewed down the mighty forests to a memory. Dean Chris spoke of the hunger of the people for education and of how they had formed the University in 1849, the year after Wisconsin reached statehood, and of how, little by little, the University had broadened its services until the whole state was, in effect, the University.

On the walls of Dean Chris's office were paintings of rural Wisconsin, and he told me that an art movement was springing up among the farm folks. Every year there was a big exhibit of rural art in Madison. And there was a theater tradition, too. The great days of theater were gone in Wisconsin, of course, when a fine German language company played in the magnificent Pabst Theater in Milwaukee and when famous American actors and actresses swept through the Wisconsin towns, barnstorming up from Chicago to the Twin Cities. Wisconsin had had the earliest little theater movement, too, when a group called the Wisconsin Dramatic Society dedicated itself to the writing and production of plays of Middle Western life. Unfortunately, the Wisconsin Dramatic Society was no more, but the University had, for fifteen years, kept workers in the field in drama, encouraging play production in the cities and in the country. True, no great plays of the people had sprung to life, but the public attitude toward theater was healthy.

That evening when I wrote to David Stevens I said that of all the places I had visited Wisconsin had done the most to establish a popular concept of drama. I said that the pioneer work had been done in Wisconsin and that there was very little need for my services there. And I went away from Madison remembering the blue lakes and the gentle roll of the country and the big barns set against the sides of the hills.

There was a comfortable feeling within me too—a feeling that in Wisconsin theater would continue to flourish. But the war came and circumstances changed, and in Canada, one Summer afternoon in 1944, I received a letter from Henry L. Ewbank of the University of Wisconsin Speech Department. He wrote:

DEAR MR. GARD:

The staff member who has been in charge of our rural extension work in dramatics has resigned. When we asked Professor Drummond to suggest candidates, he spoke of you. This morning, a committee representing the Department of Speech and Rural Sociology asked me to write to you about your availability, your interest in this type of work, and if you are interested, to inquire what salary you would expect.

Naturally you will want to know something of the position we have in mind. Some years ago the Rural Sociology Department in the College of Agriculture began to develop an extension staff in drama and related fields. In the past we have also had a full-time worker in discussion and part-time workers in music and community recreation. The dramatics and discussion specialists are also members of the staff of the Department of Speech though they have done no teaching on the campus. We are interested in promoting production of good plays by community groups. The extension worker visits clubs in various parts of the state, conducts institutes and short training schools for community leaders, plans festivals, prepares play lists and suggestions for dramatic directors, etc. We want someone who has a genuine interest in making the drama a social and cultural influence in our small towns and rural communities. We have made a good start, we feel. We would like someone who would stay with us for a number of years and eventually do for Wisconsin what Arvold and Koch have done for the areas in which they work. I'm not suggesting that the Wisconsin development should imitate or parallel those. I realize that this description is

78

somewhat indefinite, but so is the assignment we have in mind. To a considerable extent we shall rely upon the person we choose to draw his own plans.

If you are at all interested, we would appreciate an early reply. We are interviewing other candidates and must make an appointment within a few weeks.

Sincerely,

H. L. EWBANK
Professor of Speech

When I received the letter it generated great doubts within me. The conception of a new Wisconsin position in regional theater seemed narrow to me in the light of what I had been trying to do in Canada. I had definite ideas connected with playwriting, native materials, communications, and indeed, with the whole field of the arts related to the theater. I could not conceive of myself in the rôle of a drama adviser, traveling through Wisconsin merely encouraging play production with no systematic opportunity to carry out the ideas I had formulated about folklore, local history, and the related arts. It seemed to me, perhaps unjustly, that Professor Ewbank's letter emphasized the organizational aspects of a new program more than the creative ones. In Alberta, whatever the demands of my rôle had been, I had been free of routines, fields, and scopes of educational theory, precedent. And it was these things I thought I could sense as being background to the Wisconsin job. At that time the terms "adult education," "institute," "specialist," were terms of annoyance to me. I considered the programs built through and around such terms to be noncreative, deadly, with a shallow general purpose of uplifting, without much emphasis on genuine human considerations. I had a strong antagonism to these terms, and the letter left me with the feeling that I would never really wish to work in Wisconsin.

79

However, Drummond came to Banff in the Summer of 1944, saw what we were doing in Alberta, heard my opinion on the Wisconsin position, and, I believe, encouraged the Wisconsin group to think of the position as a major one conceived on very broad lines. At any rate, the Wisconsin thinking turned in the direction of a major position requiring someone who might serve, creatively and administratively, as director of a broad program in theater with possible relation to the other arts and with a definite relationship to the materials, themes of the region. The plan was carried to E. B. Fred, then Dean of the Wisconsin College of Agriculture, and it won his approval. Dr. Fred, a noted bacteriologist, had a major interest in science but felt a growing concern for the humanities. The idea of a position in regional theater also won the approval of Dean Ingraham of the College of Letters and Science and of Clarence Dykstra, who was completing his last year as President of the University.

It transpired, then, that in 1945 I received an offer from Andrew Weaver, Chairman of the Department of Speech of the University of Wisconsin, which said in part that my efforts were to be "devoted to the development of the human and cultural resources of the state, the cultivation of a community, regional and folk drama. It is our hope that you will unify and make more effective all of the agencies available for these purposes."

I accepted the offer, but not without some misgivings. Professor Ewbank's letter had mentioned the possibility of my doing for Wisconsin what Frederick Koch of North Carolina and Alfred Arvold of North Dakota had done for their states. I knew that I could never create as these men had created. In them I sensed a great faith and a oneness of purpose which I did not have. My approach to regional drama was sensuous, semi-poetic, intuitive, and only reluctantly concerned (as far as my personal participation was concerned) with the public relations aspects of regional cultural work. I knew that Mr. Arvold was a magnificent publicist and promoter and that he was even then (in 1945) Grand Potentate of the National Shriners. And I had heard Professor Koch deliver many speeches at North Carolina University and had seen the missionary light for folk drama coming out of him and warming everyone it struck. I could not do those things in the same way. Neither Koch nor Arvold had written books which attempted to deeply define their rôles. There was no doubt of their sincerity or of their leadership; yet they had offered no personal explanations for the drives that motivated them. Possibly they had been unable to honestly define their rôles. I wondered whether I would be able to define mine. I knew, of course, that Arvold had written a book in 1922 called *The Little Country Theatre* about his work in North Dakota, but I was also very sure that I could never create a "little country theatre" in Wisconsin. I did not wish to become pigeonholed as a promoter of country drama only. Partly that perhaps, but, please God, not solely that.

But, whatever my method in Wisconsin was to be, and whatever my fears, my wife and I decided to move to Madison. We wanted roots, a home. Wisconsin might be a good place to search for these prized things. Zona Gale, we recalled, had said that Wisconsin was a land of good neighbors, friendly communities where deep, intensely human values of community life existed. A neighborhood life of which we could be a part was something we earnestly desired.

And as we entered Wisconsin from the northwest and drove through the gentle greens and browns and soft slopes of Pierce County, we felt that home was very near. Here was a friendly land, surely, and I said wordlessly to Wisconsin in general: *There is nothing between us yet. I will try to understand you and to respect your moods and appreciate your places. If I win your regard, never send me away a stranger. I want to be a part of you, and I want to do the best for you.*

Maryo, my wife, drove and I looked at names on the map. Brillion, Lake Winnebago, Forest Junction, Prairie du Sac, Black Earth, Mazomanie, Spring Valley, Maiden Rock—simple, beautiful names, surely friendly names.

I had no real knowledge of Wisconsin then, or of its traditions. I had read about the state, but I had not studied it. I knew about La Follette, and I had admired his crusades in politics and in government. I understood that under a great program known as the Wisconsin Idea he and his followers had attempted, and successfully so, to extend the principles of democracy into the life of the average citizen. I knew, too, that the Wisconsin Idea was not purely a symbol of political and social reform but that it now seemed to mean the entire state-wide educational aims of the University of Wisconsin. I was drawn, somehow, to the meanings in the Wisconsin Idea. It seemed to me to be the background against which a project devoted to the creative voices of the state might be successfully placed.

But, I understood that Wisconsin was, in a way, a major dividing point for me. I felt the undefined urgings of a drive to build—urgings that had begun in New York and Canada and that were, I imagined, focused on the expressiveness of people as a kind of frontier that I must explore, develop. I sensed that a friendly attitude toward such exploration existed in Wisconsin as a result of the Wisconsin Idea in education, and I reasoned that the Wisconsin people might willingly lend themselves to cultural developments.

The question which always confronted me, however, was what such experimenting, building, would mean to me personally. Certainly it would mean vigorous organization, speeches, a whole whirl of activity that would carry me afield without rest. Certainly, parts of a Wisconsin program would be similar to the one I had directed in Alberta. There would be publicity without end, weariness without end, self-doubts and recriminations in the loneliness of one's solitude, and, perhaps, the final death of any art that might still exist within me. I knew that my chief conflict was an inner one—a desire for creative expression of my own, with solitudes to nourish it, on one hand, and a fermenting drive to help establish the arts as an essential part of American community life, on the other.

Even as I sat there on Bascom Hill in the afternoon stillness, my mind developed charming escapes from what I faced in Wisconsin. A feeling for Alberta swept over me. It was nostalgia, as though Alberta was itself the homeland I had been seeking. I saw the prairies to the east and south of Calgary with the shimmers of light across them. I saw the foothill country with magnificent shafts of sunlight streaming down from a holed, dark sky. I saw the sparkle of the Belly River across the flats, lined with willow. I remembered with entirely unjustified nostalgia a small flat place near the river bank south of Lethbridge where old Fort Whoop-Up had stood, and I could see in my mind a dim rutting across the short grass that had one time been the Whoop-Up trail.

I shifted my thoughts to Wisconsin and contemplated the differences. The Wisconsin land was different, surely. It had a softer quality. There were no mountains. The farms were large and comfortable looking, with great barns set back, often, against the hillsides. Here was agriculture in a way that Alberta could never know it. I wondered what the farm people were like in Wisconsin and whether they considered, as the farm people in my boyhood part of Kansas had, that the arts were womanish expressions, unworthy of serious consideration in comparison with the realities of agricultural production. The great farms, I thought, would seem to indicate such an attitude.

Had I known what had happened culturally in rural Wisconsin, my fears and self-doubts would surely have been magnified. I would have been tremendously more nervous about "adult education," "institutes," and the like, and a new cultural program would doubtless have seemed to me pretentious, perhaps unnecessary. I would have been even more confused had I been aware how the threads of men and ideas influential in creating a regional concept of drama in Wisconsin were twisted and interlaced. Professor Ewbank's mention of Koch and Arvold would certainly have had more meaning for me if I had known how these men had shaped the direction of Wisconsin thought toward the kind of project I had been brought to Wisconsin to initiate. I would have been astonished and certainly awed, too, had I been wholly aware of the tremendous background of University state-wide work in theater and allied arts in Wisconsin before 1945.

The spiritual soil in Wisconsin has been exceedingly good for the development of the cultural arts. It has had a rich heritage of nourishment from old world cultures brought to the state by people of many nationalities and by a high type of settler from New York State and New England who carried with them a high regard for a cultural side to their lives. Many were the pianos and melodeons lugged into

Wisconsin in its border and early statehood periods at tremendous sacrifice. During the early years of the twentieth century the political and social ferments produced or drew to Wisconsin an extremely high type of leader capable of great idealism and filled with a drive aimed at making the cultural arts important in the life of the average citizen. One such leader was Thomas Dickinson.

Dickinson was, in 1910, a professor in the University of Wisconsin English department. In 1910, the influence of the Wisconsin Idea as a democratizing factor in Wisconsin life, was at its height, and Thomas Dickinson's ideas and developments reflected the spirit of the times. In many ways Dickinson was a key figure in what occurred later in Wisconsin, and his development of the Wisconsin Dramatic Society demonstrates what wide effect a small group of people with a dynamic creative idea can have on future events.

The formation of the Wisconsin Dramatic Society was not encouraged by the University. Professor Dickinson, for his own amusement, had written a few vaudeville skits that were being produced regularly on one of the circuits. This, of course, he kept under cover so that it would not impair his good standing with the English department faculty. However, when his play *The Unbroken Road* was produced by Harrison Gray Fisk with Bertha Kalish in the leading rôle, Mr. Dickinson was given recognition, and the University submitted to the point of letting him teach a course in contemporary drama.

Today we might have a hard time visualizing a university curriculum without such a course, but at that time it was a very distinct innovation. The idea of contemporary theater as an academic subject was almost unheard of in American universities. Mr. Dickinson believed, however, that a play was not just a piece of literature; in fact, it was not a play at all until it reached the stage and was given a production by living actors. So he proposed to produce a few plays on a very minor scale right in his class. This idea was given an overwhelming favorable response by his students.

Mr. Dickinson reported that when he presented this startling plan of producing plays in class with student actors the class remained seated after the bell had rung and formed the nucleus of a formal dramatics organization. But when the University administration was presented with the plan, it refused the use of rooms and equipment for dramatic meetings or productions. The group, therefore, went outside the University and immediately found great popular support.

The formation of the Wisconsin Dramatic Society was no doubt tied up to the whole feeling of democracy in action apparent in Wisconsin in 1910. Mr. Dickinson, now retired, wrote on May 6, 1952, to one of my graduate students, Miss Talie Handler:

There is absolutely no question of the organic association of the spirit of our work with La Follette progressivism. My chief interest was in the outworking of democracy, of which I considered the theatre the workshop. While not primarily a theatre man, I knew the theatre well enough in all its angles to be aware that its chief bottleneck was the audience. You in this generation have no conception of this. The key was the quotation "to have great poets you must have great audiences too." For this reason I fought, sometimes in our group itself, against associating our movement with politics on the one side and theatrical professionalism on the other. Thence what you call intellectualism. Under this intellectualism some pretty practical work was going forward and in areas in which there were no patterns save in Ireland ... All this seems trite now, but believe me, it wasn't so trite then, when these things were cutting through the fog.

86

La Follette believed that there could not be effective democratic government without a people educated for democracy. Dickinson believed that audiences must be educated for theater. Mr. Dickinson (just as La Follette had done) ploughed right ahead with his theory. As Kenneth MacGowan has remarked: *

The year 1911 saw the gathering of forces for the first definitely conscious Little Theatres. In January, in Madison, Thomas Dickinson—a far more important factor in our dramatic progress than many realize—created something that proved almost as varied as the Neighborhood Playhouse and continued until 1929 as the Wisconsin Players of both Madison and Milwaukee. It was called originally the Wisconsin Dramatic Society; at Madison it was shepherded by Dickinson, then a professor in the University of Wisconsin, and at Milwaukee by Laura Sherry, . . . Thomas Wood Stevens, Zona Gale, and William Ellery Leonard coöperated with them. The first year there were 3 productions, sold to the public at 15 cents apiece, the next year 8 at 50 cents. Besides the usual financial and technical features of little theatre activity, the Wisconsin Players went in for the cultivation of original local plays, tours, lectures, a publication *The Play-book*, and the reading of plays.

Reflecting the interest of the Wisconsin Dramatic Society in regional themes was the production of the drama *Glory of the Morning* written in 1911 by William Ellery Leonard, who was a professor in the University of Wisconsin and one of Wisconsin's outstanding poets. The play concerns an Indian woman, her trader husband, and her two half-breed children. The husband returns from a hunting expedition to tell his Indian wife that he is going back to France and that he is not returning again. He wants to take his children with him. Given the choice of going or remaining, the girl chooses to go with her father to France, to grow up as a

* *Footlights Across America* (New York: Harcourt, Brace and Co., 1929), pp. 50–51.

white woman, and the boy chooses to live as an Indian with his mother in the Wisconsin woods. This play was produced in 1912 at the Fuller Opera House in Madison and was then taken to the Davidson Theater in Milwaukee.

Zona Gale's play *The Neighbors* was written shortly thereafter. It is probably the most famous play to emerge from the group. It was on March 10, 1912, that Professor Dickinson wrote to Miss Gale in Portage.

DEAR MISS GALE,—

To save our lives write us a simple scene, wound around a single episode beating with one human emotion taken from the simple life of a village. Not a long play—only one act. Don't bother about plot. Put in a lot of your characters all interested in one situation, and bring that situation out at the end with just a little tear and a smile in it. Quit anything else you're doing and do it now. Send it to me. Believe me when I say the faster the better. We want these human things. How much you are the only person who can take the next step for us, and how I'll curse you if you don't.

Leonard's play was produced and was all right. I don't know whether to send regards or not.

THOS. H. DICKINSON

Zona Gale wrote *The Neighbors* very quickly and sent it to Dickinson. He answered her on April 8, 1912.

DEAR MISS GALE,—

The play does. Have just read it with delight. We should produce it this spring. What part do you think Mrs. Sherry should take? I have my idea and I want to compare with yours. You won't object to my tinkering with the play, will you?

I feel like giving you a medal for the quiet and expeditious way you had of going and doing it.

Good cheer.

Faithfully yours
THOS. H. DICKINSON *

* Thomas H. Dickinson letters to Zona Gale, from the Zona Gale manuscript collection in the Library of the Wisconsin State Historical Society. Reproduced through the courtesy of the Society.

I have already told how Zona Gale's *The Neighbors* impressed Drummond and how the play became his headliner at the New York State Fair. It can be safely assumed, I think, that the Dickinson movement through Zona Gale had an influence on Drummond and on his work in the creation of a New York State regional theater. Drummond's own ideas and philosophy had tremendous effect on me, and I completed the circle, in a way, when I came to Wisconsin to initiate a project similar in idea.

The Wisconsin Dramatic Society was one of the foremost cultural manifestations to be related directly to the Wisconsin Idea, and the theory generally accepted by the Dickinson group that popular self government without indigenous art forms is incapable of civilized expression had an undoubted effect on the University in that state-wide arts programs were hastened.

The "Wisconsin Idea" was a term coined by Dr. Charles McCarthy, Professor of Political Science and head of the Legislative Reference Library in the state legislature, to describe the socio-political ferment in Wisconsin in the early 1900's. Wisconsin was, at that time, extending political democracy by passing and administering laws such as workmen's compensation laws, which have since become generally accepted throughout the country. But the Wisconsin Idea was complex: it meant the drafting of experts—such as Dr. McCarthy—in framing and administering legislation for the benefit of the people. The University naturally played an important rôle in the innovations. In education, the Wisconsin Idea meant extending the educational and cultural opportunities of the University to all the people of the state. It meant, according to the pronouncements of University President Van Hise, a classmate of La Follette, "service to the state" by the University. Dr. McCarthy was one of a small band of enlightened men who worked for the development of the University Extension Division. In 1907, the legislature approved a budget which greatly expanded the Extension Division—which actually had been started as early as 1885—and brought the Division within Van Hise's definition of service to the state.

The Wisconsin Idea in education was, therefore, well underway when the Wisconsin Dramatic Society was formed in 1910. In 1910, also, attention was turned at the University to the cultural arts as one field of service to the people. A lyceum bureau was formed to improve community entertainment, and in 1913 a Bureau of Community Music was started to furnish service to groups wishing to express themselves in music. In 1916, this bureau became the Bureau of Community Music and Drama, the forerunner of the Wisconsin Idea Theater which I direct.

By 1916, the University Extension Division had firmly established itself as a vital part of the University and had attracted national, and even international, attention for the work it was doing. In addition to the courses of many kinds offered through correspondence and in addition to institutes and short courses of various kinds it promoted, the Extension Division was conducting programs of discussion and debate and programs of community development throughout the state. And a field staff was beginning to foreshadow the immense organization that is now the "back-stage" of the University where the many off-campus services of the University are manned.

To head the new Bureau of Community Music and Drama a dynamic young man from Winfield, Kansas, was brought in. This was Edgar B. Gordon, who was to become a leading example of the Wisconsin Idea in action. The work of

90

"Pop" Gordon, as he is now familiarily known throughout the state, is worth describing. In many ways it set the social tone for programs to follow and led directly into further drama and allied arts developments.

Nowadays, Pop Gordon is one of the great cultural figures of the state of Wisconsin. He is a gentleman of short stature, with white hair and warm eyes. When he leads folks in song a great spiritual oneness seems created between Pop and the singers. Every spring three thousand or more children come into Madison in their school busses and pack the stock pavilion on the University campus. Their faces rise toward Pop standing in the middle of the crowd. He lifts his arms, a great flood of song pours from the children, and Pop's face is beautiful with the whole joy of it. I believe that, without doubt, he has been the most inspiring teacher Wisconsin children have ever had. It is easy to see that his roots go very deep into the cultural history of Wisconsin.

When he became director of the Bureau of Music and Drama in 1916, Pop considered music less for its own sake than for its rôle in a constructive program of community growth. He saw in community music and drama a means of combating juvenile delinquency and family disintegration through a kind of wholesome and uplifting recreation. He desired to see large numbers of folks working together in community programs in which the audiences as well as the casts would feel the coöperative and group nature of the work. This, of course, carried on Thomas Dickinson's idea of the need of educating audiences as well as drama casts.

Pop wished to see the schools take a leading rôle in combating the vulgar and the commonplace. He would not have anything to do with a "star" system, and he thought that community singing, especially, should be free from the stifling atmosphere of drill. He was interested, too, in encouraging folk dancing with its spontaneous color and zest.

Pop went everywhere in Wisconsin and encouraged singing, drama, and dancing. He had unique ways of solving difficulties. When he encountered problems arising from community differences he sometimes settled them through music. For instance, one time he held a singing "institute" at De Pere, which was beset by religious differences. Pop brought these differences to an appropriate conclusion through a mixed choral group that sang in a Presbyterian church under the direction of a Catholic priest.

Pop's personality was such that he was able to turn to radio successfully as a means of getting even more folks in Wisconsin to sing. WHA, the University radio station, had begun regular "telephonic" broadcasts in 1919 and characterizes itself to this day as the "oldest station in the nation." Pop became the first faculty representative to appear regularly on University radio programs. In 1922, he organized and broadcast what is without doubt the first music appreciation course ever to be heard on the air. In those days, of course, people listened with headphones, and many listeners wearing their phones sang under the leadership of Pop's friendly voice. Pop has kept up his radio broadcasts through the years, and at the present time over one hundred thousand children in Wisconsin classrooms listen and respond to his singing lessons on the "Wisconsin School of the Air."

Since he was essentially a music man, it is only natural that Pop Gordon emphasized music more than he did drama. And in the early 1920's he left the Extension Division to take a post in the University School of Music.

Pop Gordon's approach to music was essentially a sociological one. He certainly did not disregard the art aspects of music, but he considered music to be one of the cohesive forces of society; and the programs in the cultural arts that followed have also reflected a sociological outlook. This has worried me somewhat. None of the Wisconsin state-wide programs in music, drama, or art could be called strictly "art" movements. They have always been conceived within the framework of adult education or informal education and generally have placed emphasis on the group rather than on the individual. All my native inclination has been toward the individual rather than toward the group, and I have had to make major personal adjustments in Wisconsin.

The next development in the movement which ultimately became the Wisconsin Idea Theater bears the impress of Professor John H. Kolb, to whom I owe so much for advice and encouragement in my own efforts to adapt to the innovations of the Wisconsin Idea. John Kolb was a young teacher when he arrived at the University of Wisconsin in 1919 to become chairman of the Department of Rural Sociology. He has a keen analytical mind and his lips are apt to spew out fact and figures while his eyes are seeing people enriching their lives through acting, singing, painting. Kolb's grandfather was one of the group of 1848 German Revolutionists and his mother was a New England lady who had a high regard for music and art. Kolb has an intuitive sense of the worth of the arts in community life. His attitude toward them is sociological, however, in that like Pop Gordon he saw the arts as one means of making community life tremendously more worthwhile.

When Kolb came to Wisconsin he was, like other rural sociologists, under the influence of the 1908 report of the Commission on Country Life, the commission on which Liberty Hyde Bailey of Cornell and Gifford Pinchot of

Pennsylvania were key figures. It was this report that focused attention on the conservation of human as well as natural resources and changed the direction of much sociological thought. Kolb saw the importance of investigating the whole cultural background of the people and of linking such background to the arts, crafts, and to nature. The study of nationality, customs, traditions was revived and encouraged by Kolb.

Soon after his arrival in Wisconsin Kolb sought the advice of a local adviser who told him in blunt terms that "theater was theater" and should be regarded only in strict professional terms. Such opposition fired Kolb's desire to encourage community dramatics in the rural areas. He started some work in this direction but encountered great opposition by many farmers who refused to believe that drama had any place in their lives. However, Kolb found a farm woman, Mrs. Carl Felton, who could write a bit, and he persuaded her to write a one-act play. *Goose Money* was the result. Certainly, *Goose Money* was one of the most famous one-act plays ever written in Wisconsin, for it initiated a real home-grown playmaking movement eagerly participated in, eventually, by farmers all over the state. Kolb's theory that if he could get a successful play written by a farm person it would overcome opposition paid off. Thousands of copies of *Goose Money* were printed and distributed free by the University.

Kolb then got Dan Vornholt, a music specialist, to work with rural groups in singing and folk dancing, and eventually a famous book of folksongs called *The Folksinger* was published by the University, and again thousands of copies were distributed free with tremendous effect.

Kolb's rural drama and music movement finally included

94

a rural art project. These state-wide movements exist to this day.

By 1925, of course, the extension machinery of the University was running in high gear. "Service to the state" was the key phrase. But while Extension was gaining strength it was regarded as "backstage" to the major campus operations of the University. Extension was recognized as a big operation but was eyed suspiciously by many professors on the Hill. It gained, however, an enthusiastic response from the people of the state.

But, at the same time, educational extension methods had become fixed in channels, and the routines of bustle and scurry from one meeting to another were taking their toll of imaginative programming. Drama had fallen into a decline as an extension emphasis after Pop Gordon had left the division to enter the School of Music. It was the appointment of Glenn Frank to the presidency of the University which again focused attention directly on drama as a major Extension Division activity. In 1925, President Frank made a statement which I have always liked, since I read it, for its recognition of the arts by an administrator:

There's a gap somewhere in the soul of the people that troops into the theater but never produces a folk drama, that crowds into the concert hall but never throws off the spark from a folk song like a spark from a glowing iron. The arts are vital, if in the years ahead we are to master instead of being mastered by the vast complex and swiftly moving technical civilization born of science and the machine. The education for the future must, in addition to the more obvious disciplines and diets of the mind, include those stimulations and disciplines that sensitize and enrich men's capacity for worthy emotional aesthetic response to some of the overlooked needs of modern life. The art of the theatre, like the art of literature, has been damned by professionalism. We have wandered far from the days of

95

folk drama when even the great souls of simple folk found expression in the dramatic form. The next great dramatic renaissance in America will come when the theatre is recaptured from the producers by the people, when we become active enough in mind and rich enough in spirit to begin the creation of a folk drama and a folk theatre in America.

Soon a Bureau of Dramatic Activities was planned, and in 1927 it was actually initiated as part of the University Extension Division. An extremely sympathetic Dean of Extension, Chester Snell, had appeared on the scene and gave whole-hearted support to Glenn Frank's attitude toward drama.

Thomas Dickinson comes into the picture again here, though he had been gone from Wisconsin since 1915. One of his students at the University in 1910 had been Miss Ethel Rockwell, who had been also a member of the original Wisconsin Dramatic Society. From Dickinson she had caught the spark and had dedicated herself to the development of a native American drama. She had become an outstanding director and writer of pageants, and was, in 1927, in charge of the Dramatics Division of the Extension Service, University of North Carolina. Here she had been associated with Frederick Koch and from him had drawn added enthusiasm and a missionary attitude toward regional drama development. Dean Snell of the University Extension Division was also a North Carolina man, and it was only natural that President Frank and Snell turned to Ethel Rockwell as the person they wanted to head the new bureau of Dramatic Activities.

The Bureau of Dramatic Activities existed at the University of Wisconsin from 1927 to 1940. Many of these years were the depression years when the minds of the people turned toward the cultural things as a release from their

96

economic worries. Under Ethel Rockwell's leadership a series of local pageants and plays were conducted, a lending library was built up, drama programs were activated in communities, and a state-wide dramatic organization, the Wisconsin Dramatic Guild, had a wide and enthusiastic membership. Her program attracted nation-wide attention, and several volumes of plays were published as a result of her work. At the high point of the work of the Bureau of Dramatic Activities there were over one hundred organized community theater groups in Wisconsin.

Had I known in 1945 the actual extent and accomplishment of the Bureau of Dramatic Activities, I surely would never have had the courage to attempt another project that could only appear to be similar and thus subject to many unfavorable comparisons. Indeed, an outline for a state-wide project in community drama drawn up by Miss Rockwell and submitted to University officials in 1934 covers many of the major aspects of a "Wisconsin Drama Plan" which I submitted soon after my own arrival in the state. According to Miss Rockwell's outline, the objectives of the project were to:

Promote and encourage dramatic art in all of the communities both rural and urban in Wisconsin;

Introduce to adults of the state a pleasant, wholesome, cultural recreational activity that will engage their leisure time;

Demonstrate to special units (churches, industrial groups, social and fraternal organizations) the value of dramatics in maintaining and advancing themselves;

Encourage dramatics in the schools and for children's groups as one of the most worthwhile activities which can be carried on into adult life and thereby greatly enrich it and add to its enjoyment;

Cultivate a greater appreciation of all the arts and literature through the drama and thus develop a finer taste and culture;

Encourage creative work in playwriting and other allied arts,

97

thereby arousing an interest in folk drama and other folk arts. Wisconsin offers a fine opportunity to develop such work among the various racial groups that make up the state's population. Many great plays could be written based upon traditions of their native lands and upon their new-world experiences;

Help communities to organize and operate little or civic theatres;

Teach the art and technique of play production and play writing through classes, institutes, lectures, and demonstrations throughout the state.

These objectives indicate real breadth of scope and understanding of the University's rôle in a cultural arts program. They reflect, too, the distinctly sociological approach to the arts that had been so apparent in the work of Pop Gordon and John Kolb and to a lesser degree in the aims and motives of the Wisconsin Dramatic Society. I, too, have taken a sociological point of view toward the development of regional theater and allied arts in Wisconsin, and perhaps the chief difference between the project I formed under the program title Wisconsin Idea Theater and other sociological-arts programs of the University is that I have attempted to work toward the creation of a soil wherein the arts may grow, rather than with large programs of theater production activity. The difference is reflected in my radio and television programs "Wisconsin Yarns," "Creative Wisconsin," and "Wisconsin Is My Doorstep." The difference is also reflected in research programs which the Idea Theater conducts through which community attitudes are sampled and through which systematic attempts are made to relate and combine theater with the other arts.

After Ethel Rockwell's appointment as director of the Bureau of Dramatic Activities a next major step in the Wisconsin Idea approach to the arts was the selection in 1936 of the great regional American artist, John Steuart Curry, as the first artist-in-residence of a state university. Curry's appointment was arranged by Dean Chris Christensen of the Wisconsin College of Agriculture.

Dean Chris came to the University in 1931, bringing his belief that it was just as important, if not more important, to have books, pictures, and music in the home as it was to buy the adjoining "80." He had a dream of forming a great "Folkschool" built around the farm short course at the University in which young farm men would be exposed to technical agriculture, to the social sciences, and to the cultural arts. He and Kolb worked endlessly to make the dream come true and to carry the idea of the better life into the state. When Dean Chris got John Steuart Curry to come to Wisconsin as artist-in-residence, he was opposed by the University art departments, which held, at the time, that art was for the special few—never for the many. The powerful Dean, however, went ahead with his plan, and after Curry was appointed art received further recognition by the University when Grant Wood was given an honorary degree by the University. Through Dean Chris's arrangements, Kolb, a sociologist, accompanied the famous artist across the platform. President Glenn Frank said, in speaking of the Curry appointment, that "in launching this new educational venture, we are undertaking to give emphasis to regional art as a force for rural as well as urban culture in the Middle West area."

Curry was to paint creatively, just as others were to teach and conduct research. He was bald, jolly, pipe smoking, and liked to wear overalls. He averaged ten hours a day in his campus studio, where students, rural and town folk, could drop in for advice and assistance on art careers or creative painting or watch him at work. On occasion Curry took a few pieces of his work out in the state and talked about them, or lectured to students in the Farmer's Short Course, or spoke to meetings or conventions.

His desire, however, was to impress upon Wisconsin citizens the rural beauty of their own state. He was keenly interested in the layman who had a desire to paint and an interest in painting the things about him. He was able through this feeling for rural art and rural artists to inspire others not only to express themselves on canvas but to attain a greater idealism toward the open country. Curry held that art belongs in the realm of everyday life, that it should be comprehensible, and that comprehensibility should be motivated by genuine love and affection. He believed that artistic form is not something to be confined to an object but that it is the object itself. He held that it is the artist himself who creates his own standards of artistic excellence. He is to be judged by these alone and not by outside canons or stylistic measurements.

In 1940, the rural art show was initiated as one of Curry's main projects. John Barton, trained at Yale and in Denmark, had been brought to Wisconsin to aid in the folkschool idea. He performed the major share of the work of organizing and planning this first exhibition.

Barton has told me that the idea took shape in the minds of the Wisconsin delegates attending the American Country Life Conference at Pennsylvania State College in September, 1939. Among these delegates were Curry and Dean Chris Christensen. When they returned to Wisconsin and Dean Chris broached the subject of an art show to a University committee there was some real skepticism expressed as to whether farm people really had the time or inclination to paint pictures and, indeed, whether the pictures they would paint would have much native quality. However, a search for rural paintings and painters was instigated, and, Barton wrote later, "it is no exaggeration to say that a three month search conducted in 15 of Wisconsin's 71 counties unearthed enough good paintings, water colors, pastels, to form one of the most unusual collections in the history of this region. So far as can be discovered it was the first exhibition of its kind in the history of Wisconsin, perhaps even in the whole country."

Since 1940, the rural art shows have been held every year with an increasing number of people participating. The University has purchased a certain number of the paintings each year and now has a permanent collection of the best rural painting done in the state.

Curry died in 1946, and in 1948 Aaron Bohrod, well-known Chicago modern artist with regional inclinations, came to be artist-in-residence. The rural art shows have been continued with Bohrod's aid and with the active field organizational genius of James Schwalbach, who travels the state constantly.

Had I known all the history of these notable programs that afternoon on Bascom Hill in 1945, the knowledge would doubtless have added perplexity to my moody conjecturing. Had I known that the Bureau of Dramatic Activities was cut off in 1940 by an unsympathetic administrator after thirteen years of worthy service I would certainly have found much to ponder about. I would have wondered how long it would be before the terms "frill" and "unnecessary" would be applied to any new work I might begin in Wisconsin, and I would have wondered whether the kind of community-rooted culture I had visions of nourishing in Wisconsin could ever have long life. One started something up again, and it was the same wheels turning in the same ruts with bitter-eyed people (not too many, but some) watching and saying: It's been done before. Nothing new here. It will pass, this new work of yours, and you will be only a name in the old file boxes.

But I did not think about it like that, because I did not know the events of the past in Wisconsin. What I feared was that the attitude would be almost too friendly, too eager. People would be saying: Now friend, we are all behind you. But, what are you going to *do?* You are the new leader; so produce.

A great faith would have overcome such fears and imaginings, but I had no great faith. I had, instead, an anticipation that only tightened the muscles of my belly. I feared as I had in Alberta the chief conflict within myself— the creative urge struggling against necessity to promote, to accede to the demands of the public, to surrender my native inclination toward individualism to group activity. I feared being pigeonholed in a welter of educational detail. But always there was the search, the restless drive to discover the feeling of places, the desire to help nourish the beginnings of a movement in native arts, and I knew, that afternoon, that the restless drive would always be in me. Possibly the drive itself could become my faith and overcome my fears. I found the thought comforting, and presently I arose and walked down the hill. But the echo of my footsteps against the darkening University buildings sounded empty and lonely.

Chapter four

THE WISCONSIN IDEA THEATER

To go backstage of the Wisconsin Idea in action at the
University of Wisconsin is an unusual experience for a
stranger unacquainted with Wisconsin traditions. Indeed,
not many of the faculty of the University know the extent
of this great backstage, which is really a vast assembly
depot on an educational battlefront where immense piles
of mental ammunition are made ready and fired at the
people from cannon of many degrees of loudness and strik-
ing power.

Certainly, most of the students on the Madison campus

are unaware of the backstage. The students linger on Bascom Hill, walk along Lake Mendota in the quiet of an evening, make love on Observatory Hill, or have refreshment in the Wisconsin Union and realize nothing at all about the feverish arrivals and departures, the scanning of timetables, the plans and campaigns that often keep a hundred lamps burning in a hundred cubbyholes, nooks, warrens, and corners of the University until late at night.

The backstage has a relationship to life on the campus, but the relationship is hard for the average citizen or faculty member to see—perhaps because the units of the backstage are so scattered. The backstage exists in curious places related spiritually to one another and to the University but unrelated geographically. It exists, for instance, in part of a building continuously roaring with the verbal blasts of a tremendous battle between University Extension and Home Economics—a battle which Extension has lost. The backstage exists in a converted monument works, in a side of the football stadium, and in huts and basements.

In the warrens of these places is the material of tremendous educational schemes in almost every subject. Here are Great Books programs, citizen's forums, leadership courses, vast schemes of audio-visual development, plans for education by television, plans for workers' enlightenment, hundreds of correspondence courses taught by green-eyeshaded men and women who read manuscripts and mark papers in the warrens and never see the students they correspond with. Here is a department that answers questions about any subject. Here, in special institutes, is professional education for mail carriers, firemen, preachers, town clerks, traffic officers, factory foremen, recreational leaders, district attorneys. Here is an office to book entertainment for high school assembly periods. Here are fleets of cars, oiled,

104

gassed, ready for the road. And here are drivers, many with PhD's, to hurl the cars about the state, crossing and criss-crossing, holding the steering wheels like the reins of chargers, carrying out missions, leading a new kind of crusade.

In the nooks and corners are secretaries, sometimes sleek and young, sometimes old and full of woes, to mind the affairs of the knights, trace their journeys, tabulate their expense accounts, witness their successes, forget their failures.

In Madison, in many modest homes wives wait for their men—their knights of the Wisconsin Idea—and wish guiltily at times for quiet professorships in tiny colleges.

Travel, speed, and sometimes death are all part of the backstage of the Wisconsin Idea. Fog, slippery roads, deep snow, perpetual colds, hotel rooms, and lonely beds are the commonplace items. The knights are sober men, basically good family men, and they have a tremendous belief that what they are doing is important.

Their belief, of course, is often belief without imagination. They establish routines, set precedents, coin clichés, fashion absurd stereotypes, whirl about often in a kind of mad self-justification that is barren, really, of accomplishment. Some of them pause not at all for introspection. They do not define motives. They act swiftly, and only when they are old do they know, occasionally, that the tires of their souls have blown out against the hard sides of deep ruts. Yet with all these weaknesses they are doing a stupendous job.

After nearly ten years at Wisconsin, it amazes me, occasionally, to realize that I am a part of this vast backstage that the Wisconsin Idea has created. All the things I mistrusted: the sociological approaches, the "institutes," the programs in "adult education," the specializing, and the expertizing are all a part of me, now. I have been able to find inspiration in the idea of a whole state being a campus, or a stage. In a way I have been caught in the system of the backstage, but I have also created my own rôle within the system and have usually preserved my own integrity in the shadow of the system. The machinery of specializing and expertizing is very valuable in carrying out my rôle, which has become that of a sort of "specialist" in creating a friendlier attitude toward the theater and other arts. If my specializing is tinted with a crusading or missionary zeal at times it is probably the influence of my restless drive which would like to hurry the Wisconsin people toward a better use of the arts in everyday life.

My office in the football stadium is the center of what has been known for nine years now as the Wisconsin Idea Theater. I am never tired of wondering how, exactly, I came to the stadium. In my college days at Kansas University before I got exposed to the theater idea I tried very hard but quite unsuccessfully to win laurels in the stadium. When I turned my back on it the stadium became, often, a thing to ridicule, to deplore. It became a symbol of what I took to be mistaken public regard, an undue interest in spectator sports to the detriment of the arts. Now I am, through necessity, back in the stadium, seeking there every day the answers to cultural riddles. It is dramatic irony worthy of drama, surely.

My office has not always been in the Wisconsin stadium. For a little while, when I first came to the University, it was in a nice corner of the geological museum. After a short time the demands of the museum for space moved me out of the museum and transported me to a converted monument works where I remained for four years. As I built my staff, my own space problems grew troublesome, and when the football players no longer needed the stadium rooms for dormitories the stadium became a part of the Wisconsin Idea backstage and was occupied by a variety of programs. The working space is good, once one has successfully ascended the flights of cold concrete stairs with throat bundled securely against the fierce drafts of the stadium concourse. I rather like the stadium and its remoteness from the campus proper. It is filled with solitudes, shadows, under-the-stair crannies where one can sink from sight for a moment and reflect upon the wondrous ways of University development.

Toward my physical surroundings I am extremely tolerant, and of the great backstage I am a willing part. I attend meetings, sit on committees, conduct "institutes," make speeches, and I am able somehow to have faith that what I am doing is worthwhile. I have made of my approach to the arts a kind of personal religion. This religion is so strong that, like my colleagues in the backstage, I am able to endure without much notice the physical weariness and the handicaps that Wisconsin nature tosses in my way. My religion is more than dedication. It is simple acceptance of a viewpoint, of a method of operation. It is recognition of participation in the Idea quite willingly, not without question to be sure, but with the questions emerging from a consciousness of hope rather than bitterness.

The Wisconsin Idea Theater, which I direct, is such an expression of faith—a faith that has been achieved slowly through success and failure, through tormenting doubts. It is a faith which has no symbolization whatever in piles of stone and material properties. My corner of the stadium which I inhabit through the willing coöperation of the Department of Intercollegiate Athletics is all I have, materially, to express my faith. Yet, strangely, I find that I have all the material properties that are essential.

In retrospect, the lights and shadows of the nine years spent in the creation of the Wisconsin Idea Theater stand out clearly. The shadows were predominant in the early years. My convictions about native literature were sincere, strong. I saw a native literature emerging as in Alberta and New York from a feeling for places. But soon after I had started work in Wisconsin I understood that I could not work as I had in New York, for example, where the University theater itself furnished the center and the home base for my efforts with native playwrights.

There was no Drummondesque sympathy for native playwriting in the University theater at Wisconsin. The Wisconsin theater staff was overburdened with teaching and with duties connected with play production and had little or no time for the discussion of regional drama problems. The attitude of the theater staff was a blow which left me confused. I fear that I wasted some of this early period in futile bitterness. I believe now, however, that failure to establish a center for my work in the University theater was actually the factor that saved my program. For I was thrown toward the backstage and became familiar with the Wisconsin Idea, with the extension men, the specialists, the crusaders.

I was reluctant at first. Remembering what had happened to me as a kind of "extension" worker in Canada, I was somewhat mistrustful of the Extension Division at Wisconsin, especially when I learned the Division was to be the actual administrative unit for my work. The whole format of my project, however, was unique, and the Extension Division seemed to me, shortly after my arrival in Madison, to offer a more promising base than the University theater, which offered nothing.

My entire program was to be conducted by three separate branches of the University: the College of Letters and Science, the College of Agriculture, and the Extension Division. Financial support would be divided among the three branches, with Letters and Science and Agriculture providing one-half of my salary and the Extension Division providing the remaining half as well as office space, secretarial help, and other facilities. Although the new program was to be a joint undertaking of these three University branches it was placed under the administrative jurisdiction of the Extension Division, and during its first year, 1945–46, all budgetary matters not relating to salary were channeled through the Division's Department of Debating and Public Discussion.

One hot afternoon in September, I walked into the catacombs of the building called Science Hall where the Department of Debating and Public Discussion was temporarily housed. I presently found an office in which a fellow with a brush of kinky gray hair was working at a roll-top desk. The Director of the Extension Division, a young administrator named Adolfson, had told me that this gray-haired fellow, who was the Director of the Department of Debating, would give me an office and help me get started.

The man with the kinky gray hair was Leslie E. Brown. He had been an Iowa farm boy with a passionate hunger for education for himself, for everybody. He wanted the schoolhouses lighted at night for the men and women who had never had a chance to get any daytime education, or who wished to continue their education. He developed ultimately into one of the national leaders in adult education and became a Dean of Cleveland College. I liked him instantly. He said warmly: "You're Gard! I'm certainly glad to see you."

I sat down and we spoke of inconsequential things. Then he said, "What are you going to do in Wisconsin?"

I thought for a moment. Looking back, I knew that in Kansas Allen Crafton had opened a whole new world of theater for me; that in New York Drummond had taught me how to apply feeling for places and ideas about theater to regional life. In Alberta I had tested and developed these ideas, and, while I did not know exactly what I was going to do in Wisconsin, I thought that I could safely say that I wanted to try in many ways to stimulate and develop the creative forces in the people. I answered him the best I could then.

Brown and I became fast friends. In practical terms, I suppose that Brown's real rôle throughout our early association was to assist me in matters of University policy, to help to acquaint me with the state, and to orient me to previous activity in the drama field. But, during the time he remained in Wisconsin he was a constant source of inspiration. He was over-burdened, often tired, and sometimes sick, but he was never too tired or too sick to discuss my problems. Much of my knowledge of the early history of the Wisconsin Idea came out of my many conversations with Brown and out of his comprehension of what I hoped to accomplish. From Brown I learned that "adult education" was not at all alien in theory to my hopes and dreams about people's expressiveness, and from my association with Brown began my tolerance for the great backstage.

By late September, 1945, with Brown's help, I was ready to summarize some of my impressions, suggestions, and ideas relating to the possible development of a Wisconsin regional theater program. These were gathered together in an informal written proposal called "Notes for a General Wisconsin Drama Plan." In this paper, I observed that in the creative arts, especially, new work needed to be undertaken to relate the arts to people's lives. That the people themselves desired such a relation seemed to me to be indicated by the interest in local scene and tradition I had found in America. From such desire, I believed, a good popular art could grow. It seemed to me the undertaking I was proposing could add to the increasing awareness that our American picture was not a completed work in itself but a composite of developing regional pictures in every state and community in the nation.

My work in drama I hoped to relate as closely as possible to the Wisconsin scene. I hoped to make such work mirror the outstanding tradition and themes of the region and to develop the native talents of the state. I proposed a state-wide playwriting project in an attempt to bring the regional themes to the fore, and I hoped to relate to the field of drama some of the general experiments in the other arts being conducted by the University. I had in mind particularly the state-wide programs in painting and in music being conducted by the Extension Division.

The playwriting phase, I noted, would be conducted somewhat as the one Drummond and I had conceived for New York State. Lists would be compiled of persons interested in writing a Wisconsin play, of persons who might be able to provide regional materials for playwriting, and of persons who might be interested in producing Wisconsin plays. Criticism and instruction would be offered interested writers through correspondence, simple manuals on play construction, and through conducting one- or two-day institutes in playwriting.

Fundamental to such a playwriting experiment would be a central tryout laboratory theater located somewhere on the University campus. I foresaw the formation of an annual Wisconsin Idea Theater Conference to bring together once a year all the dramatic activities in the state, including not only the actual drama producing groups of the state but also interested individuals from all aspects of community life. I felt that the failure of drama experiments was most often brought about through setting up the play and its production as something for the few or as something only superficially connected with the everyday life of the people. I hoped to make the Wisconsin work broad enough to include a large proportion of the population.

The "Notes for a General Wisconsin Drama Plan" went on to suggest that a magazine be established to serve as a medium for the expression of ideas and as a means of offering some needed instruction. This publication would serve as a clearing house for the state-wide organization of groups and individuals. I also noted the need for research projects and hoped that I might find time for some research and writing myself. (I fondly remembered the modest success that I had had with playwriting in New York State and in Alberta, and I had pleasant recollections of my journeys in search of folklore, out of which grew my book *Johnny Chinook*.) I concluded that I considered the fundamental principles of the proposed drama plan to be a reflection of contemporary and past life and themes of the region. In this sense it was proposed as an educational service for developing the native talents of the region and for raising general dramatic standards. I hoped to make the drama a living factor in the people's lives. I noted, finally, that since I wanted to establish a lasting work in Wisconsin the beginnings of such a work must be carefully planned with the roots of the work in the people.

A number of copies of "Notes for a General Wisconsin Drama Plan" were prepared and sent to over a dozen University of Wisconsin officials whose advice and counsel were considered of importance prior to the initiation of a drama program. Early in October, 1945, a meeting of these individuals, the Deans of the sponsoring colleges, members of the University Speech department, rural sociology specialists, and others, was held for the purpose of discussing in detail all phases of the proposed plan.

Brown kept careful notes of this meeting. These notes indicate that practically everyone in attendance was in substantial agreement on the plan. It was pointed out by John Gaus (now professor of Political Science in Harvard University) that "the essence of the entire program rests on the attempt to create a favorable climate in which a worthwhile regional expression may grow." John Kolb emphatically stressed the need for better and more complete drama training in rural areas, the need for breaking down the traditional barriers between rural and urban people, and the desirability of keeping the emphasis broad in scope yet centralized at the University. Beyond points such as these I was encouraged to develop the entire program slowly and carefully and to feel free to make use of every facility within the province of the three sponsoring colleges.

By January, 1946, I was deeply engrossed in gearing the new theater project to the machinery of the great backstage. A name for the project then became a major concern. Since I was still unfamiliar with much of the earlier theater tradition in Wisconsin, I took some time at this point to probe a bit into such background. I hoped that a name for my project would emerge.

I presume that my selection of the title "Wisconsin Idea Theater" for the new drama program was the result of this probing into backgrounds. I was greatly impressed by what I had read about Thomas Dickinson and the Wisconsin Dramatic Society. The Society's purpose had encompassed a regional approach to drama very similar to my own. It was soon after I had learned the details of the Wisconsin Dramatic Society that the idea of calling the project "The Wisconsin Idea Theater" simply occurred to me as I was walking across the campus. I knew instantly that it was a far better name than "Wisconsin Theater Program," "Wisconsin State Theater Project," or the dozen other inept titles I had been considering. "Wisconsin Idea Theater" seemed to indicate a number of points about the plan, including its state-wide scope and its fundamental idea (already accepted by me as essential) of integrating the meaning of the Wisconsin Idea in education with the need for a broad penetration of the field of the cultural arts. So with the name decided, a version of the final draft was again sent to University officials, to newspapers, and to other interested persons.

It was a brave name full of brave hope. My optimism was boundless, and I could only consider that the Wisconsin people would welcome the new Wisconsin Idea Theater with open arms. And indeed, the opening publicity guns brought forth a mass of comment both oral and written which fluttered down on Leslie Brown and me and lifted us to wild dreams of a truly overpowering cultural emphasis in the Badger State. "Maybe even beyond Wisconsin," Leslie muttered one afternoon as we inspected our pictures over a tremendous front page story in an influential state newspaper. Looking at the headline which intimated that a playwriting boom was about to strike the Middle West I agreed with Brown that almost certainly our idea was on the way.

In fact, the lavish publicity became at times almost unbearable. Our statements that the spirit and tradition of the Wisconsin portion of the upper Middle West were to be investigated and turned to creative use were pounced upon by eager and inventive reporters who seemed willing to go to any length to plumb the comic news-value of my arrival in Wisconsin.

I was caught by reporters one afternoon in the rathskeller of the Wisconsin Union. A dozen coffee cups were quickly placed on the table in front of me and a quick-triggered newsphotographer caught my homely visage like a pale and doubtful sun above the small mountain of cups. A caption above the picture on the front page of the *Wisconsin State Journal* stated that "Cawfee helps a man think" and the story under the picture characterized me as a deceivingly tired-looking addition to the University of Wisconsin faculty who moved with a lope not far removed from the plowed fields and whose idea of real pleasure was to wander into the hinterland of wherever he happened to be and just "sit around talkin' and sittin' and drinkin' cawfee until he had absorbed the local folklore."

As a matter of fact, under different circumstances I might have found the reporter's idea of my mission in Wisconsin good fun, but in those days I did not do much sitting around and drinking coffee. I was after a big thing—a major cultural movement—and I wanted action. The newspapers, if one could believe the ebullient reporters, wanted action too. But even with all the tremendous build up of a press starved during the war years for cultural items, I was to learn that rapid decisions in favor of anything as seemingly ephemeral as a "people's cultural movement" usually do not happen, at least not at a major state university beset with unbelievable housing problems.

At the University of Wisconsin in 1946 about twenty thousand students were stacked into classrooms designed for a maximum of ten thousand. The University was also hard put to house its veterans, many of whom were married and had families, and no miraculous state art center sprang up on the campus as a symbol of the state-wide cultural developmental ideal Brown and I had in mind. It was from my first office in the enclosed corner of the geological museum that I sallied forth to interview this person or that whom I fancied might rapidly advance the Wisconsin Idea Theater as a phase of state life.

These conversations were, for the most part, of little avail. I found everyone sympathetic, but the developments I had in mind were large and costly in terms of materials and manpower. I wanted a large staff immediately to plunge into the task of creating a native literature, a native theater. I wanted an experimental theater. Everyone agreed that the University theater as it was set up could not be the focus for the experimental new plays laboratory I had in mind, but no one really believed that such a laboratory could be provided. I even encountered slightly disillusioned persons on the University faculty who had been waiting for twenty or thirty years for facilities in fields they were engaged in, and under the pessimistic attitudes my hope for a quick centering-up in material terms of the Wisconsin Idea Theater program dwindled away. Everywhere I was encouraged to move slowly and cautiously.

Meanwhile, regardless of the slowness of University development the people of Wisconsin were demanding the aid of the new drama project in community programs in the theater arts. The demands were consistently heavy, week by week, and reluctantly I withdrew from my futile promotional attempts at the University and assumed my rôle as a teacher and promoter of theater in Wisconsin community life.

The barren war years had sharpened community appetites for the arts. Jim Schwalbach, who had come to the University at the same time I did to help with the Rural Art project, was madly dashing from this spot to that trying to keep up with the demands made upon him. I was doing the same thing, though I desperately endeavored to keep my whole program in mind. I used the University radio station, WHA, extensively to reach the people with a "Wisconsin Yarns" series. These half-hour programs of dramatized Wisconsin stories which I wrote and narrated each week only seemed to increase the demands made upon me, and for a time I was engaged in almost a duplication of my Alberta rôle as a kind of promoter of state subjects. I made countless public addresses, conferred with dozens of theater groups, saw their plays, worked with playwrights, and reached the point, eventually, where I knew that I must have help.

The question of staff for the Wisconsin Idea Theater had not been settled. Brown and I had envisioned an extensive staff ultimately dealing with the varied problems of adult and young people's theater as well as coöperating with and helping to develop the allied arts. My conversations and promotions around the University by the Spring of 1946 had led me to believe that the Wisconsin Idea Theater was likely to be a one-man proposition with myself as director, staff, and flunky. But by this time it was also apparent that if the scope of the Idea Theater was to be maintained a staff was essential.

I was to learn how important private funds can be at the

beginning of a new program. I was also to learn that my rôle as director of the Wisconsin Idea Theater was to be that of a constant seeker after money. Dreams are costly at state universities. I had one single desire, however: to build an outstanding area plan in native literature and native theater. I therefore went after the money necessary to build a staff.

I learned that David Stevens of the Rockefeller Foundation had recently made a grant to a University committee organized for area studies, and in this committee I saw a means of implementing the research phase which I had planned. With the committee's promise of support I sought the help of a former Drummond student, Jack Curvin, to start digging out the source materials of a native Wisconsin drama. Jack arrived in May of 1946.

Leslie Brown meanwhile had persuaded L. H. Adolfson, Director of University Extension, that an assistant for the Wisconsin Idea Theater was necessary, and Adolfson moved to create the new job. For the first time I felt the potency of the University itself in enlarging and carrying forward the idea we had sketched. Junius Eddy, of Antioch College, joined the staff in the Fall of 1946 and things began to roll. We started a magazine, the *Wisconsin Idea Theater Quarterly*, which is still going strong today, nine years later. We opened up the community theater field again, and many new groups came to life. We began the Wisconsin Idea Theater Conference, now in its ninth year. I will never forget the thrill of watching the first Conference body assemble: farmers, teachers, students—a whole range of Wisconsin citizens assembling in a hot University hall in August to discuss the problems of theater in their home communities.

In 1947, the Rockefeller Foundation made its first direct

grant to the University for the specific use of the Wisconsin Idea Theater, and Martha Van Kleeck of Yale came to work with the community theaters of Wisconsin. Her presence released Eddy and me for more time with writers and for the whole job of communicating the aims of the project to the people.

From the Rockefeller Foundation, too, came our first playwright-in-residence, Ed Kamarck, who was to become a leader of the Wisconsin Rural Writers' Association. As the staff developed, University Extension became more and more important in my plans. Little by little my confidence in the Extension idea grew, and always Adolfson stood ready to help. He provided money for special lectures, for conferences, for travel. Extension—the backstage, actually the front door of the University to thousands of homes in the state—was always there, and I knew that my stability and the stability of the Wisconsin Idea Theater lay in the steady encouragement of men vitally concerned in spreading education throughout the state.

Eventually, when the Rockefeller Foundation had performed its rôle as a catalyst and withdrew from various early phases of the Wisconsin Idea Theater, Extension was able to take over and make the staff positions permanent. But it was the knowledge of the sympathy and belief of the backstage and of a few individuals that has been a salvation for me, and I trust that I have been accepted by the adult education specialists as happily as I have accepted them and what they stand for.

The whole job starting the Wisconsin Idea Theater might, I suppose, have been easier had the state Centennial not come into the picture. I was called to a meeting at the State Capitol one day in the Spring of 1946 and found a collection of state and university dignitaries. To my horror I was called upon to state what I was planning as a celebration during the Centennial year of 1948. I hemmed and hawed, made a few inane remarks, and learned later that one reason why I had been brought into the state was because of my interest in native lore—an interest which seemed suitable for a state about to take a good look back over its first one hundred years.

The Centennial took practically my entire time from the end of 1946 to June of 1948, and it was during this period that the whole beginning structure of the Wisconsin Idea Theater was being formed. These years were, in a sense, interlude years, questing years during which my ideas and feelings about native literature matured. The fortunate thing about the Centennial interlude period was that there were men eager to aid me in comprehension of my rôle and purposes. The Centennial rôle I had to play was a special thing, of course, which I will describe later. As the director of a state-wide program, however, I had a lot to learn, and I owe a great deal to the men who helped to educate me.

There was Brown, of course, and there was the rural sociologist, John Kolb, who really opened my eyes to the meanings of the arts in community life. Often I would climb to the high, wind-swept reaches of Agriculture Hall to seek Kolb out and always I would get a flash of his vision for an arts-conscious Wisconsin folk. Kolb believed, like all sociologists, in the group as a central concept. To him drama represented a kind of ultimate in group relations. He saw the values inherent in rôle-playing, but saw them as healthy expression, not as therapy. He saw in group expression through drama the emergence of values rooted deep in the culture of peoples and expressing the native traditions of many nationalities. He had traveled Wisconsin constantly in his earlier days, often in company with Gladys Borchers and Henry Ewbank of the Speech department, spreading the idea of drama and the other arts, and he knew the groups in the state.

Sometimes John Barton or Arthur Wileden of Kolb's department would join us and a whole world new to me— a world of philosophy built on the importance of the arts in community life—would be opened up. It was those conversations that encouraged and brought to life the urge I had first felt in Alberta to relate other arts to the theater program. And it was such conversations and personal contacts with men who had been pioneers in the cultural arts programs in Wisconsin that gave direction to my restless drive and search. They knew that I was a sincere worker in the Wisconsin Idea and that I was trying hard to build a good state-wide program. They came to know of my boyhood experiences in Kansas which identified me with country scenes and country people, and they knew that I strove to see behind the formal to the many informal ways of achieving spiritual expressions and sharing human experiences.

I found further inspiration from the great Wisconsin song-master, Pop Gordon, and from the state 4-H Club leader, Wakelin McNeel.

When I was a lad in Kansas I had belonged to an early 4-H Club in Allen County. The movement has since become a tremendous force in American rural life, but in the mid-1920's only a few boys in our county were members. I did not take well to the experience, and the organizational aspects of the Club plan bored me.

I never quite got over my mistrust of 4-H clubs. Still, I found that the 4-H Club program in Wisconsin had had drama aspects, and I was, apparently, expected to develop further Club drama plans.

I put it off as long as I could and finally, full of suspicion, called on the state 4-H Club leader, Wakelin McNeel, who was popularly known as "Ranger Mac." I expected to find an organizer rampant and discovered instead a deeply sensitive man who loved the woods and the solitudes. He knew the names of every plant and flower in Wisconsin, and the whole lore of wildlife was poetry to him. We liked one another immediately, and as I knew him better I understood that his feeling for places was even keener than mine. He had a sincere desire to give the young rural folks with whom he worked a sense of the importance of beauty in their lives, and before I knew it, Mac and I were making plans for young rural people's dramatic festivals. Our association led, eventually, to the formation of a great new creative writing idea for Wisconsin: The Wisconsin Rural Writers' Association.

Looking back, it seems to me that it has been the men who themselves have had the great faith who have helped me most. The faith of my friend David Stevens in the idea of developing regional culture has been of tremendous spiritual aid to me, for there has not been one moment since Drummond sent me to New York City in 1938 to see Dr. Stevens about a Rockefeller Fellowship that I have not felt the friendly force of the Foundation behind me. From such associations and from the entire operation of creating the Wisconsin Idea Theater have come added convictions of the need for higher standards of appreciation of art in American communities, of the need for finer leadership in the community arts, and of the necessity for creating friendly attitudes in the American public toward the arts.

At the present time these notions are being worked at

throughout the state of Wisconsin by many volunteer workers without whom the yearly cost of approximately twenty-five thousand dollars for the maintenance of the Wisconsin Idea Theater would be much higher. Such volunteers include Theodore Cloak of Lawrence College, Robert E. Freidel of the Milwaukee Recreation Department, Margo Herriott of Madison, Tom Hendry of Winnebago County, Fidelia Van Antwerp of Wisconsin Dells, Emily Sprague Wurl of Wauwatosa, Louis Poliere of Beloit, Alice Dauer of Watertown, Esther Brannan of Baraboo, Jim and Virginia Hawkins of Racine, John Kennedy of Evansville, Neil Greene of Muscoda, Helen Zillman of Madison, Sister Margaret Mary of La Crosse, and many others who have actually made the program of the Wisconsin Idea Theater a living thing in the state.

The great backstage has made it possible for me to work with such volunteers in their own communities. In my travels to visit them, seeking the creative stuff here and there in the far and near corners of the state, I have become keenly conscious of the state itself as the whole unit of focus of my search.

My impressions of the State of Wisconsin are, of course, selective, emotional, intuitive, and, in any real sense, non-historical. I can see no over-all trait that characterizes Wisconsin people, and my impressions are like short pieces of music each with its own tempo and color. My search in Wisconsin (as always) has been for the flavor and variety of place, and what understanding I have of Wisconsin is based on these things. Yet a portrait of place was extremely important to the whole early development of the Wisconsin Idea Theater and to me personally as its director. It was essential to my personal happiness that I establish an attitude toward Wisconsin which might make it as appealing as Kansas, or New York, or Alberta had been. Perhaps I have been able to do so. At least, the flavor and variety of Wisconsin are inseparable from the work of the Wisconsin Idea Theater, for I believe that theater and its allied arts should reflect the personality of the area, refine its lights and shadows, and define its poetic and dramatic climaxes.

A portrait of Wisconsin, therefore, became one of my chief concerns, and I searched harder and even more desperately than I had in Canada to know the face of the region, so that when I talked to its people it would be as friend to friend, or, better yet, as neighbor to neighbor.

Chapter five

A PORTRAIT OF PLACE

Wisconsin does not possess the soft insistent mystery of central New York nor the overpowering breadth of the Short Grass country of western Canada, but the state has its own appeals which, to me, are always more the result of Wisconsin traditions than of the geographical character of the land. One of these traditions is certainly the attitude with which people accept the Wisconsin Idea in education. For example, I was invited one evening "to make a talk on drama" at a crossroads town hall set at the edge of a large cornfield near Oconomowoc. The lady who invited me, Mrs. Isabelle

125

Tremaine, the wife of a prosperous farmer, had written: "Come on for supper. Afterwards you may make your talk."

I arrived at the Tremaine farm about six and was discussing rural approaches to the drama with my hostess when Mr. Tremaine staggered into the kitchen with an ugly gash in his forehead. He had smashed into a steel stanchion in the dim barn and was temporarily hors de combat. Now, cow milking in its various forms is one of the skills one never forgets and certainly I had had enough milking in my Kansas boyhood to make a permanent impression. I offered to take over at the barn and my offer was accepted easily, naturally.

The Tremaines had a milking machine, but there were certain cows who would not stand for machinery. With my head in a warm flank I meditated about a state where the rôle of a professor from the University is as natural to cowmilking as to conducting classes in adult education. The people of Wisconsin through their tradition of the Wisconsin Idea understand the necessities of milking and adult education equally well, and professors and people are generally on common ground. After I had finished the milking and had had a bite to eat I went to the hall and gave my little talk. It was accepted by the rural audience with the same ease and naturalness and understanding that my offer to milk the cows had been. With such understanding of motives and methods I, at least, have found the strong flavors of Wisconsin places pleasant to savor. I have become familiar with Wisconsin's past, and I have found the past always adding spice to present observations. Not to know the past of a region is like viewing the setting but never seeing the drama.

How empty a trip westward from Madison toward Mount Horeb and Mineral Point would be for me if I did not know that I was traveling on the ridgeroad, the old military highway which carried the heavy lead wagons rolling slowly from the mines at Mineral Point, New Diggings, Benton, and the whole southwest. How empty my journey would be if I could not imagine the rolling wagons, the drivers, their speech, the dust, the blue jackets of cavalrymen, the settlers' rigs, and the immigrants from Europe on foot plodding along the ridgeroad, seeking new freedoms of many kinds, finding new freedoms in the valleys and on the hillsides. How empty my journey if I did not know that to the north and south of the road were valleys where Norwegian names are thickly sown with, here and there, a few Irish, English, or German shoots sticking through. I know that there are other valleys not far from the road where Swiss names are as thick as Norwegian and others where German names blanket the countryside. It is warming to know where the plantings of names lie on the land and to know how the seed came to the soil.

It adds zest to my journey to know that the ridgeroad is the stamping ground of an elusive "haunt"—the Ridgeway Ghost. In 1820 near Mineral Point, a Missouri man murdered a Virginian in a quarrel over a pretty Cornish girl. The Missouri man got the maiden, but the Virginian took up a flitting, terrorizing vigil as a ghost along the ridgeway. He is seen sometimes riding a two-wheeled rig to which is hitched a splendid team of blacks (breathing fire, some say). The team and driver appear suddenly on the ridgeway at night weaving in and out of traffic, causing squeals of terror and sudden endings to midnight romance. The Ghost sometimes is said to appear riding the cowcatcher of the occasional engine which huffs its slow way across the ridgelands on the Chicago and Northwestern branch line. The Ghost is not seen so often nowadays, since many of the Welsh and

Cornish folks who lived along the ridgeway have disappeared. But an imaginative traveler can spot him. I have.

The folklore of the region is always the coloring of the region's portrait, and the response of Wisconsin people to adult education is a part of the picture, too, an inspiring part, especially when the educational program is attached to the arts. For example, Grant County is a county of low hills, farming country cut sharply by ravines and valleys and quick flooding streams. There are towns, too, which seem to me to be very mid-American. One cold March afternoon there was a meeting at Lancaster. This was a meeting of a group of Grant County rural artists. They had been called together to see the movie the State Department in Washington had made of their Grant County art activities. Many of the artists were actors in the movie. They brought their neighbors and families to see this movie which would be shown in nations all over the world to demonstrate that rural America has a culture of its own. The meeting was held in the local movie theater where there was 35 millimeter equipment. The place held about six hundred persons and it was full. Many of the business people of Lancaster came in, too. In the lobby of the City Hall next door paintings were piled and stacked, waiting to be taken upstairs and displayed. The artist-in-residence from the University of Wisconsin was to attend the showing of the movie and, afterward, to offer criticism and suggestion on many of the paintings brought in by the people. There was to be a supper, too, held right there in the display hall, and many of the farm ladies had brought covered dishes, or pies, cakes or meats.

I drove over from Madison with Aaron Bohrod, the artist-in-residence, Jim Schwalbach, the traveling Extension artist who had arranged the meeting, and a gentleman from the Rockefeller Foundation in New York, Edward D'Arms. He had come out to see at first hand some of the field work in the arts going on in Wisconsin. He was interested but a bit unbelieving. "Perhaps," he had said on the way over from Madison, "we are not ready for a people's art expression in America."

We sat in the back of the theater and saw the movie which had been produced by Julian Bryan who had done many good films. It was good, a work of art. The rural folk in the cast with their easy naturalness turned out to be some of the best actors we had seen. We were excited, and D'Arms expressed eagerness to go upstairs and see some of the paintings these rural folk had been doing.

We climbed the City Hall stairs and entered a long room. It was jammed with people, and there were countless original paintings lined up along the walls on tables. A passage opened before Aaron Bohrod as he went to the far end of the room. He was greeted with enthusiastic and friendly calls from every side. The people were not embarrassed. The fact that he was an outstanding American artist made no difference in their attitude toward him. He was one of their group. He believed in them and what they had been doing. He set up an easel and called for the first painting.

An elderly farm woman brought the first one. It was of a barn and cattle and a tree. Bohrod set it on the easel and commented with respect. He called attention to good points and bad, making his criticism always constructive and helpful. Then came a bachelor who had turned a corn bin into a studio; then came a high school girl, a feed store operator, more housewives, and a school teacher, a country doctor. More and more.

We watched and listened. D'Arms grew thoughtful. He made notes in a black book, asking for names and occupations of the people. Finally someone thought of food. Pictures were taken off the tables and the food was spread. We all sat down together. A grayed little lady sat beside D'Arms. She said to him, "Do you see why we like to live in Wisconsin?" He said, "I think I do."

One night in 1950 I was invited to a farmers' meeting that had a double purpose. The first purpose was the discussion of an economic measure near to the community's heart, and the second purpose was to discuss what that community might do through theater to draw the community into a more cohesive body. My part was distinctly secondary on the program.

The economic question was this: Our Wisconsin Legislature recently put through a law requiring that farmers have a separate milkhouse with a concrete floor and that they haul the manure away from the barns every day. There was a date set at which time all the milkhouses must be ready. Many farmers disliked the law. They were shorthanded. They had no time to build a new milkhouse. Some of them had always let the manure pile up around the barn throughout the winter and, by Gad, they would continue to do so!

This particular meeting turned into a hot one. The chair got into trouble trying to keep order, and the county agricultural agent was almost mobbed because some of the folks blamed him for their plight. This community had also summoned its state assemblyman to be present; he had voted for the milkhouse bill in the legislature. They said violent things to him. The discussion was not getting anywhere.

They wrangled for a while and then decided to call it off. They turned the meeting over to me.

I was in an uncomfortable spot, faced by anticlimax and the probable futility of trying to stimulate interesting discussion in this particular atmosphere. I knew I simply could not talk about drama in ordinary terms. It suddenly occurred to me, as I fumbled about, that the previous discussion had aspects of a drama: conflict, character, excellent dialogue. So I set about fabricating, without the people actually knowing what was going on, a comic situation in which the various factions and individuals were either for or against the milkhouse law, and before we realized it a kind of group play was actually in progress, only now it seemed in terms of comedy, exciting but laughable, for I had attempted to exaggerate the purpose on both sides and to enlarge on the innocence of the county agent and to exaggerate the well-meaning, slightly self-pitying attitude of the legislator as well as the anger of several of the more outspoken opponents of the milkhouse bill.

In the informally dramatized version of the affair that we made up there at the moment the farmer was getting his whacks at the legislator and the county agent was making his excuses but within the framework of a creative situation.

Somehow feelings seemed cleansed, purposes made clear, and actually everyone began to enjoy the situation. In fact, that particular group enjoyed it so much that they decided to put the dramatized discussion on again at a later gathering. And they did, with a big spread of good country grub, with some rural paintings hung around the walls of the hall, and with some singers from a county-wide rural chorus furnishing another aspect of the occasion.

We have tried this kind of community, or group, drama

a number of times with general good success. It is, of course, a purely presentational sort of theater in which the members of the audience are actually the actors. The play, if it may be called that, is frank theatricality with the theatrical elements simplified and frankly artificial.

This kind of dramatic expression, which could find great place in countryside life, has a body of precedent. For example, during the nineteenth century Nietzsche, Tolstoi, Rolland, and Appia developed theories of "art for life's sake" and considered a kind of "communal" drama as the art of the future. The form of the group play I have described bears a slight resemblance also to the theatrical concept of Evreinov, the drama theorist and playwright who formulated a theory of drama-in-life.

The form has special value to groups of young persons, especially, who are able to free themselves from their inhibitions and from the ordinary conventional restrictions of the realistic stage. Crowd scenes, for instance, are apt to be highly dynamic and expressive, perhaps confusing to the spectator but satisfying to the participant who is the chief one involved. It is the participant's show. Within its framework is endless scope for education on the part of a leader who may aid the participants in working out more satisfying ways of self-expression through dramatic movement and interplay with other participants.

I have traveled Wisconsin in all its seasons in my search for the flavor of the state. I recall a cold morning at the University's experimental farm at Spooner, up in the northwest corner of the state. It was November, late in the month. Snow was on the ground, and a wet, chilling wind was coming across the cutover and the swamps.

The young home demonstration agent and I paced

nervously about the room. We were wearing our heavy coats. She had had a lot of experience with north country economics, very little with theater. She looked continually at her watch. She was embarrassed. She said, finally, "Well, Mr. Gard, I sure hope *somebody* comes."

I said, "So do I."

That morning I had driven up to Spooner from Chippewa Falls over glass-slick roads. Earlier in the month we had written from the office in Madison: "Dear County Agricultural Agent: Spooner has been selected as a regional meeting place for a one-day drama training school. Would you please notify all persons in your area and the agents in surrounding counties so that interested people may attend?"

We had exchanged several letters. The Spooner office had written that there had never been much drama in that part of the state; folks were scattered out, sort of; and they didn't have much free time. It was hard to scrape a living out of the north country earth; so they hadn't given much thought to putting on plays, but ... well, if you want to come up we'll give your training school idea a go. Better wear your long underwear and carry a shovel in your car— guess you haven't been up our way.

So here I was, and it was time for the meeting to begin; and not a single person had arrived. The young home agent said, wistfully, "I *do* wish one person would come." She glanced at me and I knew that she sincerely hoped my trip would not be entirely barren.

I said, "Keep calm."

We paced some more, and finally she said, "There is a lady over in the eastern part of the county who put on a play once. They ... they said it was awfully funny."

I said, "That's nice."

She said, "After all, Mr. Gard, the weather is terrible."

133

She heard a noise, she thought, and rushed over to the window. A car was pulling into the yard. I ran to look, too. She cried, "There are *three* in that car! *Three!*" Sure enough, there were. Two ladies and a small boy. The young home agent rushed out to greet them and I thought, "Well, three is the size of this workshop." But it wasn't. More cars pulled into the yard. Suddenly the room was full of people. They entered cautiously, some of them, glancing at me as we shook hands. There were housewives and a surprising number of men. The home agent and I got chairs and more chairs. We were excited now and she was glowing, gratified. She whispered: "They are interested! I can hardly believe it! But they wouldn't have come if they weren't interested!"

Pretty soon the meeting was started. We talked about plays and community life, about local history, legends, about what they could do with their own groups, about playmaking in their own communities. I did not need, I found, to sell them on the idea of theater. Once they saw how theater was a part of their lives they carried me along. They represented church groups and schools. Several rural schools had let the kids off for a day so the teachers could attend the workshop. There were farm men and women. "Too bad weather to work outdoors much," the men said, attempting to pass off their presence as just something to do or just somewhere to go with the wife. But they were interested and showed it, especially when we got around to discussing playwriting based on themes familiar to the region.

One lady said to me: "But, Mr. Gard, we would love to do plays in our town, but we have no stage. We have a town hall, but there's not even a platform."

I told them that although there is a vast amount of the old fashioned and ordinary process of play production going on in Wisconsin, we have become aware of numerous experiments that seem to show that a new idea of theater is evolving. I told them that to some extent the old theater realism is dying out and that many plays are being staged without curtain, footlights, or even scenery. I told them that I believed the emphasis seemed to be coming at last to a real appreciation of human character and situation basic to people's lives. When plays cannot be found to fit the needs of the people, someone or some group must make up a play; in such playmaking there is a wonderful freshness.

I told them about such a play I saw that represented life on the town square at Stevens Point. I reminded them that Stevens Point is a small city in the heart of a large settlement of Polish people and that these Poles as well as others are in the habit of bringing farm produce to sell on the square. The play, I recalled, was colorful with dancing and singing—dances and songs the people sang and danced and everybody knew. The play used characters and subjects familiar to the central part of Wisconsin. The play was a hit, and I told the group that I believed that if we could again make our theater meaningful and joyful in terms of ourselves a great American people's movement in theater would spring to life.

I showed them how to arrange the chairs in the hall so that plays might be presented in the center of the room, and I discussed the movement in central staging that is finding popularity all over America. It was a new idea to most of the folks. We talked more theater and had lunch together.

In the afternoon a group of writers came in. Three of them had original novels. It was dark night when I got away from the farm. I said goodbye to the young home agent. She said, "You're sold on this stuff . . . plays and writing and art, aren't you?"

I said, "Are you?"

She said, "We'll have a drama festival up here this Spring."

One facet of Wisconsin that has made a deep impression on me is the selfless willingness of a few persons to assume impossible burdens in the service of the arts. One such person worked in Rhinelander.

Rhinelander, Wisconsin, is known chiefly as a small city of wood products industry and as the home of the Hodag, that fabulous and mythical white bulldog-eating denizen of the deep woods which a great local trickster named Gene Shepard captured at tremendous personal peril. Legends about Gene may be picked up by the bushel at Rhinelander, and I have often gone there with that purpose; yet Rhinelander is also to me a kind of fortress buttressing my faith in the cultural arts. A young woman named Maxine Cottrill struck the initial sparks.

It was a May Sunday night in Rhinelander, and the Northwoods Arts and Crafts Festival was due to open on Monday morning. There was a fearful amount of work to be done, and a small group of folks had been laboring almost all night at the Legion Hall. They had hung a couple of hundred excellent paintings done by artists in northern Wisconsin counties. They had carried a huge lithograph press (carted up to Rhinelander from the University) up a long fire escape and had set it up so that the well-known lithographer, Professor Art Sessler of the University Art department, might give demonstrations. They had rigged a pottery wheel, arranged an exhibit of the creative writings of the published authors of the region, constructed a low stage for the presentation of one-act plays. They had planned a "music day," an "art day," a couple of "theater days," and a "writers day."

The festival was the first of its kind ever to be held in the woodlands of Wisconsin. It was an outgrowth of a great local interest in the home-grown things—an interest inspired originally by a small group of people who had felt a great sense of responsibility to see that the arts and crafts flourished in their northern section of the state. The art and craft work, the plays, the music, they believed, must be put on display so that the public might sense the importance of the arts as a vital part of community life. There was one young lady, Maxine Cottrill, the Home Demonstration Agent for Vilas and Oneida Counties, who felt the deepest sense of responsibility. She was a creative writer and a painter and knew the deep personal satisfactions these things could bring. She had carried the idea of painting and sketching, of acting and singing and writing into the farm kitchens. She had sponsored art institutes and writers' meetings and theater one-day schools so that the people might have a chance to expand their ideas, enlarge their knowledge of techniques; and the people had responded.

Maxine had been one of my summer session students at the University. One day I got a letter from her asking whether the Wisconsin Idea Theater would participate in a Northwoods Arts and Crafts Festival. She wrote that she would undertake to see the festival through. I replied that we would participate and I sounded out Jim Schwalbach, of the art project, and Emmett Sarig, the music specialist, on the idea. We decided to combine forces to help Maxine demonstrate how powerful a force the cultural aspects of state life have become in an area remote from the University, where, ordinarily, one might think that the major interests of the region would be in hunting and fishing.

So plans were made with Maxine and her committee. There would be an exhibit of local painting, a crafts display, a play festival, a music festival. There would be pottery-making demonstrations, lithography demonstrations, a collection of the published writings of northwoods writers, and a collection of the folklore of the north country would be started. It was all very exciting.

No one realized how ill Maxine was, and all the work got done. The festival was a success and the seeds were sown for more creative work and a growing friendliness for the arts in northern Wisconsin. Maxine viewed it all with satisfaction and made notes on the good and bad points of the experiment. She told me that she was tired but that she had done something she had always wanted to do.

Maxine died two months later, but her faith in the arts as a necessary part of American community and individual life will not be forgotten in the northern Wisconsin country. Nor will it be forgotten by me.

There are many artists in the Wisconsin countryside who never hear of organizational programs and would not fit into them if they did. Some of these artists, rugged individualists, to say the least, contribute their own mite to my feeling for the state.

One Fall-time journey carried me into the woods country north and east of Hayward, a country of deep swamps and timber where coarse grasses rasp together slowly in the filtering breezes. It is country where a flick of movement sensed far away through and among the splashed shadows might mean an alerted deer, a country where the moss-covered stumps and the dim trails recall the days when the forest was a setting for crawling, endless motion and echoing sound. I had heard of a man in this woodland who was delicately atuned to all the sights and sounds of the forest and whose pencil, crayon, and brush had given life to the essence of the forest itself. Him I wished to visit, for the image of a woodland artist living in solitude, sketching and painting with sensitive, intimate passion the whole of his forest reality stimulated a curiosity I must satisfy.

I found his cabin, finally, and stood for a moment looking at it. It was a shack of unpainted boards with one tiny window and a low, plank door. The dooryard was a bramble patch with a path to the outhouse. Among the brambles were the skeletons of old machines, bleak, unidentifiable. There at a far edge of the bramble I could recognize the jutting arm of an old engine piston, and in a patch of thickly matted grass I could dimly make out the outline of an ancient wheel lying flat. The whole scene was interlaced with loneliness, and the ugly vestiges of human habitation filled me with uneasiness. I walked around a skimpy woodpile and approached the door.

As I came to the door I could hear a soft yet rough sound from within the shack and I paused a moment trying to define it. It rose and fell and fell and rose and was somehow echoed by the broken flow of the wind in the tops of the pines away from the clearing. I knocked at the door.

Instantly the sound stopped and a tremendous barking began. A voice said, "Quiet! Quiet, damn ye!" and the barking stopped instantly. There was motion beyond the door and suddenly it was pulled open violently. The smell came first, even before I could focus on the man who stood in the open door. It was a smell that instantly flooded my mind with memory of other bachelor shacks I had visited in Kansas and New York and Alberta, especially Alberta where bachelor living has been defined on prairie and on mountain by rigid rules of filth and convenience. As I peered at the man and at the cluttered interior I could see that he was short, that his hair was intensely black and uncombed, that he wore no trousers at all—only dirt-streaked drawers that ended in huge, thick-soled shoes. I could see at the far edge of the room his bunk out of which he had quite obviously just crawled. The bunk was occupied now by two huge hounds who looked at me steadily from the depth of human-warmed blankets.

There is a delicacy about situations such as this. Doors close so easily. Perhaps intuitively my eyes stayed on the dogs and I said, with the memory within me of dark-tan hounds in an eastern Kansas woodland on a frosty October night, "Those are fine dogs."

He moved slightly. "They are."

"They trail?"

He said, "They are good."

To break the conversational ice, I told him I had lived near a river, the Neosho, in Kansas, a great coon river, where there were mussels to be had in plenty, where there were ravines and tall cottonwood timber, where in the Fall a good dog's voice could be heard near two miles, and where when the dogs would call we would hurry through the woodlands and over the frost-stiff grass with a lantern throwing crazy shadows around us as we ran.

He moved away from the door and I went in. We fenced, jockeyed, and eventually I admitted that I was from the University, that I had heard he was an artist, and that I had a sincere desire to view his work. He quite properly denied this for a time, but eventually he reached under the bunk and pulled out a bundle wrapped in old canvas. He grabbed the hounds by the necks and jerked them off the bunk. He laid his bundle carefully on the bunk and unrolled it. There were some cheap crayons in boxes, a couple of dime store watercolor trays, some pencils and brushes and tubes of oils. There was also a roll of what looked like common white shelf paper. He lifted the roll and smoothed it out. One by one he lifted sheets of the paper and spread them on the bunk. The wildlife of the northwoods was there, suddenly, in the filthy shack, reproduced in breathtaking originality against delicate backgrounds of swamp and grasses and the dead rubble of decaying forest. I stood for a long while gazing at the pictures. Finally, I said, "I've got to be going. Thanks."

"Come back anytime," he said, and he began to gather his pictures, tenderly rolling them again for the bundle. He tied the bundle and thrust it under the bunk. As I went to the door the hounds jumped on the bed again and snuggled into the blankets.

One time I stopped to watch a country auction, and I saw the personal belongings of the last member of an old Wisconsin family being auctioned off. The auctioneer lifted from a trunk a yellowed wedding dress, and when he asked for bids there was a titter of nerved-up laughter that brushed across the audience. And then the laughter was still as a very old lady made her way from the back of the crowd and offered her small bid for the dress. It was undisputed, and she took the dress and tottered away with it. At a local gathering that night I heard the story, and it was like a play, for the dress had been worn fifty years before by one lady, but it should have been worn by the old lady who finally bought it.

A feeling for place, at least an instinctive understanding of the lore of the people, seems basic to the creative processes of anyone wishing to make sincere and honest interpretations of the regional scene. I have sought ballads of the north timber country in a cabin where an old lady pushed herself gently back and forth in a Boston rocker and sang "The Log Jam on Gerry's Rocks" and "The Little Brown Bulls" with such genuine flavor that I was there with Young Monroe when he broke the jam on Gerry's Rocks . . . greatest log jam the Wisconsin River ever saw. I was there beside Bull Gordon, the Yankee, when his log-skidding team of little brown bulls outskidded McCluskey's white spotted steers two to one!

I have treasured the quiet well-being of Walworth County in the south, settled by New York State people, mostly, in the 1840's and 50's. They came through the Erie Canal, bringing a feeling of New York State places to southern Wisconsin. And in contrast I have savored the central Wisconsin sand country where agriculture is difficult but where the places are warm, often, with the folk dances and wines of the Polish people. I have an intimate feeling for Taliesin, the low-roofed home at Spring Green of the famous architect Frank Lloyd Wright who believes that beauty should be a part of the everyday experience of everybody. And I have the same sort of intellectual intimacy with "The Clearing," the home of the great landscape architect Jens Jensen in Door County who believed that creative man could express himself best in terms of a deep and intimate association with nature.

I have felt constantly the influence of Zona Gale who has established the idea of neighborliness as a living part of Wisconsin countryside life. One morning during the Centennial year I attended a tiny country church and heard a prayer given by the young minister. He said: "Dear God, we have celebrated here today one hundred years of our state's life. Our heritage is good. We come of a stout stock. But, God, don't let us turn our eyes too much backwards. Let us remember, and let us use our memory to live more fully in the present and in the future. God, we are beset with problems our ancestors never dreamt. We are beset and alarmed, for the world is troubled. But, God, we have one thing that will see us through. We are neighbors, Lord. And as neighbors let us live."

A knowledge of the personality of the state has, I think, made me a better worker, for I am not really a stranger anywhere I go in the state. These and other experiences which I acquired during the three years I spent in preparation for the state Centennial constituted an interlude during which a sound groundwork was laid for later development in the Wisconsin Idea Theater but during which I did not grow very much through self-study. Chiefly, the Centennial period made the state of Wisconsin a friendly place for me, but the three-year preparation for the Centennial was a period during which my boat was exploring a backwater; the bigger developments were to come after 1948.

Chapter six

CENTENNIAL INTERLUDE

The 1948 Wisconsin Centennial Celebration was like a great pageant which swept the entire state up in its progression and carried it to a mighty climax that exhausted us all. It left me with the conviction that I would never again move to a state where there was the faintest chance of a centennial being observed within my time there. I had had enough of the ballyhoo, the political maneuvering, the jockeying for hunks of Centennial money to celebrate so self-consciously this or that community's existence. While it was all going on, of course, I was too busy to do much

144

thinking about it. Nobody did. It was not fashionable to question motives too closely. The state and the glorious fact that the state was one hundred years old was quite enough. Indeed, we who were working on the state-wide Centennial plans were, I am sure, often caught up in an intoxicating kind of self-laudation and willingly fabricated floats, marched in parades, wrote poetic rhapsodies about Wisconsin and read them aloud, shamelessly, to anybody who would listen. We beat one another on the back and boisterously congratulated ourselves on the success of our celebrating, and I did not realize at all that I was actually being thrust by the tidal wave of state worship high up on a beach completely removed from the main stream of my original set of purposes. I actually forgot that my mission was one of finding the germinal stuff of a grassroots theater and of making such seeds sprout.

The climax came with Statehood Day in May, 1948, and really, it was a glorious day. There was the biggest parade in Madison that Wisconsin had ever seen or that it will probably ever see again. What is more, the parade went off on time and functioned perfectly under flawless generalship. The luck of the day held into the night, and the night show, which I directed, was perfect to the second. I was vastly proud and filled with an undying kind of self-admiration as I stood like a field general and directed my forty Rotarian couriers who scurried to every corner of the field bearing the messages that carried the great performance forward. Admirals, Governors, and all sorts of dignitaries responded to my command. I had never felt such heady power. It was a magnificent sensation and lasted for two whole days after Statehood Day was finally over.

During this glorious period I relived episodes of my rôle during the Centennial. I remembered the many, many times

I visited the State Capitol and was consulted by political leaders. I remembered the ready clasp of their hands and the congratulatory pats on the shoulder. I was so wound up that I found nothing absurd in the highly ludicrous things that occurred every day. The whole machinery of the celebration obscured the tiny absurdities, the pompousness, the wild statements.

There were thirty-two subcommittees each with its own ax to grind, and during 1947 and 1948 the grinding went on constantly. One day I was asked to a committee meeting to present the transcription of one of my Wisconsin radio plays. It was a play in the current series of "Wisconsin Yarns" which I had created to focus attention on Wisconsin subjects. The play was a quiet one about Cordelia Harvey, the Civil War heroine who was known as the "Wisconsin Angel." She had, through a visit to Lincoln, caused Union hospitals to be constructed in the North away from the fever-ridden swamps where more men died from disease than bullets. Don Voegli of WHA had composed a musical background for the play and it was one of which I was very proud. The Centennial committee thought that the transcriptions of this and other plays in my series might be widely used as Centennial programs in schools.

It was a good idea and I eagerly carried the transcription player to the Capitol and set it up in the committee room. Unfortunately my transcription was not the chief business of the day and the committee functioned as usual. The chairman signalled me to start, but no matter how high I turned up the volume on the machine the "Wisconsin Angel" could not compete with a dozen informal committee "hearings" on different subjects conducted in different tempos in different parts of the room. Nobody heard a word of the play; yet when the record had finished a complete silence fell in the room. The chairman said: "All in favor of making Mr. Gard's play available say aye!" The "ayes" had it and business roared on.

My personal playwriting during the Centennial was hardly anything to be unduly proud of, but because my writing whooped up the state I let it pass as a part of the rôle I was playing—the rôle of a Centennial impresario. There was the pageant at Prairie du Chien which I had written in 1946 as one of the events leading into the Centennial celebration. It was to be presented at the famous old Villa Louis on the banks of the Mississippi. The Villa is the old home of Hercules Dousman, the early fur magnate, and each Spring the great house is opened to the public with a thumping celebration put on by the Prairie du Chien folks. My pageant was based on the experience of Dr. William Beaumont and his strange patient with the hole in his stomach, Alexis St. Martin. Dr. Beaumont had been a military surgeon stationed at Fort Crawford, which was the military name for Prairie du Chien in the early 1800's.

The pageant, *Beaumont*, was certainly no great shakes as a drama, but it was a lot better than the production which the Prairie du Chien folks gave it. It was horribly under-rehearsed and the electricians were still laying cable and putting up lights as the audience arrived. The director was slightly squiffed and arrived very late, but the pageant creaked off, finally, and for about three minutes seemed to go well. The three minutes were, I suppose, a small blaze of fever before the end, for the actor who was playing the lead forgot his lines and in terror leaped far ahead in the script, causing demoralizing confusion. Perhaps fortunately, the lights all went off at about the same time; someone had shorted a cable. The rest of the pageant was mouthed in darkness and a few voyageurs who came singing up from the river bank clad in quite colorful home-made costumes were never seen at all. The darkness covered my own retreat, which was quite swift.

Pageantry! I really must make some remarks about it. Pageantry is a special art and sometimes means, to be completely successful, the mustering of most of the resources, human and physical, of the entire community watched over by a director who must be a kind of unbending field general. There had been a vigorous background of pageantry in Wisconsin, and some communities looked upon it as the great theater. Individual citizens were apt to make more cautious expressions of opinion, and indeed some individuals breathed rapidly and shallowly in terror whenever the word pageant was mentioned. I often noticed a pallor creep into the cheeks of the people I met in the Wisconsin towns, and this pale look of fear was only dispelled when they understood that my mission was not to disrupt their economic and social lives with great spectacle plays.

There is probably no form of theater that brings forth both dramatic picture and human agony so forcefully as pageantry. Wives find no time during the rehearsal periods of a large pageant to prepare their husband's meals. Husbands find no time to conduct their business. Kids find no time to go to school. Lovers find no time to make love. Animals: horses, cows, dogs, mules, are often dragged from their quiet stables to march in pageant procession, and houses are stripped of antiques, fields of farm implements. Barbers starve because nobody will destroy his pageant personality with a haircut or a shave. The comfortably fat local banker worries off his bay window and may finally, at the performance, have to have a pillow tucked into his pants. Little boys suffer in stiff collars and little girls prance around in costumes feverishly constructed from most of mother's

148

old clothes. All kinds of temperament, before unsuspected, emerge to mar the community for time eternal. Ladies lose a week's sleep sitting up nights sewing, and the public park where the pageant is performed sometimes never recovers. The high school instructor who may direct the pageant becomes a hero, if the thing is done without too much fuss and with high effect, or he may suffer total disgrace and lose his job if the thing loses money and is a flop. It is a great business, and it can mean a closer community relationship if friendly relations are maintained or it can mean a community split that may take years to repair.

It is undoubtedly true that no activity brings forth local lore as does the pageant. A nice guy I know who has a bald head and a far-carrying voice may relate with great good humor (once he learns that he is safe from you, that you are not after his talent as a pageant performer) how he was once in a pageant that depicted the arrival of the French in Wisconsin; how he was the narrator; how he was put on top of a wooden tower, dressed up in a long white robe as Father Time. He may tell you how a kettle of Greek Fire placed mistakenly directly below his tower ignited his scaffolding and how the flame crept up, unsuspected, to fire the tail of his long, white robe. Suddenly, then, in the middle of the climax when Jean Nicolet, the explorer, was haranguing the Indians, Father Time leaped twelve feet from his perch and rushed across the field beating out sparks in his robe and emitting loud cries for assistance.

One of the famous Wisconsin pageant tales told with relish is of a fine pageant director who one day saw an old man with a wonderful long and natural beard walking down the street of the town in which she was directing a pageant. She accosted this man immediately, for she saw in him a natural bit of human architecture, a diamond in the rough, without the least need for make-up or false whiskers. She asked him to appear at the performance that evening and promised to assign him a minor rôle. He eagerly agreed, and that evening when he showed up he had shaved off his wonderful beard and had put on the finest clothes money could buy.

But so much for pageants. The comedy which I wrote with Doré Reich for the Centennial Exposition at West Allis was not too painful. The State Fair had been turned, for 1948, into a great Exposition, and the play, *River Boat*, was done in the State Fair Little Theater by the Milwaukee Players under the direction of Robert Freidel. The play was about an old stern-wheeler called the *Lally Ann* which plied the Fox River in the days when it was possible for a steamboat to churn from Lake Michigan at Green Bay through the lower and upper Fox rivers and through the famous mile-long canal at Portage between the Fox and Wisconsin. The conflict of the play was between the railroaders and the steamboat boys, and the presence of a ragged medicine show troupe on board the *Lally* furnished excuse for Freidel and company to create a wild and highly entertaining show, which was hugely attended at every performance. The bad thing was the terrible heat of the fairgrounds. All day the crowds stewed under the hottest sun West Allis had seen for many a Summer, and at night in the Little Theater people jammed together and sweated it out in true Centennial spirit. I fancied that *River Boat* must have tremendous drawing power and nobody spoiled my illusion. Only a few remarked that they came in off the midway to rest weary feet.

My rôle during the Centennial was not much dented by success or failure. Everything about the Centennial seemed wonderful. The most pertinent comment I can make now about it is that many of the men who worked so hard on the Centennial plans are dead and I am still barking and croaking from laryngitis which came upon me during the Statehood Night show.

It was when the illusion of success had faded that trouble began for me. Then the magnificent structure my pride had created came smashing down. The ball was over and in the litter of the departed celebration I began to seek frantically for reality. I gazed with unbelieving eyes, spiritually, at least, at myself cast apart, standing alone in a solitary backwash, while the mainstream of Wisconsin creative life seemed to flow in a channel far removed from where I was. With horror I knew that in a sense I had wasted about three years, for the façade that was the celebration came crashing down like scenery in a high wind, twisting and breaking and never again finding form. I scurried around from this place to that pretending to be hard at work at great plans for cultural developments, but my ear was always half listening for the bands and the blasts and the speeches and the poetic spoutings. When the idea finally came to me that the ballyhoo was over, that there would not be any more Centennial committee meetings, that my friendly reception at the State Capitol might be at an end since I was no longer a vital cog in a Centennial machine, I was filled with distressing emptiness.

Even as the Centennial had seemed to make every effort, no matter how mediocre, worthwhile, so the reaction seemed to make every activity connected with the Centennial a failure. The dream of a grassroots theater I had had when I left Canada seemed very dim indeed in 1948. For a time I tended to judge everything with terrible harshness, including my own motives. My Centennial rôle I longed to forget. I wished that I might forget everything we had tried to accomplish as Centennial features—the Centennial playwriting contest and the other attempts to celebrate statehood.

We believed that a contest in playwriting might be an excellent way to focus attention on the Centennial and to acquire quickly a body of usable scripts which might be circulated throughout the state on a royalty-free basis. This had worked in New York State and I hoped it would work as well in Wisconsin. The Centennial committee put up a thousand dollars as prizes and in February, 1947, we launched the contest.

We stated that the only restrictions on entries were that the author must be a resident of Wisconsin and that the play must be based on Wisconsin subject matter, either contemporary or historical in nature. There were separate prizes for one-acts, three-acts, and for radio plays. We circulated the prize-winning scripts with some success, but at the Centennial's end I could not see worth in any of the plays.

My black mood lasted for a time and then I shook myself and set about seeing what could be salvaged. I had to admit that there had been some worthwhile things started as parts of the basic plan for a Wisconsin Idea Theater. There was the *Wisconsin Idea Theater Quarterly*, begun in 1947, which seemed to be taking hold. We had revived, established, or aided a number of community theater groups in the state and had done some collecting of Wisconsin folklore. But from the point of view of developing a new playwriting movement of promise I saw little to be proud of.

In the Centennial playwriting contest a lot of plays had come in—radio plays and stage plays—and most of them were based completely on local history. They were, in a way, a part of the Centennial ballyhoo. It had actually been my tendency during the Centennial to think that almost any play, so long as it was on a state theme, was a kind of holy object to be tossed on the Centennial altar. Judgements I knew had slipped badly, and it was tempting, now that the celebration had ended, to class about everything that had been turned in in the playwriting contest as trash and not related at all to my meaning of grassroots theater. My meaning of the term, as nearly as I could define it, was simply the honest striving after artistic creativeness— striving in places where one would not ordinarily expect such expression to exist.

Yet when I really stopped to think it over I knew that many of the plays which had come in had a sincerity of intention which was not far from my grassroots dream. And as I thought more about it, and as the Centennial drew farther away, I grew even more hopeful. There was a play by Anne Dunst, the Milwaukee writer, I recalled to my-self—the play called *The Last Sitting*. The one about the sculptress, Vinnie Ream. It was pretty good, really. The play had something and was surely a cut above average. And there was the play called *Witches' Brood* by Miller, the young G.I. who had come to see me and said he had always wanted to write plays. His work was almost powerful in spots. Maybe there was a spark or two in these Centennial writers. The poet, Emily Wurl, who had won first prize, could certainly put words together. Perhaps she could learn to write really strong plays. These people should have a chance. They needed time. Patience. So much patience.

And the people, all the people who sent in the plays. They were young and old. Some had high school educations, but a few had not. Forty-six had gone to college. A hand-ful had taken a playwriting course, but most of them had not. We had assembled data on everyone who competed and we found that there were teachers, housewives, secretaries, lawyers, librarians, farmers, students, clerks, executives, doctors, and mechanics among the contestants. Here, surely, was a signpost pointing to a grassroots theater, for apparently many kinds and levels of people were willing to try playwriting, and in a completely free movement in which every sort of person might participate seemed to lie the sources of the kind of theater I had in mind.

And remember, I continued to tell myself, it was the Centennial that brought you into contact with Doré Reich. People like Reich are certainly part of this grassroots idea of yours. Reich had turned up in a night class in playwriting I had conducted at the Milwaukee Extension Center in 1946. Such classes were one of the means by which I hoped to develop strong Wisconsin playwriting. The general level of output from the class was average and the subjects the members of the class chose were largely from local history. The Centennial was already having influence. Reich sat in a corner, and during the six weeks of the class he said very little. I scarcely noticed him.

On the evening that the class finished he came to me and handed me the manuscript of a three-act play. He told me that he had written the play during the six weeks course. Would I read it?

I said, "I didn't even know you were working on a play."

He smiled and said, "I'm afraid it isn't much good."

We walked together through the shadows of Fifth Street to downtown Milwaukee. We went into a coffee shop. I discovered that Reich had been a successful manufacturer in the city and that his family was one of the old families in town. He decided suddenly that what he had really wanted

154

to do for years was to write plays. He had sold his business and was now going to devote full time to writing.

I was interested. A bit skeptical. I gave him the old business: Playwriting is tough. Maybe you're wasting your time. Fifty-to-one you can't get anywhere as a professional playwright in America.

He was not impressed. He looked at me and said quietly, "Isn't there a place for *good* plays in America?"

I said, simply, "Yes," and he said, "I don't mean just on Broadway. I mean isn't there a place for playwrights working in the back-country of America, too?"

Now I was looking at him in a different way. I sat in the booth and sketched through his play. It seemed strong. Good characters. A good plot. It was set in one of the old turreted houses along Prospect Avenue built by an early beer baron. The name of the play was *The Goldfish Castle*.

Little by little we became fast friends. He was interested in helping to develop other state playwrights. I got him a part-time appointment at the University. He was always on hand. Sincere. Ready to help. He wrote play after play, and I tried my best to get them produced. A few were done. He worked with other writers. He had amazing ability.

One day in 1948, the central Centennial committee called me to a meeting at the State Capitol. The chairman said: "Gard, we need a play for and about the city of Green Bay. After all, Green Bay is the oldest city in Wisconsin and we've got to have a special celebration up there. Can you get us a play? Incidentally, we will need it in one month."

I said, "A pageant you want?"

He said, "No. A play."

I said, "Maybe I can get you one."

He said, "If you will be so kind."

I called Doré Reich. "Can you write a play in a month?"

"What about?"

"Green Bay."

He said: "Maybe we can use the Tank story. You remember that Norwegian who started such an interesting colony up there? Refused to compromise when the settlers took sides against him? A real tragic hero."

I said, "Maybe you could."

He said, "Sure. I'll do the play."

In exactly three weeks Reich appeared on my doorstep. He was clutching a large manila envelope. He was pale. He shoved the envelope at me. "Here's your play." He fell asleep while I read it. I got excited; it really was a strong play. It was built on a good story and really came off. I rushed down to the Centennial committee. They rushed the play to Green Bay. The Green Bay Community Players agreed to produce it. They did. It was a success. Later on Reich collaborated with me on the exposition play, *River Boat*.

Reich has been one of my great friends and backers. I count on him for advice and guidance. He is liberal—sees all sides—but more than anything he is a writer, not widely produced or published, but a tower of strength now to his own community. He has left Milwaukee and lives in a small Wisconsin city, Watertown, where he helps to direct the Watertown Curtain Club.

The Centennial was over, and eventually I took the point of view that my work in Wisconsin was only beginning. A first task would be to pull out the Centennial plays and the six or seven hundred other plays that had drifted into the Wisconsin Idea Theater office and reread them. Perhaps we had missed indications of real worth, indications of at least a grasp at the universal among all the flag waving and undigested local history. If I were to have a hand in the developing of a theater of power and deep regional significance in Wisconsin there was plenty to do. And I had better be about it.

Chapter seven

GRASSROOTS THEATER

Emily Sprague Wurl is a Wisconsin writer who has been writing plays for a long while now without very much to show for her work. No one doubts her ability. She has won high praise for her verse and has published a very commendable volume of poetry. She was Zona Gale's protégé years ago when Emily was a young girl. Emily is interested in writing poetry and fiction, but her real interest is in playwriting. She has that intense, uncommon conviction present in a selected few writers that playwriting is her medium and that no other will do. She has been associated with playwriting schemes, plans, classes, whenever these things were in evidence. She wrote plays in the old Drama Guild days in Wisconsin when there were competitions for original plays in the state. Her work was always thought to be superior. She has been associated with the Wisconsin Idea Theater since its earliest promotion and has continuously worked for the success of the project and, she has hoped, for her own success. She has an unusual sensitivity to the sights and sounds of her Wisconsin, a sensitivity which has helped her create warm and intensely human stage characters. She is in middle years now and teaches kindergarten in Wauwatosa.

Realistically, Emily does not have much hope of attaining success as a Broadway playwright. What she has always thought might be within her grasp is a successful career as a playwright within her own state. She often looks at Wisconsin with a hopeful but rather suspicious eye, for she has received continuous rebuffs from the organized community theaters to which she has taken her plays. "We can't produce your plays, Emily," the directors tell her. "Your plays are good enough, all right. We concede that. But they're local products. Our audiences won't stand for that sort of thing. Our budget won't stand for it either. We're not in community theater so much for art, Emily. We're in it for entertainment, and our entertainment comes from doing Broadway stuff."

Emily sometimes attempts to reply: "But your community theater is the only living theater in town. You have a responsibility . . ."

"Sorry, Emily."

She has tried writing plays especially for the rural theater, too, but here she has encountered opposition of a slightly different kind. Her plays are poetic. They probe rather deeply into human motives. As a sincere artist she writes as she must and the musts within her do not appeal greatly to a country theater for which the rural comedy *Goose Money* is the prototype. Folks in rural areas want comedy, insist on it in fact, because they are unfamiliar with a fine, serious theater.

Emily knows now that rural folk for the most part expect to laugh when they attend the local plays and—well, there are parts in Emily's scripts which just cannot be laughed off, or laughed at. She hopes that the situation will change some-day. "After the educators stop putting so much emphasis on the group and work more with the individual," she says, "maybe the situation will be different. Or when there is not so much attention paid to recreation in the countryside and more paid to art. That might help, too."

The Emily Wurls are extremely important to my grass-roots theater, for in them I see the chief hope of its coming into being. They are the talented ones, the ones beyond the recreative arts. They are the ones whose expressiveness is a little beyond the levels of small community apprecia-tion, the ones who are having a bad time of it spiritually because they cannot understand why they are not made a part of a vital native theater movement. It is hard to make them believe that they are a part of my grassroots theater when there are few productions of their plays. They find it extremely hard to understand when I tell them that the communities of the region must be prepared to accept their work. They cannot understand. They are ready, but they see little in their communities that is apt to change in favor of sincere, home-grown playwriting. Yet they never quite give up hope.

My search for grassroots theater is forever a search for the Emily Wurls, the hopeful ones, the sincere, sensitive ones. And my search is also for ways to develop the responses of the region—responses tuned to the idea that fine living theater can be created by playwrights who have no desire to take their plays far away from home.

In this respect, of course, we have not won our battle with the Wisconsin communities. Most of them are still a long way from accepting the local playwright. I like to believe, however, that our attempts to encourage playwriting have at least had some spiritual effect on the state. In New York, the New Plays Project produced three volumes of original plays which have been used fairly extensively throughout the Empire State. In Wisconsin, the native materials collection which was started soon after the Wisconsin Idea Theater was initiated paid off in a new regional interest in writing that produced a great many plays.

My interest in native materials, in a collection of folklore and other archival matter upon which good regional plays might be based, did not change when I came to Wisconsin. I saw the Wisconsin Idea Theater as a program of very broad scope, and I was always looking for ways to interest people in the lore and tradition of the region and ways to make the lore live and become an active part of regional life through a familiarity of people with it. I even hoped that the Wisconsin grassroots theater movement I envisioned might grow strong through programs of informing as well as entertaining the people.

Such programs had worked well in New York and Alberta. Perhaps because of the initial work done in rural areas by the sociologists headed by Kolb and because of the work of Ethel Rockwell and the Bureau of Dramatic Activities, I could sense the existence of a grassroots theater in Wisconsin, and I anticipated that many plays would be written as a result of the Wisconsin Idea Theater influence.

The State Historical Society was very strong, too, and its director, Clifford Lord, had desires equally as strong as mine to inform the people of the state and to make state lore familiar and important to them.

It was in the 1946 Extension class in Milwaukee that both Doré Reich and Emily Wurl appeared. Mrs. Wurl's first play for me was in verse, *Reachin' for the Moon*, written in 1946. It was about a young pioneer husband who had promised his girl bride the moon if she would but leave her New England home and come with him to the Wisconsin wilds. The hard life of the frontier soon destroyed his romantic concepts but at the end of the play the moon glimmering in a pail of clear spring water reunites the couple on a highly poetic plane extremely satisfying to the young wife. Mrs. Wurl later won first prize in the full-length division of the Centennial playwriting contest with her *Rahel O'Fon*.

Reich and Mrs. Wurl have stuck with the Wisconsin Idea Theater playwriting schemes throughout the years. To me they symbolize the whole playwriting movement. Even at the start it was a movement of some magnitude in quantity, if not always in quality. It was a movement large with hope and one which traveled with halting steps, for we were never certain of the direction it should take. We wanted a fine regional expression to emerge; yet we feared too much emphasis on local history. We wanted a great new experiment in playwriting form; yet we feared that we might frighten talented persons away by too great an initial emphasis on experimentation. We wanted to find a touchstone for the movement; yet we did not know where, exactly, to search for it. Our one chief idea was to develop new plays for a revived, or refreshed, theater.

It is difficult to relate the feeling of excitement that comes from a search for new plays of merit. As the director of a project engaged in an attempt to develop playwrights, I tried very hard in the early days of the Wisconsin Idea Theater at least to keep my head and to keep a definite sense of direction. This was not easy, mostly because of the size of the operation. We opened the doors wide and invited everyone to rush in.

We certainly did not expect every lawyer, grocer, farmer, or mechanic in the state to hurry off to write a play. We did hope that persons of talent would respond in order to obtain guidance and to seek help in getting their plays produced. We opened the doors, in other words, to anyone who wanted to write plays. My job was to build theater in Wisconsin, and I saw new plays as the cornerstone. We threw open the doors in the hope that as many persons as possible might respond and that a few good plays would result from our efforts. We were not concerned, really, with the authors' motivations for writing plays. We were aware of the variations in the drive that produces creative work, but in this early period of stimulation of playwriting in Wisconsin we had no definite desire to define the variations. Our motive was simply to produce good regional plays. The fact that many plays which came in could not be considered art merely pointed up, for me, the vast job to be done. Our playwriting efforts included many attempts to make the region live for the playwrights, but our aim, always, was the transcendence of superficial, stereotyped expression. We hoped to educate stereotypes and superficiality (and indeed, the mediocre) out of regional playwriting in Wisconsin.

The stage plays that have come to us have been of almost infinite variety, and looked at in total they make a bright splash of color. We usually received the plays through the mail, but some of the authors, with scripts tucked under arm, came in person to our office to inspect us and to test our motives. Most of the first plays we received were one-acts—that difficult form of which Zona Gale said "it [the one-act play] is not so much the laboratory of the playwright as it is that form of drama which the author learns to write from writing three and four act plays." The one-act play is the bread and meat of the drama program in Wisconsin, and there are never enough good ones. Here are a few originals selected from the many that have been sent to the Wisconsin Idea Theater.

A librarian at the Milwaukee Public Library, Margaret Paulus, wrote a tender play about Solomon Juneau, who became the first mayor of Milwaukee. Josette, the half-breed girl whom he loved, had never seen a city. Juneau promised to build one for her on the shores of Lake Michigan—and he did. Margaret Paulus' play was called *A City for Josette* (1946). Another Milwaukee resident, Robert Michalica, submitted *Quiet Street* (1948), a beautiful, tragic play about women in Milwaukee's back streets. The play's theme was suggested by a painting of a room. The room looked like an excellent setting for a play, and the idea of the play grew from that setting.

From Whitewater, Mary Zimmerman sent her play *Mister Micawber* (1948). It was about frontier Whitewater, a domestic comedy, and very playable. Mrs. Zimmerman wrote when she sent the play that "being a Wisconsinite is for me a return home. Though born and reared in Chicago my roots are here, as my great grandparents were 'late pioneers' coming to Medford, Wisconsin, from France in the late seventies. My mother was born at Medford and her love of this lake and hill and forest country is bred in us. When I was younger and, of course, much smarter than I am now, I wrote a novel of Wisconsin in the seventies which everyone regretfully rejected." Doré Reich wrote *Tintype* (1950), about life in old-time Milwaukee, a pet topic with him and one in which he is better versed than anyone I know.

Mary Heidner of Hartford wrote *The Clearing* (1948), which came about as the result of her enthusiasm for local history and a visit she had with an old lady. About this visit she wrote to us: "Mr. and Mrs. Earl Reid sent their milk hauler into Hartford last spring during the telephone strike to ask me to go with them to Waukesha to visit Mr. Reid's Aunt Emma Reid. After that afternoon's delightful visit with nearly-ninety Emma Reid, I had enough notes, personalities and incidents from the past to make several plays. I chose the most play-worthy anecdote." Mary Heidner also wrote *The Foreigners* (1948), which grew out of "my personal interest in nationalities, and the fact that my children are about as international as they can get, being two-eighths German, one-eighth each of Danish, Swedish and English, and three-eighths Irish. The story is compounded of my own memories of farm life, a Norwegian hired man we once had, and my family and neighborhood stories."

Nancy Eichsteadt of Madison wrote *Laughing Last* (1948), an actable comedy about a Baraboo whiskey raid in which a group of ladies played hob with a tavern. (There is something about militant ladies and defenseless taverns that dramatists cannot resist.) Albertine M. Schuttler of Wauwatosa is the author of *Flight from Prejudice* (1948). It is a melodrama about an Underground Railroad incident of the 1850's and is set, properly, at Waukesha, Wisconsin, which was an exceedingly fashionable watering place during the pre-Civil War days and which drew the cream of Southern as well as Northern society. Miss Schuttler wrote of herself: "I have always taken keen interest in drama and the theatre because my family was interested and several were prominent in pioneer German-American theatrical and musical circles. My grandmother, on the distaff side, was the dramatic lead actress in the German stock company under the direction of Hans Balaatka during the 1850's."

Selection of a few other titles will give an idea of the wide geographical distribution of the authors of the plays we received: *Ephraim* (1947), by Genevieve Bender of Green Bay; *Nemesis* (1947), by Cecil Brown, Jr., of Milwaukee; *Songs for a Weary World* (1947), by Ralph V. Brown of Whitewater; *Helga* (1947), by Marie Barlow Buckman of Crivitz; *All Wool and a Yard Wide* (1946), by Frances R. Burt of Albany; *Room at the Inn* (1947), by Harriett Fellows of Wauwatosa; *The Glory of Spring* (1946), by Ronald Gee of Delavan; *Cowbells Are Ringin'* (1947), by Neil Greene of Muscoda; *Contour-Minded* (1949), by Sabrina Miller of West Salem; *The Man of the House* (1949), by Mrs. Hans Morken of Taylor; *A Home for Christmas* (1947), by Mrs. Josephine Noyes of Wauwatosa; *Ceresco* (1947), by James Roate of Milwaukee; *It's Always Been* (1949), by G. B. Seitz of LaCrosse; *Flax Blonde Squaw* (1947), by Sari Szekely of Wauwatosa; *Nawaka Chief* (1947), by Emily Jean Woodward of Eau Claire.

I was interested to note the great number of comedies that arrived. There were few serious one-acts. Comedy seemed to be the Wisconsin order of the day in original one-act playwriting. I have never decided why this is so. It certainly was not so in Alberta where most of the original plays were serious, many tragic, in tone. Perhaps it is a half-truth to say that the prairies breed loneliness, spiritual starvation, and often madness and that these things have an undue place in prairie playwriting; but there are lonely places in Wisconsin, too, and the cutover land and the sand country has beauty for me but sadness, too. Perhaps, as Emily Wurl says, the propensity for comedy in original plays in Wisconsin is partly the result of the sociological approach to theater fostered for so long in rural areas.

Unlike the one-acts, the full-length plays for the most part have been serious. It is interesting simply to note in passing that the authors of full-length plays almost without exception have not been exposed to the broad recreational program ideas associated with the University's programs in agriculture and home economics. I doubt that there is real significance in this fact; yet, again with Emily Wurl, I wonder whether the recreative motivations do not sometimes emphasize a false set of values.

Perhaps the best full-length play written in the present era of Wisconsin playwriting is *In Old Green Bay* (1947), the play carved out by Doré Reich in three weeks on assignment. The play deals with a double subject. First, it is the story of the noncompromising, idealistic Nils Otto Tank who established the Moravian Colony at Green Bay only to have his colonists desert him when they doubted his motives. The colonists moved up on the Door County peninsula to establish Ephraim and other small settlements. Second, Reich worked into the play the great story of the struggle by another idealist, Morgan L. Martin, who dreamed of a waterway connecting Green Bay with the Mississippi River. These two visionaries, Martin and Tank, were brought together in the play by Reich and their dreams contrasted. It is a moving story with a great theme.

There have been some other rather good three-acters. The prize-winning Centennial script, *Rahel O'Fon* (1947), by Emily Sprague Wurl, has merit as poetry as well as drama. Structurally it leaves something to be desired, but as a poetic treatment of Welsh pioneers it is worthy of mention. Rahel O'Fon is the chief character in the play. She was an actual person—the mother of Joseph E. Davies, former United States Ambassador to Russia and Belgium. Mrs. Wurl had intended to write a play about Mr. Davies, with whose family her family had been acquainted in Watertown. However, when she read an article about him in *Fortune* magazine she learned that his mother had been a successful girl-revivalist and a noted poet in Wales. She was brought to this country by the combined Welsh societies, and she became the first ordained woman minister in Wisconsin, perhaps the first in America. Recognizing the drama in the story of a woman minister and the drama inherent in a tale of the Welsh people, Mrs. Wurl corresponded with Mr. Davies, interviewed people who remembered his mother, and steeped herself in Welsh books to obtain background and descriptive material. The Welsh love of music and oratory and poetry lent themselves well to the theme of this play.

The variety of kinds of folk who submitted plays made me believe that a theater of the people was truly possible. They came from many walks of life and from many backgrounds.

In Milwaukee lives Mr. Theodore Mueller, who is supervisor of the Milwaukee County Historical Museum. He has also been a sailor; he once sailed on a voyage with Eugene O'Neill. Mueller wrote, produced, and acted in numerous German language pageants and dramas on the history of the United States for the Milwaukee anti-Nazi German-American societies before and during World War II. He also wrote an extremely creditable play called *The End of the Rainbow* (1947). The play was the story of the sinking of the S. S. *Wisconsin*, of the Goodrich line, on October 29, 1930, of which sinking Mueller was a survivor. He wrote the play to give a reasonably comprehensive picture of what happened at the time of the sinking and the reaction of individual members of the crew. He was also interested in reviving a few of the old-time sailor chanties, and he selected for use in the play an ancient mariner's song, a Great Lakes sailor's song, and a Great Lakes steamboatman's song. He also wished to express some of the types of conversations and slang used by steamboatmen when excursion time was at its height on the Great Lakes from 1900 to 1925. He wrote the play as a contribution to Great Lakes folklore.

Ralph V. Brown, a Whitewater attorney, wrote a play based on the romance between Knoxie Taylor, daughter of General Zachary Taylor, and young Jeff Davis, who was to become President of the Confederacy. Taylor was commandant of Fort Crawford at Prairie du Chien during the 1830's and Davis was his Lieutenant. Brown's play was called *The Colonel's Daughter* (1946), and was set at the time of the Black Hawk War.

Miss Margaret Suttie, Ettrick, Wisconsin, wanted to write a long play because she wished to prove that a rural play could be written about happy, contented farm life instead of the "rube" characters she observed in the majority of rural plays listed in drama catalogues. Her play was called *Seven Below* (1947).

In 1849, a great many Wisconsin men left their homes and families to travel to California to search for gold. Since Miss Calista Clark's grandfather was one of the seekers she had always had an urge to write a play about the Wisconsin end of the gold rush. Her play, *The Long Hill* (1953), was set in a cabin not far from Madison and the plot was built around a lonely young wife left behind by a gold-fevered husband. Miss Clark, who is a beloved schoolma'am in her home town of Muscoda, is a sensitive writer and her play is effective.

The Chocolate Milk Cow (1950), by Mary Zimmerman

of Whitewater, has had perhaps the most productions of any of the original three-acts. It is a "dairyland fantasy" for children, and it is based on a wonderful Walworth County cow that gave chocolate milk. Neither cow nor owner can stand the fame that comes to them, however, and Daisy goes back to giving white milk (with the help of a convenient fairy) in self-defense.

I had learned in New York and Canada to believe in the studied use of radio in furthering cultural development of the region. Hence radio naturally became a strong part of the attempt to stimulate native writing in Wisconsin. WHA had, in 1946, a creative staff which, in a smaller operation, emulated the Canadian Broadcasting Corporation's high ideals of dramatic production and regional emphasis. WHA had splendid production facilities, and I gained great pleasure from the series of weekly half-hour radio plays which I initiated with the aid of Gerald Bartell, the station's chief producer. The series called "Wisconsin Yarns" told many of the great stories of the state and attracted a considerable following. The series in fact stimulated many Wisconsin residents to write radio plays, and we were able to start a second series of original scripts under the title "The Wisconsin Idea Theater." Ray and Helen Stanley directed this series, the first of which was a dramatization of the famous battle of Cameron Dam in which a citizen of northern Wisconsin defied at gun point the powerful Weyerhauser lumber interests. Other plays were based on the lives of the French explorer, Charles De Langlade, and Zona Gale, and on dramatic episodes of life in rural Wisconsin. The play about Zona Gale, called *The Girl and the River* (1946), was sensitively done by Opal Palmer. It told the story of the famous authoress as she grew up on the banks of the Wisconsin River at Portage.

This play particularly was well received and stimulated the writing of a number of other radio dramas by persons who heard it.

During 1946, 1947, and 1948 many original Wisconsin radio plays were produced by WHA. The best ones, or the ones which were considered the best written and which gave the best interpretations of some phase of state life, included *The Greatest Show on Earth* (1948), by Fred Gerber, which told the exciting yarn of the Ringling Brothers of Baraboo and the great circus they had dreamed about. *The Literary Piano* (1947), by Mary Ellen Varney, told how the typewriter was invented in Milwaukee by Christopher Latham Sholes, who was surely one of the greatest emancipators of American womanhood. (The theme of the great Wisconsin inventors has been a favorite one in radio playwriting and many plays have been fabricated about John Appleby of Mazomanie, who invented the twine knotter which revolutionized harvesting, about Gilda Gray of Cudahy, who invented the shimmy dance, William Kurz of Appleton, who invented the hydro-electric plant, Stephen M. Babcock of Madison, who invented the test for butterfat in milk, and others of greater or lesser import.) *The Fighting Editor* (1948), by Fred Gerber, told the story of Sherman Booth, the editor who was involved in one of the most important antislavery cases. *The Baraboo Raid* (1948), by Barbara Puls, was a yarn about a determined group of ladies who tried very hard to stamp out the evil of drink in Baraboo. Their dismantlement of a Baraboo tavern would have put Carrie Nation to shame. *Radio Covers the Indian Scare* (1947), by Junius Eddy, related a famous Wisconsin story of an Indian scare in 1863.

Thunder Bell (1947), by Wesley Egan, was about that famous Ridgeway Ghost, and the play had all the atmosphere that a good ghost yarn ought to have. *The Story of the Newhall House Fire* (1948), by David Pollard, was a dramatized account of one of the most famous of Wisconsin tragedies—the burning of the Milwaukee hotel, the Newhall House. The famous midget, General Tom Thumb, was a guest in the Newhall House that terrible night, and the General also got into the radio play. *A Moses of the Mormons* (1948), by David Pollard, recounted the strange story of James J. Strang, fanatic prophet of the Mormons, who tried to establish a "Garden of Peace" in Voree, Wisconsin.

Mrs. Rust's Straw Hat (1948), by Shirley Tollefson, was a really charming little drama which told how Mrs. Rust's ability to make straw hats affected the name and location of Monroe, Wisconsin. *Wilderness Chapel* (1947), by Elaine Johnson, told about the Swiss nobleman, Count Von Benzel, and his commoner wife, Emmy, who came to live near Iola, Wisconsin, in 1851. *Ben McKusker and His Locomotive* (1949), by Martha Van Kleeck, offered the jovial tale of how an early railway locomotive made a historic journey over big Ben McKusker's great plank road running from Sheboygan to Fond du Lac.

And there were hundreds of others, such as *Thanks to Aunt Sally* (1948), by Mrs. Albert Ball of Iron Mountain; *Once in a Hundred Years* (1947), by Marguerite Barnett of Boscobel; *The Postmaster of Potosi* (1947), by Marguerite Barnett of Boscobel; *Little More Than a Cowpath* (1947), by Ray Barth of Monroe; *Green Gold* (1947), by Frances Burt of Albany; *The Old Elm Speaks* (1947), by Alla Stratton Colbo of Racine; another *Defender of Cameron Dam* (1947), by Myron Curry of Madison; *The Bridge War* (1947), by Lulu M. Dysart of Milwaukee; *The Badger Saint* (1948), by Donald Fellows of Madison; *Wisconsin Takes a Stand* (1948), by Ella B. Goodman of Milwaukee; *The Land Lay*

Sleeping (1948), by Frances Jaeschke of Kenosha; *Child of Two Mothers* (1947), by Elaine Johnson of Iola; *Man's Got a Right* (1947), by Lucille C. Kazlow of Green Bay; *The Pastor* (1947), by Pearl Kuhn of Rockford; *Not Cut Out for the Farm* (1947), by Sabrina Miller of West Salem; *Birthright* (1947), by Victoria L. Rinelli of Wauwatosa; *The Stepmother* (1948), by Dorothy Cole Schrader of Evansville; *Saratoga of the West* (1948), by Albertine M. Schuttler of Wauwatosa; *Wait for the Belgians* (1948), by Ruth W. Smith of Green Bay; *The Jovial Man of Science* (1948), by Mrs. Dorothy Svien of Waunakee; *Memory's Pages* (1947), by Milo Swanton of Madison; *Bred in the Wilderness* (1947), by Mrs. K. E. Brueckner of Madison.

I considered the radio plays a hopeful sign of grassroots theater—or at least as a potent sign of the wealth of talent. It seems to me that any playwriting project would do well to capitalize on the ready willingness (and surprising ability) of many persons to write radio drama. All things considered, I think the radio plays we tried to develop did more to stir up interest in playwriting than did our stage plays. Many persons apparently found the radio form easy to handle and as a result of their radio experience successfully overcame the problems of the stageplay form. A number of the radio writers who cut their playwriting teeth on a radio play tried their hand at a stage play later.

A vital part of our grassroots theater attempt is a new plays theater at the University. For a few years after I came to Wisconsin no theater space for the tryout of new scripts was available, and I considered this to be a serious lack in a program such as I was developing. A new plays theater could, I believed, have great significance for the entire region with the recognition given the better plays by the state University. This was, of course, part of my larger plan, for I had seen the good area-wide effect of experimental new play production by the Cornell University theater. I had seen how the prestige of the state University carried great weight in most communities, and I believed that production on even a very simple level at the University would add stature to our whole playwriting idea. This was quite beside the obvious fact that the authors would learn much from seeing their plays produced.

In 1948, David Stevens of the Rockefeller Foundation was considering a grant to the University to further the programs of the Wisconsin Idea Theater. As it developed finally, a part of the stipulation of the grant was that the University should furnish the drama project with a laboratory theater, and there were many conferences to see what might be done.

Old Bascom Theater, long abandoned as a playhouse, had been condemned as a fire hazard. Dressing rooms and stage shop next to Bascom Theater had been converted into classrooms. The great theater plant of the Wisconsin Memorial Union had been built and it was not conceived possible that Bascom Theater would be wanted for dramatic production ever again. However, the cost of securing the stage of the Union Theater was almost prohibitive, and, furthermore, it was booked to capacity most of the year by the University theater shows, by music, dance, ballet events, lectures, forums and conferences of every description. There was a tiny "play circle" theater originally designed for experimental production, but movies were shown there except for the rare occasion when a graduate student might direct a thesis production in it. As a result, no on-campus outlet was available for trying out any of the promising scripts received. My Centennial committee contacts at the State

Capitol stood me in good stead, and I was able to get the fire prohibition lifted from Bascom Theater. The Dean of the College of Letters and Science, Mark Ingraham (himself a proud Cornellian), found some money to repair the ancient switchboard, to replace the ropes, and to purchase a nice set of black drapes.

Ed Kamarck's new play, *Gopher Wood* (1949), was the first full-length script tried out in Bascom Theater, which we rechristened the New Plays Theater. Ed had been at Cornell before World War II and was generally thought to be the outstanding student playwright that Drummond had produced in several years. At Cornell Ed had written several powerful short plays on regional themes, and when Drummond suggested that Ed come to work for me at Wisconsin I was delighted to have him. I was able, with Rockefeller funds, to make him our playwright-in-residence.

He had written and put together, soon after his arrival in the state in 1948, a touring production, *Wisconsin Showtime*, by which we hoped to arouse great regional interest in native materials as well as to provide a demonstration of good theater to smaller communities. Ed did a good show with strong sketches and good music and we were able to round up an adequate cast. Unfortunately, we took it on tour at the height of the basketball season, and Wisconsin people take their sports seriously. The night we played in Menomonie some of us were talking with the old caretaker at the Tainter Theater. He was expounding on the sorrowful demise of the "road." He said that he did not see much theater these days. It was a shame. Where were the good old days? I said: "Well, Jack, here are a couple of tickets for our show tonight. We'd sure be honored to have an old-time theater man like you come and see it."

I handed him the tickets and he handed them back quick

as could be. "Boys," he said, his face brightening up, "I sure couldn't do it tonight! Tonight our Menomonie basketball team plays the All Stars! Boys, I couldn't miss that!"

The tour was a financial failure, but it was good for Ed as a writer. His new play, *Gopher Wood*, our first production in the New Plays Theater on the campus, was based on his experiences in a New York shipyard during wartime and had an important wartime theme: a mastercraftsman unwilling to compromise in the face of wartime hurry and poor workmanship. Our production was necessarily sketchy, for we had no acting company and had to recruit one where we could. University students who are used to light comedy, Broadway successes, and an occasional classic are hard to convince that new play production is worthwhile. We were able to do Ed's play, however, and it furnished him considerable enlightenment as a result. Now that the New Plays Theater is established, casts for the plays are easier to obtain, though there is still a certain amount of reluctance among University students to perform original scripts. Lately the community theaters have begun to take an interest and have demonstrated a willingness to undertake a new play for experimental production at the University.

In addition to helping with new play production at the University, the staff of the Wisconsin Idea Theater has always given as much personal help as possible to native playwrights. Plays have been criticized by mail, classes in playwriting have been held in various parts of the state, and conferences on the problems of the native playwright have been conducted at the University. Ed Kamarck, especially, has been a consistent worker with other playwrights. Through correspondence or personal conference he has aided (among others) Marjorie Bell of Racine; Marie Barlow Buckman of Crivitz; Betty Epstein of Millston; Isabel

McIsaac of Rhinelander; Mary Zimmerman of Whitewater; Frances Burt of Albany; Wally Schultz of Elkhorn; Calista Clark, Muscoda. Recently Miss Clark's play *The Long Hill* was given a tryout production in the New Plays Theater.

A playwright-in-residence is a worthwhile adjunct to a playwriting scheme. Not all playwrights-in-residence work out as well as Ed did, of course, and I remark in passing that I believe the rôle of the playwright-in-residence needs clarification. Too often these writers who become artists-in-residence at a University are given a grant of money to pay their expenses in the hope that they will get freedom to write, freedom from financial worries, freedom from obligations of every sort. I believe that this is an erroneous point-of-view. The truth of the matter is that a man or woman given money under such conditions is generally unused to these freedoms and becomes self-conscious about them. Sometimes he feels an overpowering sense of responsibility to his rôle, and without guidance this very sense becomes a terrific burden and destroys his chance to produce fine writing. He is willing to observe but not to put down roots. There is no education at present to teach the aspiring playwright that he must grow with a community, that community roots must become his roots, and that only through such merging will he have any value to that place and consequently to other places as an individual and an artist.

Playwrights-in-residence at American universities, at least, have been chosen in a number of ways. They are recommended, often, by the director of a university theater to a foundation or association able to provide funds. The initial stimulus, so far as I know, comes from an institution and not, initially, from the foundation or other financing agency. In the case of the Wisconsin Idea Theater, we have had playwrights-in-residence who were actually members of our operating staff. Stipends vary from three or four thousand dollars to five or six hundred dollars a year. I strongly believe that the playwright-in-residence should be a functioning part of the theater or institution where he is located, and not be left on his own simply "to write."

In 1952, the Wisconsin Idea Theater had two of the seven playwrights-in-residence sponsored throughout the nation by the Rockefeller Foundation. These young people, Julius Landau and Ruth Hershberger, had a distinct sense of responsibility to other writers. Landau, a really brilliant man of twenty-five, went with me often into the state to confer with other playwrights. Ruth Hershberger, an outstanding young modern poet, had the idea that she must help establish a poet's theater and engaged in a number of such experiments.

A good deal of my own time has gone toward the education of the playwrights-in-residence. I have considered their presence with us as one more means through which a grassroots theater may grow. I have believed that the presence at the University of talented playwrights who are willing to work a bit with other writers is a valuable part of native theater development—valuable, that is, if the attitude of the University playwright is sympathetic, since he becomes in his situation a kind of symbol for many native writers. Unsympathetic attitudes on his part may greatly harm the program.

It is actually rare, of course, that a playwright brings a sympathetic attitude to a project such as the Wisconsin Idea Theater. Most young writers have their eyes on Broadway and consider fellowships and other kinds of aid as mere stepping stones. In some cases I have been able to help the writer to broaden his sights, to find himself spiritually included in a dream of a great native theater of the American countryside. But in other cases I have not been able to dent the armor of defensiveness with which the writer had surrounded his personal motives and goals. In one instance, indeed, a playwright bitterly decried the lack of a true bohemian atmosphere in Madison, Wisconsin, and soon went off to Boston, where such an atmosphere was said to exist. What the writer meant, of course, was that he wished for an atmosphere congenial to his particular kind of temperament and approach to art. Some artists, I am sure, must have a surrounding of the bohemian sort in which to develop. Unfortunately, the upper American Middle West cannot provide much of this. I am personally more interested in writers like Emily Wurl who do not require bizarre surroundings or unusual appetites, who desire only a warm friendliness toward their creative efforts.

The case of Emily Wurl seems to me to lay the chief problem squarely on the table. What must be done by the universities and the other educational agencies to make the communities of America more receptive to the Emily Wurls and, indeed, to the whole idea of the arts in America? This is a tough question, but in my search for grassroots theater I have developed the conviction that we must begin to tackle the tough ones. Without a friendly soil in American communities there can never truly be a people's art or a real grassroots theater in America. Like Emily, I find it uncommonly strange that there were only three full-length original plays produced by community theater groups in Wisconsin last year. I can generalize about the reasons for such an attitude, but I want, and she wants, solutions for the problem of making the arts a serious and significant part of community life in America. In order to find some of the answers and to develop programs for creating new attitudes, I have undertaken extensive research into community attitudes toward cultural arts in Wisconsin.

Chapter eight

CULTURE AND COMMUNITY

There are some things that are difficult to understand about a big university such as the University of Wisconsin without close personal association with it. Wisconsin is a big university in numbers of students (about fourteen thousand on the campus in 1954) and big in budget. It is also big in idea. The impact of the Wisconsin Idea in education on the University as well as on the state has been tremendous. The Idea has scope, and within its scope there is room for almost unlimited expression of the dream and its resulting program. There are, indeed, many men at the University who are

181

giants in their own fields. Wisconsin has been able, because of its tradition, to attract extremely able men who in business or in any commercial field would probably do exceedingly well.

It is hard to hold back capable, energetic, and persuasive men, and veritable empires have sprung up within the University. These may be in such places as visual aids, radio-television, medicine, or chemistry. They may be in agriculture or commerce—in short, in any division of the University. And wherever the building process is going on the bigness of the Wisconsin Idea is being demonstrated. For certainly the Idea has always encouraged the individual. It has encouraged him to think big and to act big. It has encouraged such individuality of action and responsibility that occasionally the state government or the University administration itself has grown alarmed, for the cost of a state university big with idea, big with energy, is thought-provoking, to say the least.

Then there is the occasional budget clamping, the economy cries, the almost comic-frantic pleas to the people for support, the secret meetings by legislative committees, the strategy planning by University officials, the faculty committees appointed to look into the relative values of different University programs. All this is very hectic for a time, and it is very distressing to the sensitive spirits. Despair engulfs the campus. Wise old men shake their heads and pat trembling young shoulders. Students hold mass meetings on University aid. The campus newspaper makes caustic remarks about the legislature. The legislature issues sharp statements about student liberalism and irresponsibility. All over the state the weeklies and the dailies fight the battle of the University budget. Scars are left, of course, but soon the cries become fainter and fainter. A few new rules emerge "to stabilize the University financially." A dozen new report blanks are forwarded by the University administration to the faculty, to the department administrators. Paper work becomes important for a while. Justifications must be made. The facts are important.

But in the background are the younger men, the empire builders, the dreamers. The budget slash has slowed them down, but they will not be stopped. And in a way the Wisconsin people would not want them to stop. It is the drive of the University, the bigness of the Wisconsin Idea that the people cherish. Let anyone threaten to cut out the great backstage of Extension, the link between the campus and the state, and public opinion is quick to express itself. And definite. The people like their big University, and if there are young men who have ambition, ideas, talent, well, the public (unless their pocketbooks are tickled too much) considers that such builders are part of the Wisconsin tradition.

I have often tried to think what it has meant to me personally to be associated with the University of Wisconsin. In my own small way I have had a drive to build. I have wanted a big thing for Wisconsin and for America. I have wanted the arts to come into their own as a vital force in community life, and I have managed a staff, materiel, and funds to move in this direction. I am sure that my own drive has been quickened and my appetite sharpened by my Wisconsin associations and by the freedom given me by the tradition of the Wisconsin Idea. Under its influence I have assumed responsibilities, broadened my horizons, taken on administrative duties—paper work duties which have engulfed, often, my own deeper creative desires. I have willingly sat through three-hour committee meetings with a bag lunch on my knee and a half-completed play at home in my typewriter, simply because the committee meeting seemed more necessary at the moment (in terms of the Wisconsin Idea) than the play.

These comments I find extremely pertinent to the subject of this chapter. I have always considered research as a part of my larger plan. Drummond had ideas about research into native materials which I borrowed and tried out in Alberta. And I carried to Wisconsin the conviction that research into community arts development was an essential part of my understanding of my work.

At Wisconsin one cannot escape the feeling of the necessity of research. The University is known far and wide as a great research center with extensive private funds for carrying on large research programs, especially in science. I presume that the research developments I saw in progress sharpened my desire to begin my own research. At any rate, I now find myself in the rôle of a kind of leader, or facilitator, or whip, or driver of a research program aimed at discovering how the arts can assume a more important place in community life and how the talents of artists in American communities may be best encouraged.

In many ways the rôle of the director of a research program is a strange one. My own talents, such as they are, are creative rather than scholarly; yet such is the bigness of the Wisconsin Idea that I am able to assume the rôle and not find it too distasteful. It means more meetings, planning sessions, reports, and other items of burdensome detail that go with a research program. I have hardened myself to all that, however, as I have to the necessity of raising special funds. There is never enough money to do all the things a University would like to do, and cultural arts research is definitely one thing for which there is at present little public money.

What the Wisconsin Idea Theater has attempted so far in research would not have been possible without my long association with the Rockefeller Foundation which began in 1938 when Drummond asked Dr. David Stevens, then Director of the Humanities Division, whether there might be a playwriting fellowship available for me. Stevens replied favorably and expressed a desire to meet me. So on a May morning I boarded a Lehigh Valley train at the Ithaca station and, clutching my best play, sat through the slow miles in fearful anticipation of meeting this man in the big city who seemed so remote from my own prairie origins.

I found my way to 49 West 49th Street—an address that has been very important in my work—and to the fifty-fifth floor where the Foundation's offices are located. I stated my mission to a pleasant, one-armed man at the desk inside the door and sat down to wait. I had no idea what was to occur and feared that Dr. Stevens would read my play on the spot with results unfortunate for me. In a little while I was shown to his office.

Dr. Stevens is a firmly-made, clear-eyed man, not tall, yet with an impression of bigness about him. As he greeted me his eyes warmed up wonderfully. He said, "You're a Kansas boy?"

"Yes, sir."

"Like your home town?"

"I surely do."

"Been home lately?"

"Not for quite a while."

He gave me a pat on the shoulder and said: "All right. If you're going to stay on at Cornell this year you should go home for a little while. We'll pay your expenses to Kansas and back to Ithaca. You'll have to fill out an application for the fellowship, now, before you leave. It's been nice to meet you. I know that you'll have good luck. Good-bye."

And that was all there was to it. I was dazed by the quickness of it all, but there was something about David Stevens that made me know that if I had not impressed him he would have refused me a fellowship as rapidly as he had granted me one, and, of course, he had Drummond's recommendation.

During my years with Drummond, working on the New York State Plays project, I became increasingly aware of how little, really, was known about the arts in community life. I carried away from Cornell, as I have said, several basic ideas about theater, especially, but embracing the other arts as well, and I was able to test in Alberta several of these ideas in an informal way. These informal testings were concerned with public acceptance of a collection of native materials and with the stimulation of a native literature movement. The Foundation supported my work in Alberta, and while the project there could not be strictly called research still it sharpened my conviction that more systematic attempts must be made to determine the most effective methods of conducting regional cultural arts programs and to gauge the place of the arts in community life.

When I went to Wisconsin this idea was a dominant one with me, and it eventually worked out that a series of research projects actually got underway. These projects included work in uncovering Wisconsin native materials, an experimental program in three counties to discover better ways of developing native theater, an attempt to discover what type of person actually participated in a creative writers' movement, a report on the rôle of the University in off-campus arts programs, and, finally, a broad community arts research project to determine levels of taste, leadership, and other pertinent factors in community arts development. These investigations were possible largely through coöperation of the Rockefeller Foundation.

Soon after I took up residence at the University Dr.

Stevens made a grant in 1946 to a Wisconsin Studies committee whose particular interest was the investigation of the cultural backgrounds of the state. The group included Merle Curti, Pulitzer Prize-winning historian of the University, Clifford Lord, director of the State Historical Society, and other scholars. They were sympathetic toward my idea of delving into the native materials of Wisconsin with the aim of assembling or of pointing toward basic subjects and themes in state life which might be of value in stimulating a native drama revival in Wisconsin. My own appetite for such material was well known through my radio programs. Indeed, I had found the Wisconsin lore so fascinating that when the committee approved my idea I eagerly looked about for someone to conduct such a native materials project—the first of the several preliminary steps toward a community arts research. I discovered that my old friend from Cornell, Jack Curvin, would come to Madison. Jack, who like myself was a Drummond student, had been born and raised in Medina, New York, almost on the banks of the old Erie Canal, and through his boyhood associations with American small-town life and through his father, who was a country general store keeper in the best old-fashioned meaning of the word, had acquired a sensitivity for places and peoples. He was a fine actor and theater director, and he had a liking for scholarship.

Curvin and I shared space in the geological museum where schemes were worked out for collecting native materials. I was extremely hopeful that a unique and important aspect of the Wisconsin Idea Theater would be the result. In order to stimulate interest in the area and to encourage native playwriting we planned a Wisconsin humor contest and a catalogue of unwritten Wisconsin plays.

Jack traveled the state, broadcast a humor series on the

radio, interviewed old-timers, and for a while, I think, greatly enjoyed the job. It really did not work out, though. There was no space to keep the stuff he collected. Indeed, on our next office move (to the converted monument works) Jack did not even have desk space and simply hung out in the Historical Library with no real home—an extremely important consideration to a scholar who needed his materials about him as well as quiet and solitude to work on them. Quiet and solitude were, however, items which the University simply could not provide in the period 1946–47. There was not enough space. The Wisconsin Idea had suddenly grown too big and was expanding too fast. Building was a decade or more behind the developers.

I worried a great deal about Curvin's program, for it was obviously one in which I had a deep personal interest. My own job, however, was more and more demanding. Centennial preparation was in full flower. I could not help Jack enough to satisfy either of us, and eventually he accepted a position in the University Department of Speech—a teaching berth for which he was well suited. I was glad, of course, to see him permanently located, but I was sorry, too. It is not easy to keep well-trained men in the broad cultural idea which I personally have found so important.

Curvin turned over to the Wisconsin Idea Theater the collection of regional materials which he had assembled. Much of this material has been used in some fashion by creative writers, and I anticipate that it will continue to be used as more Wisconsin folk turn toward the local scene for creative themes. The small collection is housed in the Wisconsin Idea Theater offices, and someday I presume it will become a part of the regional collection of the State Historical Society. At present the Historical Society has very little Wisconsin folklore in its fine library. A dream I have always had is of a state arts center which might house such a collection. Special archives are to me a vital part of my plan.

The controlling notions I had developed earlier became evident in the materials collection and the other steps in the building of the community research program at Wisconsin. Looking back, I believe that my ideas have not changed materially from those outlined in New York and demonstrated in Alberta. One of the notions I had then was the necessity for broad development of theater interest.

In 1948, the Rockefeller Foundation approved a fifteen thousand dollar grant to the University of Wisconsin to try out aspects of the Wisconsin Idea Theater program. The money permitted us to begin experimenting with new plays on the campus. It also enabled us to conduct a unique tri-county theater project in Winnebago, Washara, and Waupaca counties, in which area we kept a man steadily for more than a year trying various techniques of stimulating theater interest. This specialist, James W. Mitchell, was a tall, personable man who had a natural ability to work with and to win the confidence of people. His job was to concentrate Wisconsin Idea Theater aid in a small area and to test the effect of such concentration. Unfortunately, a year was not long enough to allow conclusive results. His concentrated three-county effort, however, produced a remarkable upswing of theater interest and led me to believe that concentrated area work might be more valuable than broad, state-wide programs. Mitchell used films, public lecture, special theater classes, and large county-wide theater revues successfully to educate audiences to appreciate and participate in theater. One result of his efforts was the Winnebago Rural Drama Association composed of drama-minded leaders in Winnebago County (county seat,

189

Oshkosh). This is a group of people with a primary interest in native playwriting. Last year, 1953, some thirty original one-act plays were written and produced in Winnebago County as a result of the Association's work.

Dr. Stevens encouraged me to solidify my ideas and to think in terms of research which somehow might shed a little light in the dim places where the arts are scarcely known, and I determined that I would try to work out some new research phase of the Wisconsin Idea Theater. I had learned to analyse my own personal rôle, but now it seemed that I must analyse the rôle of my entire project both in respect to the people of the state and to the University. The University of Wisconsin Graduate School had funds for research, and I applied to the Dean for assistance. The Graduate School had stature and immense respectability within the University, and it seemed to me that a research link to the Graduate School would lend the state-wide arts programs a prestige which they badly needed. My plea for assistance brought James H. Herriott, Associate Dean of the Graduate School, to my office. I discovered that he was a Kansas man, and we were immediately on friendly ground. He had been born on a Kansas farm near Salina. After swapping a few Sunflower State yarns he helped me obtain a small grant to do research into the Wisconsin Rural Writers' Association. This was in 1951, and if I could have foreseen that by 1954 I would be the administrator of a rather extensive research program involving constant fund-raising drives, supervision, and travel I doubt whether I would have taken the initial steps, for the research has been to me a very heavy burden. However, the Rural Writers' grant was for a modest study, and I could foresee no future developments from it. It was designed to throw general light on the rôle of the University in connection with a writers' movement and to study the type of individual likely to associate himself with it.

Ed Kamarck was put in charge of the project. He studied five hundred members of the writers' group and gleaned quite a lot of information. Seventy-five per cent of the members studied were born in Wisconsin. The average member had lived about thirty-eight years in the state. I was interested in this fact, for it seemed to indicate that the organization was really deeply rooted in Wisconsin life and that it was a truly indigenous movement. The bulk of the writers were between the ages of twenty-six and sixty. Again this was a significant fact to me, for I had anticipated that the largest number of writers would be people beyond sixty—retired folk with plenty of leisure or younger persons of school age. The largest group, indeed, was in the thirty-six to forty age bracket—in the age group, in other words, that should ordinarily be most heavily engaged in child raising, business, and other prime-of-life pursuits.

It was interesting to me to observe that over 25 per cent of the five hundred writers studied by Kamarck actively participated in the theater parts of the Wisconsin Idea Theater's plan as well as in the writing parts. They acted, directed plays, or performed some other theater activity. This tended to support one of my hunches: that a person interested in one art is very likely to be interested in others and that the development of one arts movement is very likely to bring the whole arts idea forward.

The reading habits and tastes of Wisconsin rural writers are interesting. The average rural writer in Wisconsin subscribes to about 5 magazines, takes a daily newspaper, owns 133 books, and reads about 25 new books a year. Ninety-five per cent of the writers particularly enjoyed reading poetry, books, and plays which dealt with the small town or rural scene. Familiarity with the subject matter seemed to be the chief reason for their enjoyment. Among the magazines subscribed to, the news magazines rated very high, with the women's magazines, the digests, and the fiction publications such as the *Saturday Evening Post* riding close behind. It would seem that the average writer is quite well informed about current events but is generally unfamiliar with the better contemporary poetry and fiction. Favorite poets most often given were Longfellow and Tennyson, and O. Henry and de Maupassant led the short story authors in popularity.

All this has pertinence to me in judging the writing done by the Wisconsin authors. Obviously tastes are influenced to a major extent by literature studied in school. Eighty per cent of the writers studied had high school educations. Only 20 per cent had been to college. This perhaps means that the big backstage ought to jump in here and give a dose of adult education by working out programs to give these people a greater familiarity with tastes and trends in art. Imaginations need to be freed from literary types studied in high school. Indeed, if high school is the extent of the formal education of most of the writing folks of Wisconsin, the high school English people ought to be seriously concerned. The kind of formal education which the average writer may have had possibly has great influence on the development of a grassroots literature.

We found that 83 per cent of the writers wrote for self-expression. That is, they felt a sincere need and desire to communicate thought and emotion in literary form. Only 7 per cent thought of writing as a hobby. This, of course, encouraged me. It is out of the self-expression group that a native literature will come, I believe. It is there that art exists. The hobby-recreation motive is not as important.

The rural writer survey constituted another step toward a larger research plan, and it broke new ground. The state-wide cultural arts program of the University had never before engaged in any plan of systematic research of itself. A next step, therefore, was the assembly of a complete historical record of the cultural arts in the state of Wisconsin. We knew that this would be a large task, for there had never been any attempt to pull the history of the cultural arts movements into focus.

There had been, of course, regional studies elsewhere which had included the arts. Of these perhaps the Montana study financed by the Rockefeller Foundation and directed by the American philosopher Baker Brownell was the most notable. Experimentation with pageantry and large group plays was one focus in Montana. The regional writer Joseph Kinsey Howard was utilized in the Montana study to draw attention to regional themes and writing. His fine book, *Montana: High, Wide, and Handsome*, published in 1944, was the first result. The Montana study, however, did little to delve into the potential development of a region-wide art consciousness through community research.

In Wisconsin little was known about the effect of state-wide cultural arts programs. To *do* had always been considered sufficient, largely because to do was about all that could be done with the public funds available. Self-justification was often the key to activity. The University had been more concerned with the creative individual or group than with the cultural level of the community, hoping to affect the latter through the former. It seemed to me that a question of increasing importance was: How does all this state-wide activity affect the community as a whole?

As our research into Wisconsin's cultural history progressed, a report on past programs was assembled by several graduate assistants working under the direction of Ronald Gee of the Wisconsin Idea Theater. The Rural Art project and the Extension Music department also provided studies in their own fields similar to Kamarck's work with the five hundred rural writers. The report, assembled, bound, and suitably noted by University administrators, is an impressive document. It is over six inches high and weighs about five pounds.

I found the report immensely illuminating. It defined the rôle which the University of Wisconsin had actually played in the development of a cultural arts consciousness in the state. It was apparent that the University had been genuinely sympathetic toward the cultural arts interests of the Wisconsin people and that it had played the rôle of teacher by offering many kinds of program aids. By recognizing and accepting participation in the arts as a perfectly natural and desirable kind of behavior the University had given status to the local artist. The University had developed numerous programs shaped to the particular interests or specifications of particular University administrators, and this development had the effect of giving the history of the state-wide cultural arts schemes a feast-or-famine kind of aspect. The report showed how dramatically and dynamically the state University could assume a rôle of leadership, given the presence within the University of men of vision who were willing to take chances, create programs, and bring the forces of the University into line with community cultural problems.

The great University President Van Hise was one of these leaders, and so was President Glenn Frank, who came a couple of decades later. Dean Chris L. Christensen of the Agricultural College was still another outstanding example, and so was Dean Snell of the Extension Division. When the administrators favored the state-wide programs in the arts they had spectacular effect. The trouble seemed to lie in the absence of long-range planning, which gave the whole history of the arts developments a scattered and hit-or-miss appearance. University prestige was greatly damaged by the withdrawal of such programs as the Bureau of Dramatic Activities, which Ethel Rockwell had directed, by the discontinuance of the community music development when Professor Gordon shifted to resident teaching from Extension, by the departure from the University of Dean Christensen which left a gap in the Agricultural College arts leadership. A generalization which I drew from the report was that University leadership in the cultural arts must be kept constant, for such is the fountainhead nature of the state University's rôle as an influence in community life that alterations in that rôle can disrupt and cripple local leadership and attitudes for years after a program is dropped.

A kind of hit-or-miss pattern of University promotion and leadership is what I came into in Wisconsin. Undoubtedly the University had done excellent things for the arts because of the presence of such leaders as Gordon, Kolb, Curry, Rockwell, and Dickinson. These individuals in their own times were outstanding in the notion of the vital place of the arts in community life. Yet even their leadership created dangers, for they tended to teach and encourage in great peaks lighted by their personalities and they left, often, the plains and valleys filled with shadow. The shadowland is where I have tried to walk, but it is disheartening, often, and dangerous, too, to succeed heroes. In arts cultivation the heroes plow magnificently but tend to miss the corners, the hillsides, the bogs.

The report pulled the whole Wisconsin Idea in cultural arts education into a single picture for me, and I understood the Wisconsin Idea in a way I had never before understood it. The picture which began with the various kinds of people who had settled the state and which reached completion through the many leaders who furthered the idea of the arts as vital part of family, individual, and community life emerged strikingly. The report presented a magnificent case for the arts in Wisconsin.

While the report was being assembled during the academic year 1952–1953, plans were being laid for actual field research to test the effectiveness of contemporary cultural arts programs, including the Wisconsin Idea Theater, the Rural Art project, and the Extension Music project.

I had always had a natural opposition to social science and had held the personal opinion that an artist might make more valuable judgements on art matters simply through intuition and artistic insight than social science might ever hope to accomplish through elaborate tests and controls. The position of social science is so strong now, however, and the results of its research have been in many areas so impressive that it seems ill-considered of the arts not to see whether there is anything in social science methods of value to themselves. Probably one of the weaknesses of community arts programs is that they have not been able to gauge their proper place in the community, to judge the tempers, inclinations, and potentials of the community, and to fit themselves, through proper public relations, to community life.

With personal aversions to social science yardsticks sticking somewhat insecurely in my back pocket, therefore, and with a hearty belief that social science did not have all the answers I submitted myself to the public opinion expert Burton Fisher. In the nature of my cross-departmental setup at the University I was able to seek the aid of many University facilities. I discussed the problems of the community arts with Fisher, a member of the Anthropology department, and he drafted a document which led eventually to an actual research program. Professor Fisher outlined in detail the kinds of information that should eventually be sought from the participants in the arts programs as well as from the general public, and with his document as a basis for discussion a University Cultural Arts Research committee was set up with Dean Herriott as chairman. Seven departments and divisions of the University were represented.

I have no idea how many committees it takes to handle the vast detail of the Wisconsin Idea in education. I do know certain faculty members who spend almost their entire time going from committee meeting to committee meeting. It seems a dreadful waste of time and talent to me, although I know there are individuals who have developed committee personalities which bloom under no other conditions than those found in a smoky committee room. These souls are lost in limbo, and when the committees cease, life will surely end for them.

At the present time, however, committees are the ways in which the business of the Wisconsin Idea is largely carried out. So we formed another one. The Cultural Arts Research committee gave our idea a sort of official status in the University. It was decided that aid would once more be sought from the Rockefeller Foundation, and in January of 1952 I wrote to the Foundation asking whether they would sponsor the research we had in mind.

David Stevens had by that time retired as Director of Humanities for the Foundation, and Charles Burton Fahs, a keen-minded young man—a specialist in Near East history—had taken his place. He replied cautiously, stating that the Humanities Division had a theoretical interest in such research and suggesting that someone from the Foundation visit us at Wisconsin. Edward D'Arms, the Associate Director of Humanities, came out in March, and we escorted him on a whirl about the state, showing him programs in progress. He reacted favorably, and late in the Spring a proposal was submitted to the Foundation. After considerable alteration and modification of the proposal a grant of ten thousand dollars for a beginning year's research in community culture was made by the Foundation to the University.

The University committee and I decided to base the research plan temporarily on two basic assumptions: (1) that the University of Wisconsin by its various cultural arts programs sponsored by General Extension and Agricultural Extension and furthered by the generous coöperation of many other University agencies and departments has made a significant contribution to the levels of appreciation and degree of participation in the arts in Wisconsin, and (2) that the communities of the state may attain satisfactory levels of art appreciation, and community studies should be started to discover how such levels might be attained. The report on the state-wide cultural arts programs of the University, the results of the research finished and drawn into final form under the Rockefeller Grant, furnished the springboard for the community projects to come.

My committee was greatly disturbed by the fact that not enough money was available to set up adequate controls for field experiments, but the committee finally agreed to a single area test study on a purely observation basis. For this study Washington County (county seat West Bend, population 5,000) was chosen. It was fairly representative of many of the counties in Wisconsin in that it had large communities and small ones. It was primarily agricultural, but there were also several large industries in the area. The county was close enough to the University to permit staff members to travel frequently to the area for meetings and consultations. It also had an interesting, dramatic history, and the large percentage of persons of German extraction provided a valuable side-consideration of an ethnic group and its relation to the cultural arts. In addition, the rôle of a large metropolitan center, Milwaukee, in stimulating cultural art activity in its environs could be estimated, it was thought.

We planned to work with the county in developing or carrying on interest in music, theater, painting, and creative writing, using the same methods for developing participation programs in these fields as we would ordinarily use in any community in which we might work. We hoped to employ one full-time, trained social scientist to live in Washington County, preferably at West Bend, and to observe what went on. The study was to be a short-term one, and we knew that the observer's impressions would doubtless be general. I was certainly somewhat skeptical; yet I could see the value in having sociological techniques applied to the problem of estimating public reaction to the things we were accustomed to do.

We obtained the coöperation of a group of city leaders, including newspaper and radio representatives, school men, librarians, the county agricultural agent, representatives of the woman's club, and various other individuals known to have an interest in the arts. We were fortunate, too, to acquire the services of Bernard James, a young anthropologist with artistic inclinations, who had recently made important studies on the Menomonie Indian reservation in north-central Wisconsin. He moved his family to West Bend, and the study got under way in the Spring of 1953.

Many things underlie a study of this kind, and I think a word about underlying factors is needed here. It is a temptation to start a community culture investigation with the assumption that the average Middle Western town is comparatively undeveloped from the standpoint of the cultural arts. But, then, one always has to ask: comparatively with what? I seriously doubt whether West Bend, the town in question, is culturally more undeveloped than most towns of its size in other American regions. As nearly as I have been able to observe, the levels of appreciation are pretty low everywhere one goes, and, unfortunately, very little is being done in most communities to raise cultural appreciation levels. It is well known that most small community schools do not have art teachers and that the number of full-time dramatics teachers in small communities in Wisconsin can be counted on the fingers of one hand. Children are simply not getting the kind of training in the elementary and high schools that would help them to appreciate the arts more. A good deal is accomplished, perhaps, through radio and television programs devoted to the problem, but the effect of this type of education can hardly be as effective as the direct teacher to pupil relationship which a couple of generations ago produced strong respect for poetry and art in a way that modern educators are apt to write off as simply old-fashioned. I have been struck on visiting Great Britain by the respect for poetry which most British school children as well as most adults seem to possess, purely, I suspect, as the result of educational method and tradition. This may be one of the reasons why more than one hundred repertory theaters are able to survive in British communities and why the British countryside is more thickly sprinkled with arts festivals and art centers than ours is.

Then, too, we are not much aware of the oral values in

literature, and this perhaps may be a reason why small community theater productions are not often appreciated as much as they ought to be. We are not a reading nation in the way that we were once. The family circle being read aloud to in the 1880's (as my grandfather read to his family in Kansas) developed appreciations and tastes that were never forgotten. Families do not read together much now, I am afraid, and instruction in reading aloud is practically non-existent in the small community schools I come into contact with. I have often met with groups of young persons and adults in towns the size of West Bend who have been interested in play presentation. In asking members of the group to read aloud I have found that it is the rare individual indeed who can stand on his feet and read aloud with fair understanding and clarity.

Adult education is important here, of course, and adult educators should take account of this lack of oral reading ability. Indeed, the field of adult education in relation to the community arts is wide open and adult instruction could do much to correct present conditions. One such condition is that indicated by the question of democracy in arts groups. This factor causes the disintegration, still, of many groups devoted to the arts. Middle-class attitudes are apparent in these towns of the Middle West, and theater groups, particularly, tend toward cliques and closed organizations, perhaps not as a general policy but through the dynamics of group development. In our work with community theaters as one method of advancing an area-wide theater interest I have often observed that a certain group of persons does the bulk of the work in these organizations and that a kind of undemocratic system is evolved, not from choice, perhaps, but from necessity. The necessity grows sometimes into a convention, or a mode, and the nature and broad purpose of the group is often destroyed. Such narrowing of focus of the art group can come about sometimes through the presence of a small central nucleus of semi-professional or professional artists who dictate policy and method and insist on a kind of star system of their own. The professional artist within a group who is willing to act as a sincere teacher without attempting to dictate the kind of art a community should have is a tremendously valuable asset.

Our study of the rôle of the University of Wisconsin in the cultural arts made us particularly aware of the importance of local leadership in arts programs and bred in me at least the conviction that the University ought to make a careful analysis of the kinds of arts leadership available in communities before attempting to develop programs with the people of those communities.

The problem of local leadership is greatly complicated in America by the number of activities available in nearly every community. One is amazed at the things there are to do every night in the week if one wants to do them. The big point is, of course, the communities are over-organized; from every side one hears the same cry: "There is too much going on in our town. Too many things. Every night is taken up. There isn't, simply isn't room for anything more." What is to be done about it, I do not know. The number of organizations is certainly a hazard to arts development. To take another example from abroad, in a number of places in Scotland (and notably in Galishiels) a kind of art center has been developed which includes most of the organizations of the town within its fabric. That they are not strictly art or creative groups in purpose apparently is not important. The important thing is that they are a part of the center and therefore give strength to the arts by their very presence. It is said to work well.

Community arts research must take such considerations into account. Bernard James, our young anthropologist, found them pertinent in his West Bend observations. These considerations also were pertinent to the fact that the Wisconsin Idea Theater in association with the other arts programs was able within five months to stimulate the formation of three cultural-arts organizations and assist in reviving one other group.

During the Spring the Wisconsin Idea Theater worked with a partially defunct community theater—the West Bend Community Players—and was able to revive it to some extent. The Rural Art project worked with a group of artists who planned and developed a five-county Rural Art show. A sizable body of amateur creative writers was organized by Kamarck as a unit of the Wisconsin Rural Writers' Association. The Department of Extension Music provided a choir directors' training clinic and helped establish a county-wide band and a homemaker's choral group.

The Wisconsin Idea Theater and the other cultural arts workers from the University effected the participation of 150 to 200 persons in the Washington County area. Bernard James watched closely the whole process which developed the county art activities. He attended all the meetings, talked with the individuals involved. He hung around taverns, libraries, stores, filling stations, and clubrooms, listening to gossip, asking subtle questions, and getting as complete an idea as possible about the way the average citizen regarded art activities and the people who participated in them.

What he reported was in general what I had assumed to be true as a result of my own experience here and there. According to what James heard and saw in West Bend, the place of the cultural arts in the daily lives of those who participate in them is pretty much determined by class attitudes. The dominant class attitude, of course, is that of the American middle class, although there are traces (in the choice of subject matter for writing and painting, for example) of the operation of farm and urban working class viewpoint and values.

Amateur theater in particular is shot through with the ideas of the middle class regarding the kind of world that ought to be portrayed on the stage and the problems to be treated there. Painting is also largely dominated by similar sentiments. The amateur writing and painting examined in Washington County exhibited only very slight evidence of socially critical or "bohemian" attitudes. Most creative efforts conformed rather closely to the prescriptions of our mass entertainment and educational media. The cultural arts in general are viewed by the general public as pursuits for the few, as heavy with prestige overtones, and for the most part are conducted against mediocre standards.

I have been saying for years that mediocrity is the standard in most American communities. This is especially so in play production where one poorly-chosen and ill-produced script leads to others of the same kind. Most communities see no living theater except that locally produced, and communities accept standards and place values in accordance with what is seen. Mediocre standards may be the single greatest drawback to the spread of the living theater idea as a force in community life.

James observed another phenomenon in Washington County that is common over the country—the dominant rôle of women in the arts. The arts, he noted in his report, were defined by residents of the area as a woman's world, and this definition, of course, held male participation to a minimum. Many times have I addressed large groups of womenfolk on theater subjects and deeply longed for the presence of just one strong masculine face in the audience. I cannot doubt that American women have a sincere sense of responsibility to see that the community arts idea gets ahead, but participation by men in carrying out the idea is badly needed. I am sure that there can be no vital and widespread consciousness of the arts in America until the American men rally behind the idea. In many places men do accept the arts and often the artist in ways they have not done before; yet only a relatively few men participate in arts activities. The sports idea is still dominant with American males and is probably apt to remain so for a long while.

In connection with the lack of male participation in the arts I am struck by the difference in attitude between Wisconsin and Alberta. In Alberta I had the experience of witnessing a large male participation in the native materials program and theater movement I helped to establish. I attribute such participation now to the linking of the programs with the frontier. The frontier in Alberta was much nearer in time to the people of the region than it is in Wisconsin, and since my approach in Alberta was from the point of view of the frontier materials it naturally attracted males who still, in that part of Canada, respond to frontier motivations. The frontier has little meaning as a living symbol in Wisconsin.

I do not think that we have found the touchstone for an art movement that can appeal to large numbers of males. If we could discover one we might break down attitudes characterizing the arts as womanish or nonvirile. In the smaller places particularly these attitudes do persist. However, James reported that the leadership of the arts groups in Washington County seemed to be male, and I certainly accept this as a definite sign of encouragement.

James was struck by the strength of what he has called, for want of a better term, a "happy-ending, pretty-picture" sentiment. The cultural arts are supposed to soothe and please, not stir uneasy emotion or stimulate thought. It is the kind of sentiment which one visitor to an art show in West Bend expressed with regard to a very realistic rendering of a kitten: "Now that to me is good art. Look how fluffy that little kitten looks. Isn't that nice. You just want to hold that little thing in your lap." It is the kind of sentiment which prompts many of the women involved in cultural arts to collect shelves of pretty trinkets and "antiques." It immerses women in a world of "nice" things—delicate doilies and harmless thoughts.

If this is so it certainly demonstrates how far we have come from the folk arts that flourished on the American frontier. Apparently only tenuous connections exist between the old folk culture of Washington County and the present culture.* Leadership which James saw in action was rather sophisticated and much of it was imported from metropolitan centers, principally Milwaukee.

Personally, I, too, respond to the "folk" approaches, and somehow I wish that James had observed something hopeful for the folk arts in Washington County. From my own observations in Wisconsin and elsewhere, however, I fear that he is correct in saying that the "folk" arts have no real meaning and function in American daily life, except of course as recreation. There is going on in America a revival

---

* In our Washington County research we were, of course, aware of the Montana study conducted in 1944–45 under the direction of Baker Brownell. This was primarily a program to stimulate cultural growth generally by group attention to local history, local civic problems. The Montana study is not easily compared with the Washington County research, but we found little evidence of "folk" tendencies and interests reported in Montana.

206

of the "folk" notion, and there is a spreading cult of "folk" singers (most of them with guitars) in practically every college community in the nation. In England and Scotland also I have observed large and rapidly spreading movements in folk dancing, and in Scotland especially the wonderful "Scotch feet" are coming back into their own. The recreation people in America have built practically a whole recreative philosophy on folk and square dancing. In many communities the homespun arts of rug weaving, pot making, and wood carving have had a tremendous revival but with commercial overtones.

Unfortunately I cannot believe that this kind of synthetic "folk" tone has much to do with the kind of theater and art movement I have been trying to develop. The folk dance programs, the copied "folk" forms in the homespun arts are very nice, very pretty. Sometimes they are moving and actually arouse nostalgia. They do in me. But except as recreation and commercialization, they have served their purpose. The seeds of a vital art movement for our time are not in them. We must seek the answers within ourselves and in terms of our own time and being as individuals and as a nation. The absence of a true folk concept or necessity in the arts in community life explains, perhaps, why the gap between the arts and the daily lives of average persons is very great today. This gap is the challenge to modern education and cultural art development.

James recounts in his report an incident that occurred during the Washington County research period which serves to illustrate the problem. A gentleman involved in the organization of an art show in Milwaukee expressed his opinion of popular art and mass participation. His argument ran as follows:

"Frankly, I am a snob. I believe shows like this are for a

minority and the people that come to shows like this are a minority. Do you realize that less than 5 per cent of the people of Milwaukee are interested in art? But the door over there is open. Anyone can come in. But it makes no difference to me what 95 per cent of the public thinks about this show, whether they think that it's crazy and artists are all nuts. And I wouldn't go out on the street to try to convince them to come in here. It makes no damned difference to me."

Such a statement shows plainly to me the breakdown of communion between the artist and the public. Many of the modern artists aggravate the breakdown of rapport between themselves and public by failing to make clear the nature of new developments in art. If the average interested art show audiences were told "why" Mondrian painted rectangular planes of pure color which "don't look like anything" or "why" artists cannot simply go on repeating the styles of the past, they would undoubtedly become more receptive to experimental and abstract work. And, of course, more attention by the community to the whole question of public taste would help in many ways.

West Bend has had, on occasion, special speakers giving talks at the library and to women's groups on literature, politics, and current affairs. But as one of the women active in these programs said: "We just can't get people to come. Even though it costs nothing, they simply don't care to learn anything." But when a West Bend women's organization sponsored a guest speaker for one of their public lectures, they chose an eastern publisher who had gained some notoriety on a television quiz program. Ostensibly, the lecture was to concern "How TV and Movies Influence or Affect Literature." In fact, however, the lecture amounted to rambling chatter about "show people," their wonderful personalities, *Time* and *Life*, and a Wisconsin Senator. The whole affair was punctuated by stale and slightly questionable jokes which kept the audience giggling and tittering. The audience was comprised exclusively of well-dressed middle-class persons. Comments in the lobby suggested that a lot of the people who attended felt "much enriched" by the experience. Such incidents suggest how social sentiment and attitude can in some ways become an enormous obstacle to cultural art development.

However, I do not consider such attitudes unsurmountable obstacles. To me it remains a matter of education and a part of the whole idea of native arts development of which I have dreamed. Appreciations must be given adequate chance for expression, and I personally consider it the state University's responsibility to see that such expression may occur. As long as University Extension remains a backstage operation with hit-or-miss community programs in the arts, the bulk of the communities of the state will not raise their standards of appreciation very much. The University cannot do the entire job, of course, but long range plans involving the really vast resourses of the University would certainly help.

The churches could greatly help increase appreciation levels, too, if they would take a dynamic point of view toward the arts in the community and make arts programs a living part of church experience. Certain denominations in America, such as the American Baptist Association, are at last recognizing the contemporary worth of drama in the church. In England, the Church Drama Society is conducting a national program in experimental theater, one of the most interesting drama manifestations now in progress in that country. In Edinburgh, the Church of Scotland actually owns and operates a professional experimental theater—the Gateway Theater—with a resident company and a Church of Scotland minister as manager. There are also movements in certain church denominations both in America and abroad which are taking a strong favorable point of view toward the arts in general. Within the churches may lie real hope for changed public attitudes toward the arts.

The whole reason and purpose of the community arts study is, of course, to develop and further the arts themselves. Research is never an end in itself in a plan to nurture grassroots arts expression. The art, or the search for the artists and the preparation of a compatible soil for their growth, is the main consideration always. The big structure of the University, the whole complexity of the backstage, furnishes the means of search. The institutes, the car fleets, the lists of names, the mailing routines, the duplicating machines, the coöperating agencies, the instructions by mail, the movie projectors—these items and a hundred others have been my tools for searching, for developing the arts idea. Without them the Wisconsin Rural Writers' Association could never have come into being as a grassroots literary movement with strong community ties. In a way, the Rural Writers' Association is a tribute to the all-encompassing Wisconsin Idea.

Chapter nine

RURAL WRITERS

When I was about eighteen the creative writing bug stung me. It stung me on a late Fall night when I was walking home from Iola, Kansas, to our farm which lay on a hill about two miles from the courthouse. The night was moonlit, and a heavy, still mist lay in all the low places. I kept noticing the shapes of the mist and the gaunt forms of trees and the patterns of faint moonlight and shadow and mist.

It happened that father had taken in just that day, as part of a fee for a bit of legal work, an extremely battered old Remington typewriter. It was sitting on the kitchen table, and when I came in I simply sat down at the ancient machine and picked out a poem about the mist and the shapes in it. I am sure it was not a very good poem, but to me it seemed the most wonderful thing I had ever done, and the idea of writing became completely fascinating and irresistible. It has remained so with me ever since and has, I am sure, motivated my interest in helping to develop the creative writing talents within the areas where I have worked. The thought that many rural persons might experience the same keen pleasure I discovered as a farm boy on that misty night in Kansas is a warming one. I have had this dream of a native literature growing from a deep sensitivity to things, to places, and now, perhaps, it has become with me a drive as well as a dream. I never tire of searching for the deeply creative person.

To discover the few, of course, one must work with the many, and this too can be satisfying. It seems to me that the idea of creative writing can unite people into a great force capable of creating within itself a grassroots literature such as I dream of.

I had an unformulated notion when I came to Wisconsin that a state-wide program in creative writing must be one of my objectives. As time went on I studied the possibility more and more. A conscious stimulation of wide interest in creative writing had never been attempted in the rural areas of the state. Playwriting had been emphasized by the University from time to time, but the whole idea of creative writing as a countryside movement had not been dealt with. Besides its worth to the individual, I saw in creative writing a stepping stone leading toward the public consciousness of the arts I visioned as a possible major result of all our work in Wisconsin. I saw creative writing as one intensification of the home-based or home-grown culture ideal. And I saw the Wisconsin Idea Theater, more and more, as a kind of center around which a campaign to encourage and develop home-grown theater, art, and literature might be conducted. I sensed intuitively that a free literary movement in rural areas might spread and grow quickly, since writing did not necessarily require the same group focus characteristic of theater participation.

The Rural Art project had grown from thirty exhibitors in 1938 to fifteen hundred in 1948, and I saw no reason why creative writing might not be equally well received as another creative facet of Wisconsin country life. From what I had observed in other places of the widespread desire to write, I guessed that the Wisconsin countryside was ripe with poets and that the sheets of all the original short stories and plays written each year in the state would probably paper all the rooms in all the houses of at least a small Wisconsin town.

For a long while I had wanted to open the creative writing idea up, expand it beyond just playwriting, and at last I determined that this must be done. I realized that there were several considerations one must make in developing such a literary movement. My aim was not only to awaken people to the creative factor in their lives but also to stimulate them to the ultimate production of literary art forms. I recognized the values of a self-expression program on a broad sociological level in keeping with the general principles of the Wisconsin Idea, but I also envisioned fine books and plays and stories arising out of the broad movement through a few particular talents. The third notion inherent in the idea of a people's literary movement was, of course, that of area interpretation. I hoped for poetic or deeply sensitive writing about home themes superior to that brought out by the State Centennial.

All these considerations I had mulled over, but by the Summer of 1948 no actual plan had materialized. The opening up of a creative writing idea developed without warning. I had discussed many times with Wakelin McNeel, "Ranger Mac," the naturalist and 4-H Club leader, the possibility of encouraging the writing of more good short plays for young people's use. We knew the great need for a sincere, creative dramatic literature within the performing capabilities of young rural folk, and we thought that perhaps an appeal made directly to the leaders of 4-H clubs in the state would have merit. We hoped that several of the more creative leaders themselves would write plays which might be widely used by many groups. I volunteered to meet in Madison for a few days with any of the leaders who might wish to come and participate in a kind of writers' roundtable with the specific purpose of developing rural-life plays. Wakelin McNeel made the offer known through his office channels, and a few weeks later on a hot June morning when I had almost forgotten about the proposal my phone rang. It was McNeel and he said:

"There are nine people from rural Wisconsin here to see you."

"What for?"

"They want to talk about that writing."

"The rural plays?"

"Sure."

I said, "I wish I'd known they were coming today. I'm pretty busy."

"One of the women has thirteen children."

"A farm woman with thirteen children has time to come to Madison and talk about writing?"

"She's here," he said.

"All right, I'll see them right now. Where?"

"Bascom Hall. There's a classroom reserved."

I went up the Hill to Bascom. I found the nine people in a hot room that looked out on the slope down to Lake Mendota. There were eight women and one boy. The boy was about eighteen years old. One of the women was tall and gray, two were young, one was fat and jolly, one was quiet and serene, one was dark and small, two were middle-aged. They waited for me to say something, and as I paused a moment looking at them, for no reason at all, I began to remember the happy and careless life I led as a kid in the Neosho River Valley down in Kansas. And it seemed that my early experience had had for me the un-shackled quality of complete freedom, the gaiety, the un-reasoned and complete savoring of the goodness of earth and sky, the unquestioning appreciation of neighbors and music and dancing. And with the memory of the free wild-ness of my youth running through me these folks who had come to see me were transformed. I forgot that they had come to Madison to talk about the technical processes of creative writing. They became, instead, a symbol of a group of my neighbors in Kansas or of people I had encountered on my wanderings, people who knew a wordless apprecia-tion of the theater that was life.

Then I said to the eight ladies and the one boy: "You are like a group of my neighbors when I was a kid down in Kansas."

The tall, gray one said: "You remind me a little bit of a neighbor of mine up in Manitowoc County. He's a farmer. Not really a very good farmer."

"Why did you come?"

"I don't know exactly. Except that we've heard that you want people to write about their own places and the folks they know well. I think I could do that."

I said to them: "Tell me about yourselves. Where did you come from and what kind of places are they?"

And then began one of the most incredible experiences I ever had. These nine persons stayed at the University for three days; and every day about 9:00 in the morning we would start talking together. And as we talked our lives and the struggle in them emerged to lie against the whole fabric of our native places; and as we talked, hour after hour, a kind of fantastic play that was like life itself began to emerge and to encompass us all within its spaceless and formless self. There were times when we would speak, not as ourselves, but as imaginary characters that grew from our talk of people and events that were as real as the earth itself. The whole affair was a kind of dramatic ecstasy in which we were both the actors and the audience, the dancers and the music.

When the three days were over, it was as though a kind of dream had ended, with no more explanation than that with which it had begun. Then we awoke suddenly and realized that we had hardly mentioned the processes of writing at all and that, instead of a partly completed manuscript tucked in pocket or purse, we had only a confused but terribly exhilarating sense of something that had stirred our lives.

When the group was ready to leave Madison, I said: "I have met with hundreds of groups like this one, and I have seen hundreds of plays, but I have never had a deeper sense of theater than we have had together."

The tall, gray lady said: "I think it was because we all had something to express, and we did express it, and maybe the memory of it is somehow better than the written play."

"I wish there were more persons like yourselves."

216

"Mr. Gard," said the tall, gray lady, "there are hundreds and thousands of rural men and women who live on the land and love the land and who understand the true meaning of the seasons and man's relationship to man and to his God."

I said: "If that is so, the plays they send to me don't reflect such an appreciation."

She replied that she thought one reason the plays reflected little poetic appreciation of the area was because everything was made to seem too complex, too technical, too difficult. She said there must be a great, free expression. If the people of Wisconsin knew that someone would encourage them to express themselves in any way they chose, if they knew that they were free of scenery and stages and pettiness that the plays we do seem so full of, if they knew that someone would back them and help them when they wanted help, it was her opinion that there would be such a rising of creative expression as is yet unheard of in Wisconsin and it would really all be a part of the kind of theater we had had these past three days, for the whole expression would be of and about ourselves.

The eight ladies and a boy went away, but I could not stop thinking about them. And that same Fall we launched a new kind of organization—an organization that was really not an organization, for in its beginning it was never really organized. As machinery for the launching we used the backstage of Extension in all its parts. The car fleets, the duplicating machines, the promotional devices were all brought into play, as well as a considerable amount of financial backing. The title was "The Wisconsin Rural Writers' Association." It cost nothing to join, everybody was eligible, and the only rule was that a person must submit creative literary evidence of appreciation of familiar scenes and faces.

Edward Kamarck, who was then our playwright-in-residence, took over the actual direction of the Association and in 1948 wrote an invitation to membership. The invitation noted that the rural scene in America seemed to be neglected in the literary field. It was hoped that this organization would be able to seek out the talent existing in this state and that through the Association it would be possible to gather the writings of our people and encourage them to tell about their particular section of the Middle West.

There was some confusion about the word "rural" in the Association title, and indeed there is still. We did not have in mind a policy of excluding near-urban or even urban writers, and despite the fact that we were oriented in the main toward an interpretation of what is generally regarded as rural life, we were not rigid in excluding other scenes and locales. The significance of the word "rural" lay in the fact that it defined the field of interest of the organization; it gave us a common subject matter; and it provided a common aim—the honest interpretation of that subject matter. The word was included in the name deliberately for the encouragement of rural people who might, otherwise, have thought that the organization was not for them. City folks were more than welcome to membership so long as they had a sincere regard for the land. However, the focus of the Association was kept rural because of the general lack of cultural opportunities in nonurban areas.

The Wisconsin Idea Theater acted as a center for the movement. We had no idea of how people would react to it. I did recall the healthy response to playwriting invitations dispensed in New York and in Alberta as well as in

218

Wisconsin, and I had a hunch that quite a few folks would respond to the Rural Writers idea. I was really quite dismayed, however, to find how loaded our mailboxes were each morning with manuscripts. To the horror of my already overburdened small staff, over one thousand poems were sent in in a few days' time. There were short stories, too, and a few plays. The curious thing was that the material for the most part was quite above average. There was some bad verse, but most of it had at least an honest ring. For a while, until I could get special help, we were all reading innumerable manuscripts every day, at lunch, at dinner, at night, and all of us would usually be walking from this to that task with several rural life poems or stories or plays sticking out of our pockets.

In attempting to make sense of the seemingly phenomenal popularity of this movement I have arrived at a number of apparently contributing factors. Writing is an art that can occupy the mind while the hands are busy with other tasks. It can engage the subconscious while the conscious mind is intent on other things, thus offering an opportunity to slip away from the routine task even while busying oneself with it. It is an art that does not require an outlay of money for its enjoyment; a pencil and paper are all that is required. It concerns itself with the substance of everyday life; new fallen snow, a stony field, the harvest, a neighborhood rumor, a church supper—any of these may be the germinal idea for a poem, a story, or a play. Receptivity has been made easier, too, by ventures in other arts stemming from the University—the Rural Art project, rural music, and correspondence courses offered by University Extension, and by the encouragement and active interest of the Wisconsin Idea Theater and the whole prestige of sponsorship by the state University. There is, of course, one final main reason for the popularity of the Rural Writers' movement: the itch to write, which is apparently universal.

Some persons could not understand what a theater project was doing fooling around with poets and story writers. The fact, however, is that during the course of a year nearly one thousand rural people aligned themselves with the Association and a good effect began to be noted in playwriting. The plays that were sent in were certainly improving, and I took this to mean that playwrights could see themselves as part of a freer literary movement. The scripts contained fewer stereotypes and clichés and I began to see that the development of the creative impulse, no matter what its outlet, was of common benefit to all the arts. The increasing number of plays containing strong central idea or good conflict led me to believe that the Association might become one of our best methods of encouraging new playwrights. No one knows how many talents lie buried for want of exposure to the thing for which they are talented. The broad approach of the Association may reach many talents which would otherwise remain undiscovered.

A board of directors was formed, and in 1950 the board stated its broad objective as follows: "The Association can perform an extremely valuable function by encouraging the preservation and recording of the rich and colorful state lore: folk tales, local history, and the manners and mores of the rapidly vanishing older communities. In addition to its aim of encouraging and stimulating writers, the Association should set itself a broader aim: that of helping to build a fuller cultural life in the state, the creation of a sympathetic and understanding atmosphere for the flourishing of all the arts."

I welcomed this statement as an illustration of the relationship of all the arts—an idea that had been building up in me since New York days. As director of the Wisconsin Idea Theater I believed and hoped that the writers' movement might be one major integrating force between the arts in Wisconsin. And in a small way this seems to be working out. For instance, at Evansville, the Community Theater has produced a half-dozen one-act plays by Evansville writers who got their initial stimulation from the Association.

While Kamarck supervised the actual work of organizing and furthering the creative writing plan begun by the Rural Writers' Association, my rôle was always that of a kind of spiritual guide. I was forever reminding the Association, through written communications or speeches, of the necessity of honest interpretation, of spiritual satisfactions, and I never lost an opportunity to play down the commercial possibilities inherent in creative writing. The idea of commercialization of literary effort was, naturally, extremely appealing to many of the writers, and no matter how I pleaded with them to be faithful to the art ideal first and let the commercial tail follow if it would, a few jumped completely on the "sell your stuff" band wagon with, I felt, corresponding declining quality of their work. The reasons for this are too well known to brood over. The patterns, the stereotypes, are apparent in the bulk of the publications aimed at by amateur writers who consider slick publication at whatever spiritual cost the criterion of success.

The "sell" motive, however, is not the dominant one with the average rural writer. What the movement means to the individual was summed up as follows by a writer from Baraboo, Wisconsin:

The writers' movement has focused my attention on the life I know best, and it has helped me to recognize the wealth of material right here in my own community. From that viewpoint I have acquired a greater understanding of my neighbors and their problems.

The writers' movement has erased the inferiority I felt, arising from my limited education, and has paved the way to continued knowledge. Too, being associated with so many others in the state has removed the stigma of eccentricity from writing as a hobby, making it at least as respectable a pastime as crocheting bedspreads or hooking rugs. My "hobby," in turn, has given me an emotional outlet to supplement the monotonous routine of housework and has probably made me a more interesting and certainly a more contented person.

This lady's husband is a farmer who always rather tended to disapprove of his wife's writing projects. But lately the stuff she has been writing has taken on a lot of personal meaning for him, because a lot of her writing is localized around their farm. Last Christmas, without saying a word about it, he went to Baraboo and bought her a new writing desk and a new typewriter.

The Rural Writers' Association has a sort of creed which was made up by a lot of folks who sent in their notions of what the Association was, or ought to be. When the major ideas were put together it was apparent that a cultural movement was in progress. Sharing experiences, belief in one another, emphasis on the individual artist, recognition of creative writing as one way to an understanding of the democratic process, sympathy for the folklore of the area, and desire for more education were ideas of outstanding importance expressed by the organization. Attracted to the movement have been a number of dynamic leaders like Fidelia Van Antwerp of Wisconsin Dells. Fidelia, who is a retired school teacher of commercial subjects, appeared one summer in my regional writing class at the University and worked intensively on a collection of short stories based on the lore of the Wisconsin Dells region. She heard from me about the Rural Writers' Association and immediately became a member. She became increasingly interested in the project, and since 1949 she has given the Association her full time. She has done more than any other person to develop the rural writing movement and to sustain its ideals. She travels the state constantly in behalf of the writers' movement, and there are not many localities in Wisconsin now where Fidelia is a stranger.

Mary Zimmerman is another leader who understands the broad objectives of the writers. In 1947 I was giving a lecture one night to a nice group of ladies in Elkhorn, Wisconsin. I cannot recall what the lecture was about, but after it was over my hostess took my arm and pointed across the room to where an animated and just slightly plump lady was talking with three or four other ladies. My hostess said: "That is Mary Zimmerman from Whitewater. She writes."

"Really?"

"I mean it. She's a real writer."

I thanked my hostess as graciously as I could for the information and tried to forget Mary Zimmerman. It was impossible. In the next three or four weeks, indeed for the next three or four years, her name kept popping up. At first it would be on a poem some place, then on a play she had written for the State Centennial, then on a children's story, and then on the letters she began to write to me at the University. I finally said, "I must meet this lady, pardon me, this writer," and I did.

Mary Zimmerman is a vital spirit, and her pen is as facile and talented as her conversation. She has pleased my simple professional heart with many literary gems, and recently she has written a book of poems called *A Gallery of Women's Portraits*. In the very first poem is the tiny rhyme

> As other women dress a bonnet,
> She trims a heartache with a sonnet

which demonstrates Mary's whole outlook. I know that she understands what I am trying to do in Wisconsin. She is one of the most inspiring leaders of the Rural Writers' Association.

There are several professional writers in the Association whose devotion to the group is inspiring. Katharine Green, who resides at "Bonnie Oaks," a lovely old farm north of Portage, is one of these. She has been in big time publishing and is able, through gentleness and deep understanding of the reasons behind the movement, to guide many others of the Rural Writers' group to a deeper consciousness of the "whys" of the organization. And there is Helen Smith, of Evansville, a mother, a legal secretary, and a successful creative writer; she is an unselfish giver of herself, her time, and her talents to the Association. She believes completely in the effort to develop a fine native literature, and so does John Lonsdorf, of Birnamwood, who acts as treasurer. If you can find the Lonsdorf gate on a country road near the village of Birnamwood and trudge or drive over his private trail for half a mile through sweet pine woods you will come to a log cabin in a clearing on the bank of the Plover River. The cabin, which is spacious and homey, was built by John, who worked in the surrounding woods until he had enough timber and then somehow got the great logs into position. John and his wife have lived in the woods for four winters. They are both poets. Recently John completed an epic poem which recites the whole basis and soul of the American tradition.

Another gifted leader is Louise Leighton of Baraboo, an established poet and artist. Her most recent volume of poetry, *Journey to Light*, is illustrated with cuts from her own paintings. Mrs. Leighton has always been actively interested in the cultural life of the community and the state.

Because of her experience and ability and her willingness to assist others and her idealism she has been of inestimable help to hundreds of struggling young poets in the Association.

These and other leaders have worked closely with Kamarck and me to make the Association have local as well as state-wide appeal. Many county and community groups of rural writers have been formed, and the members are finding stimulation, encouragement, and social joy in one another. There is considerable diversity among these clubs, both in organization and activity. In some the organization is informal, while in others much importance is attached to such matters as officers, dues, and a planned program for the year. Activities take many forms. A number of the larger clubs publish a mimeographed bulletin, which appears more or less regularly and prints news of the club and the best work of its members. Among these are the Lakeshore Writers, the Evansville Writers, the Sauk County Club, the Wausau Club, and the Rhinelander Club. For its December, 1953, project the Manawa Writers' Club issued an attractive sixteen-page booklet of Christmas verse, the work of its members. And some time ago the Evansville Club gathered together the best writings of its poets and had them published in a bound anthology. In the communities where these groups operate a new awareness of creative writing is taking place.

All over the state the creed of the Wisconsin Rural Writers' Association is being exemplified, strengthening the belief of its authors that writers can grow by working together coöperatively. Within the local clubs members share writers' books and magazines, discuss common problems, and offer their manuscripts for constructive criticism and suggestions regarding possible markets. Some groups have organized local writing classes and have sought instruction from the University. Others have enrolled in correspondence courses in creative writing offered by the University Extension Division; and an excellent correspondence teacher, Ralph McCanse, who instructs in poetry writing and other things, has had a profound effect upon many individuals. Ralph goes out sometimes to see his students, and this personal touch makes the correspondence instruction tremendously more worthwhile.

It is interesting to conjecture as to why a rural writers' movement was not started years before the Wisconsin Idea Theater began. Creative writing courses had been offered for a long while through University Extension correspondence study, and there was at least an indication of the widespread interest in creative writing among the people of the state. The field was waiting to be opened up, but nobody took the trouble to open it. It was easier, less dangerous, more comfortable to sit at a desk, green eyeshade pulled low, and correct papers than it was to make a few trips away from the campus. It was a great deal more in keeping with routine to correct commas and mark new paragraphs than it was to meet in some cold country schoolhouse or town hall with a small group of people eager for the personal attention of a University instructor. The correspondence instructors were paid to sit in offices and correct papers, and the professors in the University Department of English were perhaps too conscious of tradition, classrooms in Bascom Hall and with the whole field of literary criticism, or they were too busy with their own research schedules to pay much attention to the people of the state. Not that they were (or are) unsympathetic to the rural writers' movement. Indeed, of late years some of the very best known English professors have instructed at Rural

Writers' Association meetings. Helen White, known equally well for her historical novels and for her scholarship, has gone a number of times to work with writers in their own communities. So has Helen Patterson, the fine teacher of feature writing in the Department of Journalism. When such teachers go into the field it is a worthwhile event for the people. Unfortunately it does not happen nearly often enough.

At the start, we kept in touch with the members through a newsletter which began as a mimeographed bulletin. Later an attractive cover was added, and the publication, sent to everyone on the list of members, helped to hold the Association together. An annual Rural Writers' Contest has been held each spring, and cash awards have been made for the most meritorious entries in poetry, short story, and drama. An additional prize has also been presented to first place winners.

A large movement like the Rural Writers' Association is bound to attract wide attention, and in the six years of its existence it has woven itself into the cultural fabric of the state. The name of the Association is synonymous with sincere creative writing now in almost every community in Wisconsin, and the Association has attracted the interest and aid of many kinds of people. The founder of Kraft Foods, the late J. L. Kraft, was much interested in the Association. His own particular hobby was working in jade, which he cut for ring settings and other ornaments. His home at Elcho, Wisconsin, was always open to members of the Rural Writers' Association, and on one Sunday evening each year he would invite a group of the writers to give a Sunday evening "service" in the chapel on his estate. They complied by reading some of their best poems and other work. In 1949, Wakelin McNeel arranged with Mr.

Kraft to present jade rings made in his own workshop to the winners of the annual Rural Writers' Contest. This practice was continued until Mr. Kraft's death in 1953. Since 1953, Ira L. Baldwin, Academic Vice-President of the University of Wisconsin, also an enthusiastic lapidary, has continued the tradition started by Mr. Kraft. Winning one of the rings is now considered the highest honor that can come to a rural writer.

The University has published three annual collections of the best writings of rural authors who submitted their work in the annual contests. These collections, called *Pen and Plow*, were published by the Agricultural Journalism department as extension bulletins. Printings of five thousand for each issue were made, and each printing was exhausted within a few days. The cover of each issue carried the legend: "Here is rural Wisconsin—the land, the people, the winds, the faiths. This is Wisconsin in terms of people who understand the true meanings of the seasons and man's relationship to man and to his God."

The material in these collections threw the state into relief. There were the poems of Inga Gilson Caldwell of Waupaca County, that stone-filled part of Wisconsin where it would seem unlikely that a sensitive and sometimes powerful poet would be found. Nostalgia for the old days was a part of the collections, too, but personally I felt that the nostalgia was not sentimental. The collections illustrated many important state themes, such as neighborliness, transition from forest to agriculture, adjustments in the new concept of rural and urban. All this was good. Power was the item most lacking, perhaps, for there was nothing in the collections that really stung, shocked, or astonished. The great aesthetic impacts were absent.

228

I suppose, though, that I enjoy the writings of the Association members because they often recall dramatic episodes from my own experience. One summer while I was harvesting wheat in western Kansas a cyclone roared through the countryside leaving a ten-mile-wide path of almost complete destruction. The memory is still very real, and I was, therefore, greatly interested in Wilhelmina Guerink's story, *The Twister*, which was sent in for the first Rural Writers' Contest in 1949. Later it was published in the first issue of *Pen and Plow*. *The Twister* demonstrates the faithfulness with which rural writers treat their material and illustrates one of the outstanding themes used by Wisconsin authors: nature as a chief antagonist of man. In Alberta this theme was widely used, too, and there it was generally man against drought, roots, dust, cold, and natural catastrophes such as the Frank slide, about which I wrote in Canada.

In rural Wisconsin the best pieces seem to be the ones devoted to man striving against cyclones, stone, sandy soil, cutover forest areas, fires, and floods. Mrs. Guerink's story *The Twister* is one of these, and the yarn has another theme also very typical of Wisconsin: the theme of neighborliness. Zona Gale set the neighborly tone for Wisconsin with *Friendship Village* and *Neighbors*, but such writers as Wilhelmina Guerink carry the theme along.

The Rural Writers' movement in Wisconsin has seemingly greatly furthered a consciousness of the worth of the arts in the state and has strengthened the position of the creative artist in community life. Neighbors are proud of Wilhelmina Guerink. One rather good poetess from southwestern Wisconsin told me not long ago that before the Association was formed she would rather have told her neighbors that there were bedbugs in her house than to have admitted that she wrote poetry. Since it is known now, however, that many rural people are writing poetry, she feels that she can freely admit her interest.

My own desire that many rural people know the joy of simple creativeness, has, I think, been fulfilled. They have paid me back, too, in many ways: in personal loyalties, in a wealth of home-made pies and good Wisconsin country cooking in a hundred or more farmhouses, as a great spiritual force which I feel, somehow, at my back.

The Wisconsin Rural Writers' Association has recently been incorporated as a legal organization of the state. It is practically completely self-supporting now, but it could never have become so had it not been for the channels of the great backstage. The University opened up the idea and furnished the staff of instructors and organizers who toured the state. The University paid for publications, postage, gasoline, hotel bills. It paid a stenographer to type letters, a clerk to send out contest materials. The University, through the backstage, has brought a movement into flower and little by little has ceased the number of its services. The people have willingly assumed the responsibility in material terms, but the spiritual bond to the University is still very strong and will, I think, remain so.

Not long ago I heard that the Association was thinking of beginning its own magazine. They had plans for a quarterly which would appeal to readers as well as writers. Now, a new literary magazine is almost always a fine idea, but it is also most always doomed to failure. I had helped start a little magazine (*The Gale*) in Kansas, and one in Alberta (*Alberta Folklore Quarterly*). Both had high ideals, fair material. Both flopped in a year. I considered *The Gale* quite successful, since it lost only eighty dollars. I was fearful for the success of the Rural Writers' magazine venture, and

Kamarck and I reminded the board of directors that the University could put no money into it. Our pessimism made no difference. They would have a magazine and it would be called *Creative Wisconsin*. How would they publish it? Well, time would tell.

First of all the various groups pitched in and earned some money. The Baraboo Club held a "silent auction" of many articles stripped from a multitude of homes and a nice sum of money was assembled. The Columbia County Writers' group had a food sale. The Manawa Club printed a Christmas booklet containing the writings of members, and they sold out a whole edition to a local public. The Evansville Club led by the tireless Helen Smith conducted a "make dollars grow" plan. Each member contributed a dollar and contrived to make the dollar grow into more. Helen Smith bought a dollar's worth of mimeograph paper and did a job of duplicating for a local customer. She took the money from that job and bought more paper. By adding more paper and getting more jobs she soon had more than fifty dollars for the new magazine. And so it went.

Al P. Nelson, a quiet, talented professional writer from Delafield took hold as editor. Since *Creative Wisconsin* was to be a publication devoted to a home-grown literature, the board considered it proper that a home-based creative method of printing it should be found. The method was Mrs. Erma Graeber, a member of the Association from Rhinelander. She was a talented artist and had worked out interesting methods of silk screen reproduction. Also she had a printing press in her basement. She had never done any printing, but she was willing to teach herself. She taught herself on the first issue of *Creative Wisconsin* and turned out an extremely attractive publication. Her printing from hand set type was even and her illustrations were excellent.

It took her two months, working approximately twelve hours a day, to get out twenty-five hundred copies. Somehow she did it, and the Association launched its magazine.

I am proud of the rôle played by the University in connection with the Rural Writers' Association. It seems to me quite proper that the University should act as a catalyst and then withdraw, leaving the project to capable leaders. But often it is not possible for the University to withdraw from a program without causing its collapse. The key, of course, is local leaders who will shoulder responsibility. The Wisconsin Idea with its great backstage can cause many things to come into being, but without strong leaders among the people themselves nothing can survive. This I think has been one of the hardest lessons I have learned from my work in grassroots arts movements.

Chapter ten

CATALYSIS AND LEADERSHIP

I know that I have been a wanderer, that I have had an itching foot since my Kansas boyhood days. The urge to see new places, to discover the sparks of creativeness existing in new places, has been one of my major drives. The University of Wisconsin, with its backstage devoted to spreading the boundaries of the campus, has encouraged and enlarged my itch to wander. I have been completely free in Wisconsin to go where I pleased, when I pleased, and means have been furnished me with which to go. I have wandered literally in every county in the state, and I have

233

talked about the arts in kitchens, living rooms, auditoriums, town halls, schools, and even on back porches. I have sat in many a restaurant late at night after a community play, going over the good stuff and the bad with green but terribly keyed-up community actors. I have sought out grassroots playwrights and artists in their own communities.

Through my wandering I have become a loyal son of Wisconsin. I am loyal because the willing wanderer sees things and intuitively knows things that others may not, and the whole sight, sound, smell, the poetic being of landscape, area, state, become powerful magnets to the wanderer and breed in him a kind of loyalty to place that his awareness alone makes possible. My awareness of Wisconsin and the rôle I have played in the state has given me scope of idea and sense of importance of my program that has been in many ways fantastic. My rôle at times has seemed somewhat like that of a wandering seer so hopeful that what he is attempting will succeed that he fancies he has a prerogative to issue visionary statements. With me the statements have concerned the bloom of culture in America, the fine plays being written, the million or so Wisconsin folks who seemed to be engaged in the creation of a huge grassroots cultural movement.

These visionary expressions have had some basis in reality. My wandering and my rôle have given me a sense of the Wisconsin people—a knowledge that for the most part they are back of my efforts to stimulate, educate, and develop the cultural arts. This knowledge has made me heady, confident, and often blind to the cycles within the very fabric of the thing I have been so close to: the Wisconsin Idea in education.

The ups and downs of the cultural arts portions of the Wisconsin Idea have been very plain. There have been times of prosperity and of famine. I have worked in Wisconsin for nearly ten years now, all of it in a time of comparative prosperity when the great backstage and all that it represented expanded faster than at any other period. To be sure, private funds were necessary for many experiments, but state money was relatively easy to get, and there were no real worries over budget. As a wanderer in Wisconsin I knew that the people expected certain things of their University. They had become, after fifty years, used to the Wisconsin Idea and all that it could mean in their lives. I believed that my accomplishments were worthy enough to justify public expenditures. The very nature of the thing I had set out to do demanded funds. Spreading an idea such as my major notion of developing talents in many places is expensive.

When the prosperity period ended in 1953 I refused to believe that it could happen. It was not easy for me to recognize financial cycles, and as I went on about my wanderings, stating my hopes and visions, I discovered that visions are extremely good game for legislators armed with sharp fiscal knives. My visions were slashed and my pride was hurt when the rumor filtered down that a total cut of the Wisconsin Idea Theater's budget was in prospect. Later the cut was reported to be 50 per cent. Finally, the budget was left almost intact, but to me the whole process was disturbing, spiritually. Eventually, of course, the crisis pointed up for me some very important considerations, namely, that ways must be developed to train local leaders to carry out community arts programs on their own. It also led to some serious sifting and winnowing on my part of the University's own contribution to arts leadership.

But in its first stages the budget crisis which began in the Spring of 1953 left me feeling quite alone and very depressed. I had had no comparable experience upon which to base judgement. At Cornell and at the University of Alberta my work had been supported completely by private funds; so the general budget developments had never affected me. The sight, therefore, of a great state university threshing and gasping in the throes of a major economy move opened my eyes to the skirmish line position the Wisconsin Idea Theater occupied in the University's perpetual battle for funds. The arts are the easiest parts of the University's program to brand as frills and unnecessaries. They are the facets of the backstage most easily pointed to by unsympathetic economizers as unnecessary parts of the University Extension work. As a skirmisher in the front line I was acutely aware of my own position. I knew, of course, what the University as a whole was going through, and I knew that there was tautness in almost every department. I observed with pride and hope how the people of the state were responding to the plight of the University, especially to the backstage. A threat to discontinue thirteen University Extension centers led to such a storm of protest that the notion was dropped immediately by those advocating it.

Nevertheless, the whole affair of the University budget took on a personal focus for me, and for a time my wanderings were fraught with unhappiness, bitterness, and perhaps a little self-pity. The fact that the Capitol and even some branches of the University administration appeared to doubt the worth of the arts in community life seemed to me an impossible development; yet the whole history of the cultural movement in Wisconsin, which I had discovered in the research carried out by the Idea Theater, pointed to the tremendous prestige that had come to the University because of its national leadership in this field. Even such historical evidence did nothing to deter the threats of program extermination. The ancient battle between art and economy was, apparently, as hot and bitter as ever.

The thing that took the sting away from my own wounded feelings was the response of the people. Many letters were sent to the legislators, to the Governor, to the University administration urging that as little tampering as possible be done with the arts projects. And letters people—some of them strangers—wrote to me gave me a powerful lift that helped eventually to clear away the fears and depressions that a big budget struggle at a state university can cause. But while the budget hearings were actually going on I fell lower and lower into a kind of spiritual bog, out of which no amount of wandering in the places I had come to love could seem to lift me. Everything boiled up together. I had no perspective. My itching foot told me that I needed a change, a big one, and I looked around for something I could do, somewhere I might go. Maryo, my wife, said: "Why don't we go over to England. That man wanted you to come."

In the Fall, Martin Wilson, the Secretary of Education for Shropshire County, England, had visited us. He seemed to see in the Wisconsin Idea Theater something hopeful for the arts abroad as well as in America. He had said: "If you will come to visit us in England, perhaps you may clarify your ideas. A visit would make your achievements seem more concrete by comparision with ours."

As I thought it over it seemed like a good idea. My itch especially liked it—the call of new places again. I also hoped that the journey might do something to lift the despondency that the budget crisis had placed upon me. As always, the Rockefeller Foundation rallied to my aid. The Foundation could see value to the Wisconsin Idea in a visit to Britain. Therefore, as a part of their cultural arts research grant to the University they would send me to England. Perhaps in Britain I might measure my dreams, efforts, results, against those of others. Eventually I was on board a Grand Trunk train running toward the boat waiting at Quebec.

It was July, and the budget battle was over. The University had emerged fairly intact, but the hangover was strong upon me. Many curious and unhappy thoughts flashed and grumbled in my brain. The train was running through Indiana and Michigan. There was a blue flower growing along the tracks—miles and miles of blue. A memory of blue flowers arose in me, and I was a child again picking them along the Tulsa branch of the Santa Fe track behind our house in Kansas.

I remembered that I had carried the flowers to my mother who had said something about the wild blue, the endless blue, the sighing blue. This was a delicious thread. I clung to it, swayed on it, plucked it for strange, nostalgic sensations. I stared out the train window. Blue flowers along hot tracks stinking with tar. Blue flowers in Indiana, Michigan. Blue flowers in Kansas. But there were no blue flowers in my brain for Wisconsin. From Madison to McFarland, Janesville, Walworth there were only voices mumbling in my thoughts: "Well, how do you justify the arts?" "I, sir?" "Yes. How can you justify them?" "Why, I refuse to try. The arts are as old as mankind." "You refuse to answer?" "Yes, sir. The answer would sound slightly silly." "Well, it's my opinion that it's a mistake for the state University to be dabbling in this theater stuff, this writing stuff. It's dangerous to let the people express themselves. Besides, what good is it? What money does it bring the state?"

But blue flowers, blue flowers, blue flowers, was the rhythm that lulled me as I left the Middle West, and as the

238

blue flowers along the tracks disappeared I grew less bitter. There were no uneasy thoughts at all in Canada, only a feeling that the backstage was far behind me. Adult education, institutes, special classes, one-day workshops, group activities, the wheels crossing and recrossing the state, the meetings, the local committees—all the routines of the backstage glimmered farther and farther away. Later there was the trip down the St. Lawrence on the ship *Scythia* from Quebec, down the great, beautiful river past Belle Isle. Later still there was the beauty of the British countryside and the excitement of wandering returned in all its allurement.

My purpose in visiting Britain was to see as much as possible of the ways in which the British develop native theater, art, and music. I went everywhere and saw practically everyone who had a vital interest in the arts as an essential part of British life. I was introduced to the programs of adult education conducted nowadays in some of the great houses of England, and I stayed for two weeks at Attingham Park, one of these converted estates, at Shrewsbury.

There were thirty of us at Attingham Park, and we were from almost as many nations of the world. We were young and middle-aged and old, representing many different professions and occupations. We were the guests of Shropshire County, where Martin Wilson and his warden, George Trevelyan, operate the great house. For generations, of course, Attingham had been the meeting place of the local aristocracy. Now that the aristocracy were no longer able to afford to use the house, this new aristocracy of the mind seemed a fitting last duty of the dwelling. Here the thirty of us—college professors, students, newspapermen, farmers, factory workers, museum directors, and artists—discussed the arts in Canada, Britain, Australia, South Africa, New Zealand, Germany, France, and Denmark, and when the two weeks were over my stability had returned and the small scars which the slashing knives of the budget cutters had left on my sensibilities had healed.

I went throughout England and Scotland searching for the leaders, the arts festivals, the craftsmen. I journeyed to Wales, where I heard the Welsh people singing at their National Eistedfodd. I went to London and visited with the men and women who ran the great national programs of drama for the British Drama League, the Townswomen's Guilds, the Women's Institutes, the Church Drama Society. I scribbled a great many notes and I moved so rapidly that I had little chance to absorb what I saw and heard. I was, however, particularly interested in the leadership principle in the British system of encouraging the development of the arts. The budget cut at Wisconsin had made me aware of the necessity for strong leaders in the community—leaders who were trained for their job of guiding the arts in community life and who could carry on when University aid failed. England seemed an excellent place to study the growth of the arts in community life, for of course the English Universities were not at all engaged in great backstage operations like Wisconsin's. The bulk of the work in developing community projects was done through the education authorities of the various English counties. Field personnel in drama, music, and, occasionally, in the arts and crafts were maintained in many counties, but it seemed to me that the burden of continuing programs was placed more squarely upon the individual communities than in Wisconsin where the University was often looked upon as the real leader in community arts movements.

It was in Somerset that I found an outstanding example of

leaders working directly with the county authorities on a continuing arts program with roots deep in community life. There was something about Somerset—the hills, the moors with their great reaches of blooming heather—that stirred me. The villages in many ways were like some of the tiny places in New York State and in Wisconsin where I had seen and savored the germinal stuff of native literature.

I was met in Taunton by a young drama advisor, Rosa Ewing, who carried me about the county in an ancient English Ford. She had been born and raised in Somerset, and she was aquainted with everybody. We visited folks on the farms and in the villages, and everywhere the people talked about drama as though it were a normal part of their everyday lives.

I began to feel again a great excitement in me, for here, it seemed, was evidence that a people's movement in theater could actually exist. When I expressed my keen interest in what I saw and heard, Rosa told me how a special plan of leadership training had been developed. The county had developed "tutors" for theater production and education. These tutors were people who had expressed a deep interest in drama and who had demonstrated that they were willing to carry a load of responsibility for a theater plan in their own places. The tutors were first thoroughly grounded in theater theory and practice and then given a stiff examination. If they passed they were accredited by the county education office and might then offer theater classes in their own communities, for which the county paid them a fee. There were sixty-three such tutors offering active skilled aid in theater in Somerset.

Rosa said that the tutors could not handle the demand for their services. Plays were being produced everywhere and produced extremely well. Standards were high and getting higher. "The leaders," Rosa said as her rusty Ford panted up a tremendous hill near Simonsbath, "are the secret, always the secret."

The Somerset Education Authority was doing things, though, to help the leaders. The educators had a dream of twelve fine playhouses to be built in different rural sections of the county. These buildings were to be real theaters, and though they were to be included within new school buildings they were to be constructed as theaters with the look and feel of a real playhouse so that the people of Somerset would know what a beautiful theater was like. One had already been constructed at Wiveliscombe as the theater community center for the whole countryside.

A Somerset county playwriting plan was in operation, and a number of excellent plays had been written and produced by the local theater groups. In Glastonbury, a medium-sized city, I met Kenneth James, a talented young poet-playwright who had convinced his home town that poetic drama written locally and produced by a fine company was just about the most wonderful thing that had ever happened there.

"What are you doing about native theater in Wisconsin, Mr. Gard?" asked Rosa. Her question was as though a hand had suddenly shaken me awake. I thought again of the plaque on the front of Bascom Hall—the plaque about sifting and winnowing. I knew that I had arrived at a time of sifting and winnowing in my search and that all I had been seeing and weighing was a part of it. My spirit lifted. I saw my own Wisconsin playwrights, the Wurls and the Reichs, struggling in their own communities, and suddenly their struggles seemed as worth while and as heroic as the battle Kenneth James had waged in Glastonbury. I explained to Rosa what I had tried to do in Wisconsin as well

242

as I could, but I was eager to return to my home ground where the things I had witnessed abroad might have more clarity.

So back in Wisconsin in October I plunged into wanderings that had a new appeal for me. I was entirely free of the depressions of the budget, though I had not forgotten the lesson.

Wisconsin is an area about the size of England. When I recalled the vast programs in the arts I had witnessed there the magnitude of my job emerged for me. On the University field staff in theater, visual arts, music, creative writing, there were six full time persons—six field workers, attempting to do a job similar to the one for which hundreds of workers were engaged in England. There is, to be sure, a great difference in population; yet even so six workers for the fifty-six thousand square miles of Wisconsin necessitates a great deal of moving around.

I have some favorite spots in the state to which my wanderings often carry me. One of these is Sugar Bush Hill near Crandon, about two hundred miles north of Madison and the University. Sugar Bush Hill is the highest elevation in Wisconsin. Once in a public address I made the terrible blunder of remarking that Rib Mountain near Wausau was the highest point in the state (as indeed it was once thought to be). A native in the audience arose, placed the tip of his long finger under my nose, and stated bitterly that if I had not been a "foreigner" I would surely have known that Sugar Bush was fifteen feet higher than Rib Mountain. There was no denying his triumphant correctness, and, foolishly, Sugar Bush Hill has been ever since an eminence which invites me to ponder my small difficulties or puzzlements in regard to the state or the University. When I am in the vicinity I never fail to stop at Sugar Bush and cogitate a bit. Hilltops looking out upon whole areas have been important to me ever since Drummond taught me to romanticize the hilltops of New York State. From the firetower on Sugar Bush the forest lands stretch away and away and it is not at all difficult to imagine the whole state lying at one's feet.

Driving from Rhinelander to Green Bay one October day after my return from Britain I paused at Sugar Bush. The whole flame of the mighty forest claimed attention, but beyond the forest were the Wisconsin communities and my long look was at them. I was pondering once again the development of the community for the arts. I knew that the development of a community attitude friendly toward the arts was a Herculean task that must be faced. Finding ways to accomplish the task was a search that had underscored many of the experiments I had tried and one that had made me understand that the entire community must develop attitudes friendly to culture, especially drama.

Baker Brownell, the American philosopher who has frequently grappled with the problem of the arts in community life, wrote an article for the August, 1948, issue of the *Wisconsin Idea Theater Quarterly* in which he said that drama should be the formulation of the integrative unity of man in his community. The drama, he wrote, should be the formulation of this spiritual core in life and should be expressive as only art can be of the deep answers in common men to the perennial threat of disaster, human dissolution, and community disintegration. I knew that these deep answers which Baker Brownell speaks of must somehow be made more apparent to the people, or they must see the arts as one means through which such answers can be obtained. Pondering over these questions on Sugar Bush Hill I

244

realized that at the present time the arts do not represent deep spiritual answers and satisfactions to the common man. I had seen the possibilities of it in some of the experiments I had tried—experiments such as the Rural Writers' Association—and yet I knew that my efforts could not be said to have touched off in Wisconsin a great and deeply expressive movement in the arts—a movement which touched everyone.

Many persons, of course, take the point of view that such a movement is not possible and perhaps not even desirable. But in Wisconsin we adopt the attitude that an arts movement touching all classes and influencing all levels of human beings is a possible and desirable goal. We believe that we have made steps toward such a movement in Wisconsin, but we recognize that we have a tremendous distance to go.

It seems to me that a part of the problem is the lack of community symbols of art. I do not mean that we want more museums—places of defunct art—but rather that we need community arts centers in the small communities as well as in the larger cities where art may be witnessed and participated in. Such symbols as we once possessed have almost disappeared, although their relics and the ideas they once symbolized are still to be found. For example, in Menomonie, Wisconsin, on the banks of the Red Cedar River stands a remarkable building. I do not mean remarkable in beauty, for the Tainter Memorial in Menomonie is not beautiful; in fact, externally there is little to distinguish it. The place sprawls, its stone is dull-hued, and it now houses the Menomonie Library. A sign on the front of the building reveals that. Inside one is perhaps even less impressed, unless the pleasant lady who works at the library desk is present and opens a certain door with a sometimes long-sought-for key on her well-tenanted ring. With the opening of this door, however, another world is revealed, for here is a jewel of a theater—intimate, beautifully designed, with auditorium and stage all of a piece, so that the carefully turned-up chairs seem occupied, somehow, by the laughing and weeping personalities who witnessed comedy and tradegy here throughout the bygone years.

Yes, a beautiful theater. The carpeting of the 1890's is on the floor; the furniture of the lounge is just as it was arranged sixty-five years ago. Drops hang from ancient lines above the stage; the paint frame has probably carried no burden for many, many years; yet it hangs waiting. One walks to the edge of the stage and reaches across a corner of the orchestra pit to caress tenderly the grand drape. (Yes, it is the original.) Idly one looks at his fingers—black. Smoke, grime, dust, accumulation of years and years. And suddenly, as though awakened by a shot, one realizes the meaning of this emptiness, this grime, this air of futile waiting. Since this theater was so lovingly built in 1890, great changes have come to Menomonie, to the lives of the people, to the destiny of the wonderful building. The emptiness of this beautiful theater is terrifying. It means the death of the road. In the past many great actors and actresses played here in this small town in northern Wisconsin, played through here, perhaps, from St. Paul to Eau Claire, Madison, and Chicago. The emptiness of this theater means the sickening and death of the stock company, hardy troupers, playing a week, two weeks, then moving on.

Here in Menomonie, when this theater was in the bloom of its worth and beauty, the people knew about good plays, fine acting. What do we have left? In or near Menomonie, the home of this wonderful theater, there are young people who have never seen a real play, whose sole knowledge of the theater is the canned entertainment offered by the movies. Further, there are many young persons in or near Menomonie who do not even know of the existence of the Tainter Theater, to say nothing of all that it meant in the half-forgotten life of that place. Sad? Yes. And tragic, too, for the doors have been closed to the development of a theater appreciation in the children, and that means the doors have been closed to the fascinating characters of the world's great dramatic literature.

Community symbols are important, but so is leadership. The fact that on this October day I can sit and think on top of Sugar Bush Hill in northern Wisconsin two hundred miles from the University is significant to me. I am conscious that in a sense my freedom to wander carries with it a responsibility to the men and women in the University and the state whose hunger for culture made it possible for me to be here. Those men and women who expressed the hunger of the citizens of Wisconsin for culture were of course few. They were the great names, the leaders. But they were the voices of the less articulate citizenry into whose homes I have gone so frequently. Ways must be found to train more leaders, more voices. There are always the few who will carry the load, and I, at least, have been guilty in the past of relying too heavily on the willing few, rather than facing up to the job of training new leaders.

For instance, I would have had a sorry time in Wisconsin if it had not been for Bob Freidel, upon whom I have leaned heavily for guidance and help. Bob works in Milwaukee. He is head of the Milwaukee Recreation department's division of drama. He is a tireless worker in the task of establishing better home-grown theater in his own place. Here are some of the things he does: he directs the Milwaukee Players (a community theater group), directs and stimulates drama activity in the Milwaukee schools, directs a summer theater (the Hayloft), directs and develops a children's "trailer theater" which plays the various playgrounds in Milwaukee, builds audience appreciation through classes and lectures on theater, conducts a program of radio drama over a Milwaukee radio station, and is a key figure in the Greater Milwaukee Children's Theater committee that develops better theater for the kids in the Milwaukee area. Bob Freidel is a tremendous worker; but it is unfair to place all the burdens of leadership in his community upon him. Communities need many such leaders as Bob.

Another of our drama leaders in the school field, Neil Greene, of Muscoda, recently wrote an article for the *Wisconsin Idea Theater Quarterly*. He wrote that no town is too small, too poor, or too remote to be completely devoid of some sort of artistic expression; and no town has people who are too destitute, too ignorant, or too uncultured to gain artistic or spiritual values from theater experience if a way can be found to bring into their midst a single individual with a deeply-rooted devotion to drama. He need not be a master of drama or a staid patron of the arts; neither should he attempt to impose the strict principles of his dramatic creed upon his disciples; rather let him remain unpretentious and humble throughout. For drama is an art which in its infancy cannot withstand the intensities of superiority; only with patient indulgence and nurturing will it attain a high degree of perfection and worth.

It is always the question as to how the University can train such leaders. It is certainly true that the University recognizes the type of person needed. There are inevitably a few exceptional people attracted to the University. These few infuse a kind of dynamism into the staff of the University which attracts them. At Wisconsin there have been the Pop Gordons, the John Kolbs, the Ethel Rockwells. Yet the

248

University has trained no Drummonds, no Frederick Kochs, no Alfred Arvolds, no Edward Mabies, or Allen Craftons. Those men became great leaders in native theater in their schools, but because of the smallness of their number and because of the tremendous scope of their jobs, they were, as single leaders, almost alone in what they visualized as theater developments for their own areas.

Perhaps because of the demands upon such men, because of the very complexity of the things they attempted, they did not bring themselves to write down their experiences, let alone their dreams. Consequently, the wealth of their experience has not been returned to the people. Who knows how American theater might have flourished had the people been able to comprehend the dreams these men had dreamed for them or what developments of native playwriting and native literature might have been accomplished if the people had not only comprehended but had actually been able to put such dreams into practice. Somehow it is only by flowing it back to the people that experience and idealism can mean anything. It has gone back of course to some extent through their students. Unfortunately, not enough students have been able to grasp successfully the great scope and importance to the nation of their teachers' ideals.

In general, the students who have grasped the main ideas for community arts development from a great teacher or who have developed a firm sense of responsibility for the arts through a broad education become the best of the local leaders, and they are all too few. They continue to look to the University for help, for understanding, and for articulation of their desires. The Wisconsin Idea was and is still the expression of the people's desire for the benefits of education, and the University of Wisconsin has succeeded in many areas in bringing to the people of the state the fruits of research in agriculture, science, and business administration. In the cultural arts, however, it is a different matter. Here there are fewer "results" of "research," fewer tangibles to show the effort spent. Then, too, there are few, if any, immediate results of efforts to encourage theater, music or art. And it is difficult to make the need for the development of leaders in the arts seem acutely necessary.

So far, it seems to me, the universities have left the development of the Drummonds, Arvolds, Mabies, Kochs and Craftons to pure chance. This seems especially incongruous with the traditions of the University of Wisconsin, which has certainly understood, through its great backstage, how desperately the people have needed sensitive, talented guiding hands. The University fabricated the backstage for the people; yet it has been quite willing to leave the future, the sustaining part of the backstage, to chance leadership.

It seems to me that a stream of fine new community arts leaders should be issuing from the University of Wisconsin and, indeed, from all the universities and colleges of the nation. The universities and colleges are training artists, many of them, and training teachers. The theater departments are training actors, technicians, directors, and writers for whom there is at present at least little place in the profession for which they are being trained. No consideration is given to the fact that a profession might be developed in community life in theater. The young person graduating from the university has little concept of the scope of the theater to be developed, of the delicate social problems involved in fitting himself and his talents successfully into community life. He is too frequently a failure when he attempts it.

There are, however, tremendous satisfactions in store for him personally if somehow his attempt can be successful. I know the leaders in Wisconsin who have made themselves successful community focal points of the arts, and I know that their idealism has enriched them as well as the arts they have nurtured. From my perch on Sugar Bush Hill the picture looks far from hopeless. I only wish that the universities might be turning out many leaders with the idealism of Tom Hendry of Winnebago County, for example, who gives weekends and evenings in order that a home-grown rural playwriting plan may flourish, or like Isabelle Tremaine of Oconomowoc who endlessly teaches drama in her community to young people as well as adults. There is Alice Kelly of Rhinelander striving to raise the standards of a small group of creative writers, and there is Hugh Albert, agricultural agent of Rock County, immovably determined that a fine theater movement should flourish there. There is Fidelia Van Antwerp tirelessly beating around the state, usually at her own expense, in the cause of the Rural Writers' Association. There are others who lead writers', or musicians', or artists', or theater groups. There are Marie Barlow Buckman of Crivitz, Marie Kellog Kolb of Delavan, Jean Maccus of Oconomowoc, Bea Kietzer of Wautoma, Hatti Sorensen of Rhinelander, Betty Anderson of Prentice, Alice Dauer of Watertown, Margaret Means of Manitowoc, Margo Herriott of Madison, Virginia and Jim Hawkins of Racine, Dean Flegel of Racine, Harvard Smith of Kenosha, Louis Poliere of Beloit, Harvey Becker of Rhinelander, Clarence Westphal of Oshkosh, Dr. Irving Clark of Janesville, John Kennedy and Mark Bruce of Evansville, Herb Selissen of Green Bay, Jo Kading of Watertown, Dorothy Patchett of Burlington, Robert Sullivan of Oshkosh, Mrs. John Fritschler of Superior, Edward Helminiak of Milwaukee, Howard Rich of Sheboygan, Everett and Coyla McNeill of Kenosha, and many more.

Somehow the ideas which have become apparent through

the efforts of the American pioneers in the movement for a grassroots theater and allied arts must be spread more thoroughly back to the people. The group of leaders in Wisconsin, for example, is far too small to awaken the arts consciousness of over three and one-half million persons. What is needed is more idealistic wandering, more work, more ideas, the marshalling of more force for the cultural arts. Such activity means more fine teachers willing to devote a part of their time to their area, their state. It means administrators and legislators willing to spend more funds on new ideas and on the arts in general. It may mean, eventually, a whole new concept of the university in which the backstage becomes the forestage.

For me, personally, the answer I seek is not necessarily in Wisconsin or New York or Alberta or even in any one place. It is, for me, within myself simply in a will to continue my wanderings, to maintain faith. Whatever the results, the drive, the restless seeking, the searching into dim corners is the great thing. The sproutings of artistic expression, the coming to life in a thousand places, the places where people strive honestly for the spark of an art impulse, are my satisfactions and the results of my search.

Here on Sugar Bush Hill the wind blows hard. The forest lands stretch away and away as far as I can see. But beyond the forests there are the farms, the towns, the cities of Wisconsin, and beyond and around Wisconsin is all America waiting for the spreading back of the grassroots arts idea. The Wisconsin Idea is only a seed of an America whose expressiveness awaits the wanderers to search it out. The roads lead far and in many directions.

INDEX

Index

ADOLFSON, L. H.: and University of Wisconsin Extension Division, 109; and Wisconsin Idea Theater, 118; and Rural Writers' Association, 119
Adult education: importance of in community arts, 201–2; in England, 239
Albert, Hugh, 251
Alberta Folklore and Local History Project: establishment of, 48; as stimulus to regional writing, 64–65; and Wisconsin Idea Theater, 70–71
Allen, Andrew: and Canadian Broadcasting Corporation, 64, 67
American Country Life Conference, 100

Anderson, Betty, 251
Anderson, Maxwell, 35
Appia, Adolph, 25, 26, 132
Appleby, John, 171
Aristotle, 25, 26
Arvold, Alfred: and country theater, 80–81; mentioned, 84, 249, 250
Attingham Park Conference: and encouragement of cultural arts in England, 239–41. *See also* Somerset County, England

BABCOCK, Stephen M., 171
Bailey, Liberty Hyde, 93
Baker, George Pierce, 14
Bakshy, Alexander, 25
Balaatke, Hans, 166
Baldwin, Ira L., 228

New York State Fair Country Theater: established by Drummond, 13; performances of Zona Gale's *The Neighbors,* 15; mentioned, 14, 17, 19

New York State New Plays Project: establishment of, 33–37; production of *Cardiff Giant,* 43–44; mentioned, 53, 161

Nietzsche, Friedrich Wilhelm, 132

Northwoods Arts and Crafts Festival, 136–38

Notes for a General Wisconsin Drama Plan, 111–13

Noyes, Mrs. Josephine: *A Home for Christmas,* 166

O'NEILL, Eugene, 168

PAGEANTRY: in Wisconsin Centennial, 147; art of, 148–50; in Montana, 193

Palmer, Opal: *The Girl and the River,* 170

Patchett, Dorothy, 251

Patterson, Helen, 227

Paulus, Margaret: *A City for Josette,* 164

Pharis, Gwen: and Banff School of Fine Arts, 67; as regional playwright, 67–68; letter from, 68–70; and Alberta Folklore and Local History Project, 70

Pen and Plow, 228. See also Wisconsin Rural Writers' Association

Phillips, Walter, 47

Pinchot, Gifford, 93

Playwright-in-residence: in Wisconsin, 119; in American Universities, 177–78; and Wisconsin Idea Theater, 178–79

Poliere, Louis, 123, 251

Pollard, David: *A Moses of the*

Mormons, 172; *The Story of the Newhall House Fire,* 172

Puls, Barbara: *The Baraboo Raid,* 171

RADIO plays: in Canada, 66–67; importance of, in regional writing, 67, 170, 173; in Wisconsin, 170–73. See also Canadian Broadcasting Corporation; WHA

"Ranger Mac." See McNeel, Wakelin

Ream, Vinnie, 153

Regionalism: and feeling for place, 3, 24, 33, 71, 141–42; Zona Gale's use of, 16, 17; A. M. Drummond on, 17, 18–19; standards of, 26; in New York State plays, 36–37, 53–54; materials of, 45, 64, 134, 161; in Canada, 47–48; rôle of leader in, 51–52; and frontier spirit in Canada, 54–61; definition of, 61; and Wisconsin Dramatic Society, 87–88; use of radio in developing themes of, 170

Reich, Doré: *River Boat,* 150; as regional playwright, 154, 162, 167, 242; *The Goldfish Castle,* 155; *In Old Green Bay,* 155–56; *Tintype,* 165

Research in cultural arts: necessity for, 184, 186, 189, 210; and Wisconsin folklore, 187–88; and Wisconsin tri-county theater project, 189; and Wisconsin Rural Writers' Association, 190–92; and Wisconsin cultural history, 193–94; in Washington County, Wisconsin, 198–209

Rhinelander Writers' Club: and Rural Writers' Association, 225

Rich, Howard, 251

matic Society, 85–86; origin of term, 89; scope of, 89–90; in education, 90, 125–26, 181–84, 249–50; and Bureau of Community Music and Drama, 90; approach to arts, 98; and University Extension Division, 103–5; as basis of Wisconsin Idea Theater, 114; in Wisconsin cultural history, 195–96, 234–35; mentioned, 71, 107, 110, 121, 197, 210, 213, 232, 252

Wisconsin Idea Theater Conference, 118

Wisconsin Idea Theater Quarterly, 118

Wisconsin New Plays Theater: establishment of, 173–75; first production in, 175–76; acting companies in, 176

Wisconsin Rural Art Project: established, 100; and John Steuart Curry, 100–1; growth of, 213

Wisconsin Rural Writers' Association: organization of, 122, 217–18, 221–22; purpose of, 218; development of, 219–21, 227, 229–30; creed of, 222; publication in *Pen and Plow*, 228; magazine, *Creative Wisconsin*, 230–32; mentioned, 119, 225, 232, 245, 251

"Wisconsin Yarns," 117, 170

Wiveliscombe, England: and theater community center, 242

Wood, Grant, 99

Woodward, Emily Jean: *Nawaka Chief*, 166

Wright, Frank Lloyd, 142

Wurl, Emily Sprague: as regional writer, 158–60, 179–80; *Reachin' for the Moon*, 162; *Rahel O'Fon*, 162, 167–68; mentioned, 123, 153, 162, 242

ZILLMAN, Helen, 123

Zimmerman, Mary: *Mister Micawber*, 164; *The Chocolate Milk Cow*, 169–70: *A Gallery of Women's Portraits*, 223–24